Archbishop Justin Welby:
Risk-taker and Reconciler

Archbishop Justin Welby: Risk-taker and Reconciler

Andrew Atherstone

DARTON · LONGMAN + TODD

First published in 2014 by
Darton, Longman and Todd Ltd
1 Spencer court
140 – 142 Wandsworth High Street
London SW18 4JJ

A catalogue record for this book is available from the British Library

ISBN: 978-0-232-53072-8

Photypeset by Kerrypress Ltd., Luton, Bedfordshire.
Printed and bound by ScandBook AB, Sweden

For Catherine, the love of my life

Contents

List of Illustrations   ix
Acknowledgements   xi

Chapter 1: Politics and Privilege   1
Chapter 2: Kenya   21
Chapter 3: Cambridge   27
Chapter 4: Career and Calling   41
Chapter 5: Growing Churches   67
Chapter 6: The Ministry of Reconciliation   105
Chapter 7: Liverpool Cathedral   141
Chapter 8: Durham   161
Chapter 9: Canterbury   185
Chapter 10: Sex, Money and Power   211
Chapter 11: A Global Communion   237
Chapter 12: Speaking for Jesus   255
Index   261

List of Illustrations

1.   The archbishop's father, Gavin Welby, formerly Gavin Weiler, as a child.
2.   Gavin Welby's campaign leaflet in the 1951 General Election.
3.   Jane Welby and Justin.
4.   Justin Welby, aged four.
5.   At St Peter's preparatory school, in Seaford on the Sussex coast.
6.   Engagement to Caroline Eaton, June 1979.
7.   Wedding at Holy Trinity Brompton, December 1979.
8.   With his conservative evangelical mentor, E. J. H. Nash (centre), and a Cambridge friend, Nick James (right).
9.   Caroline Welby and Charlie Arbuthnot posing as tourists in Prague during their Bible-smuggling expedition in 1980. Justin is behind the camera.
10. Group Treasurer of Enterprise Oil, aged 30.
11. Monitoring the stock market in Barclays De Zoete Wedd's trading room in the City of London.
12. Ordinands and tutors at Cranmer Hall, Durham in 1991. Justin Welby is at the centre of the back row.
13. Ordination as priest at Coventry Cathedral, July 1993. With the family are Welby's mother and stepfather, Lord and Lady Williams of Elvel.
14. The rector of Southam.
15. Collation at Coventry Cathedral before Welby's installation as residentiary canon, 2002. Bishop Colin Bennetts and Dean John Irvine are wearing the yellow copes.

16. Welby and Andrew White on satellite phones in the compound of Saddam Hussein's palace, Baghdad, May 2003. With them is General George Sadda, author of *Saddam's Secrets*.

17. Palm Sunday, 2007, in the ruins of Coventry's medieval cathedral. The robes were designed by John Piper.

18. Welby and White at the re-opening of St George's, Baghdad. With them are the caretaker, Hanna Younan, and his daughter Marriam.

19. The Dean of Liverpool with Nicky Gumbel at an Alpha International Conference.

20. Abseiling down Liverpool Cathedral, in aid of the cathedral centenary fund.

21. Sorting food at Sunderland Minster for 'One for the Basket', an ecumenical food bank in Durham diocese.

22. Seated in the chair of St Augustine at Canterbury Cathedral, March 2013.

23. With Prince Charles at the enthronement ceremony.

24. Reading Psalm 15 at the Western Wall, Jerusalem.

25. Sharing a joke with the Archbishop of York at General Synod.

26. With Archbishop Mouneer Anis at the Al-Azhar Al-Sharif mosque in Cairo.

27. Flying from Nairobi with the Mission Aviation Fellowship, with Caroline Welby (second left centre), Joanna Udal (centre), and Archbishop Eliud Wabukala of Kenya (second right).

28. A welcoming party in Dodoma, Tanzania.

29. Praying at a mass grave in Bor, South Sudan.

30. Barefoot torchlight procession on the 'Holy Mile' to the Anglican Shrine of Our Lady of Walsingham, during the annual youth pilgrimage.

31. Children at New Wine pray for the archbishop, July 2013.

Acknowledgements

An earlier version of this biography, *Archbishop Justin Welby: The Road to Canterbury*, was researched and written at break-neck speed in ten weeks flat. The research began on 9 November 2012, the day Justin Welby's nomination as the one hundred and fifth Archbishop of Canterbury was announced by Downing Street. It was drafted by Christmas and published in March 2013 in time for his enthronement at Canterbury Cathedral. This new book tells the story of Welby's life and ministry in fuller detail, in the light of further research, up to the end of his first year in office. It is far too early to assess the likely legacy of his archiepiscopate, a task which will fall to future historians, but some trajectories are already clear.

This biography, like its predecessor, is unauthorised. Justin Welby and his current staff team at Lambeth Palace declined invitations to be interviewed, though the archbishop happily and graciously allowed me to speak freely with his wider circle of friends and colleagues. I am particularly grateful to Lady Williams of Elvel for details of the family background and for access to some of the letters and photographs in her private archive. Thanks are due to many others who have provided insights into the archbishop's character and contexts, in particular to Charlie Arbuthnot, Simon Barrington-Ward, Tory Baucum, Stuart Beake, James Behrens, the late Colin Bennetts, Simon Betteridge, Myles Bowen, Francis Bridger, Mark Bryant, William Challis, John Collins, Ken Costa, Jo Cundy, Adrian Daffern, Martin Davie, CJ Davis, Paul Dembinski, Jeremy Duff, David Fletcher, Jonathan Fletcher, David Ford, Andy Freeman, Bernie and Jean French, Andrew Goddard, Jonathan Goodall, Pete Greig, Ian Grieves, Clive Handford, Jamie and Anne Harrison, Terence Hill, Nick Hills, Josiah Idowu-Fearon, John Irvine, J. John, David Jones, Phil and

Anne Kelly, David Kennedy, Graham Kings, Ben Kwashi, Susie Leafe, Dorrette McAuslan, John McClure, Frank McHugh, Sandy Millar, John Moore, David Moxon, Fiona Newton, Bernard Ntahoturi, Hank Paulson, Paul Perkin, Marilyn and John Perry, John Philpott, Anthony Priddis, John Pritchard, Jackie Pullinger, Michael Reiss, John Risdon, David Runcorn, Alan Russell, Ian Russell, Chris Smith, Michael Stockwood, Chris Sugden, David Urquhart, Eliud Wabukala, Tim Watson, Jo Bailey Wells (before her appointment as archbishop's chaplain), Andrew White, David Williams, Rowan Williams, Jonathan Wilmot and Tom Wright. For access to archives, thanks especially to Phil Kelly for his letters from Kenya; Jonathan Smith at Trinity College, Cambridge; Julia Durand-Barthez at St Michael's, Paris; John Collins for a run of *The Brompton Magazine* from Holy Trinity Brompton; David Goodhew and Claire Readey at St John's College, Durham; Frank Seldon and Alison Perkins at Chilvers Coton parish church; John Armstrong and John and Ruth Tresidder at Southam parish church; Don Brewin at Sharing of Ministries Abroad; David Porter and Sarah Watts at the Community of the Cross of Nails, Coventry Cathedral; Abigail Rhodes at Holy Trinity, Coventry; and Val Jackson and Stuart Haynes at Liverpool Cathedral. I am grateful also to Ed Loane for help with references, and to Charlie Arbuthnot, Martin Davie, Andrew Goddard, Jamie Harrison, Phil Kelly and Nick Moore for reading various chapters of the book in draft. The interpretation of Justin Welby's life and ministry presented here remains, of course, my responsibility alone.

Andrew Atherstone
Wycliffe Hall, Oxford
Easter 2014

Chapter 1

Politics and Privilege

Justin Welby is a scion of Britain's political, military and educational establishment in the middle decades of the twentieth century. The family tree on his mother's side boasts an array of civil servants, academics, soldiers and clergymen. One great-grandfather was Sir Montagu Butler, who made his name in India as Governor of the Central Provinces 1925–33, and was afterwards Lieutenant-Governor of the Isle of Man and Master of Pembroke College, Cambridge. Two of Welby's great-uncles were Knights of the Garter, England's highest order of chivalry, which is limited to the monarch, the Prince of Wales, and 24 companions. One of them, Viscount Portal of Hungerford, was Chief of the Air Staff during the Second World War overseeing the strategic operations of the Royal Air Force.[1] The other, R. A. ('Rab') Butler, later Baron Butler of Saffron Walden, held three of Britain's great offices of state as Chancellor of the Exchequer, Home Secretary and Foreign Secretary in the 1950s and 1960s. Only the premiership eluded him.[2]

Welby's mother, Jane Portal, was born in India and sent to boarding school in England, at Cambridge and Wantage. She wanted 'passionately' to go to university, but her uncle Rab Butler took her aside and said, 'Forget that! Learn to type, learn to drive a car and, if you can, learn to cook, and you'll be perfectly all right.'[3] Butler put her in touch with Sir

---

1   Denis Richards, *Portal of Hungerford: The Life of Marshal of the Royal Air Force, Viscount Portal of Hungerford, KG, GCB, OM, DSO, MC* (London: Heinemann, 1977).

2   Anthony Howard, *RAB: The Life of R. A. Butler* (London: Jonathan Cape, 1987).

3   Interview with Lady Williams, 13 January 2014.

Winston Churchill for whom she worked from December 1949, aged 20, as the most junior of his five secretaries. Her main task was typing his six-volume history of *The Second World War*. Although Churchill was in his mid-seventies, he remained Leader of the Opposition and soon Jane was assisting him at the House of Commons, taking dictation of his speeches, and at Chartwell, his home in Kent. In October 1951 the Labour government fell and Churchill was re-elected as Prime Minister, which brought a move to Downing Street and Chequers. Jane travelled with the premier to summit meetings with President Eisenhower in Bermuda and at the White House during 1953–54, though she recalled that for Churchill's young staff it was 'one long party', including midnight bathing at the beach. When Churchill stood down in April 1955 in favour of his Foreign Secretary, Sir Anthony Eden, he asked Jane to go with him to Sicily to help finish his *History of the English-Speaking Peoples*, but she flew instead to the United States to be married to Gavin Welby.[4]

Jane Portal was introduced to Gavin Welby, a wealthy businessman and aspiring politician, through her friend Piers Dixon, a merchant banker working in New York and son of the diplomat Bob Dixon, Britain's permanent representative to the United Nations. Although Welby was well connected, his background remained mysterious for many decades even to his new family, and his son recalled:

> He told lots of stories but one was never really sure what was true and what wasn't. ... He was a great keeper of secrets. I think he told people the stories that he wanted them to believe and kept the rest quietly to himself. ... He was a great raconteur. ... There is no hiding the fact that he was a complicated man.[5]

Justin Welby was brought up, for example, on stories that his paternal grandfather was an adventurer who was killed

---

4   Interview with Lady Williams, 11 February 1986 (audio recording), Churchill Archives Centre, Cambridge, CHOH 1/WLMS.

5   Jason Lewis, 'New Archbishop: Secret Life of My "Alcohol-Dependent" Father', *Sunday Telegraph*, 25 November 2012, p. 1.

in South Africa, though actually he was a businessman who died in a nursing home in Torquay. Gavin 'found it very, very difficult to talk about himself and his private life, his past'.[6] Only after his son's nomination as Archbishop of Canterbury in November 2012 was light shed on his origins, romantic liaisons and business career, chiefly through the investigations of the *Sunday Telegraph* which described him as 'a man of mystery, with a flair for reinvention and a story to rival that of the Great Gatsby'.[7]

Gavin Welby was born Bernard Gavin Weiler at Ruislip on the outskirts of London in November 1910. His father, Bernard Weiler, was a Jewish émigré from Germany in the 1880s and an ostrich feather merchant, importing plumage from South Africa as luxury accessories for the European market. In September 1914, seven weeks after Britain declared war on Germany, the family abandoned the surname Weiler in favour of the anglicised Welby.[8] Gavin was sent first to Stratton Park preparatory school at Great Brickhill in Buckinghamshire, and then to Sedbergh School in Cumbria, but left in 1927 when his parents split up after his father had an affair.[9] This pattern of family breakdown was to be repeated in the next generation. Gavin blamed his parents' divorce for depriving him of the opportunity to study at Cambridge University.[10] After his father's death in 1930 he sailed to New York, aged 19, and in later life enjoyed telling stories of how he had run alcohol with his 'Italian friends', the mafia, as a bootlegger during Prohibition.[11] Welby became import manager in 1933 for the National Distillers Products Corporation and was

6   Interview with Lady Williams, 13 January 2014.
7   For the best research, see Jason Lewis, 'A Master of Reinvention Who Hid Gatsby Lifestyle From Son', *Sunday Telegraph*, 25 November 2012, pp. 6–7; Jason Lewis, 'German Jews Who Fled the Nazis: Secrets of Archbishop's Family Tree', *Sunday Telegraph*, 2 December 2012, p. 19
8   *London Gazette*, 25 September 1914, p. 7634.
9   For details of Bernard Welby's affair and Edith Welby's petition for divorce, 1927–28, see National Archives, J77/2488/7563.
10   Reference from British Consulate-General, New York, 22 October 1942, attached to Gavin Welby army record, Ministry of Defence archives.
11   Lewis, 'New Archbishop', p. 1.

married the next year to Doris Sturzenegger, a factory owner's daughter, though the relationship did not last.[12] In New York he enjoyed a lavish lifestyle amongst the business elite, residing in hotels, and attending debutante balls and dinner parties for ambassadors. He dated a string of beautiful and rich young women. According to the gossip columns, during 1937 Welby and Wimbledon tennis champion Kay Stammers were 'volleying letters across the Atlantic'. By 1942 he was a rival with Errol Flynn for the attentions of millionaire heiress Doris Duke.[13] Halfway through the Second World War, in January 1943, Welby was commissioned in the Royal Army Service Corps responsible for transportation and supplies for frontline troops. As part of the 21st Army Group he served briefly in Normandy, Belgium, Holland and Germany, before being deployed in Kenya as a staff captain with the East Africa Command.[14]

After demobilisation, Welby settled back in Britain and invested his wealth in two whiskey companies in Glasgow, Gavin's Distillers (incorporated 1946) and Coulmore Distillery (incorporated 1949) of which he was managing director. His leading brands, Gavin's Gold Blend and Gavin's Liquor, averaged sales of 100,000 bottles a year. He also turned his attention to British politics. Baron Queenborough introduced Welby to Harold Mitchell (vice-chairman of the Conservative Party) and in March 1945 he sought selection as a parliamentary candidate. His application form explained: 'I am a Conservative because (1) I believe it embodies the best in character and brains of any party, (2) is the most socially Progressive from a sound and stable viewpoint, (3) and is – spiritually speaking – the most Christian.' His dream was to secure a rural constituency, purchase a country estate and

12   *New York Times*, 28 January 1934, p. 26; 13 May 1940, p. 28.
13   Tom Leonard and Steve Bird, 'An Unholy Bounder!', *Daily Mail*, 12 December 2012, pp. 30–1.
14   Gavin Welby army record.

begin farming.[15] Welby failed to secure the nomination of any local Conservative association for the general elections of 1945 or 1950, but his chance came in October 1951 when he was chosen to fight for Coventry East against the sitting Labour MP, Richard Crossman. Welby's campaign literature accused Clement Attlee's Labour government of presiding over a series of economic and foreign policy disasters:

> We have suffered from lack of foresight, lack of experience, lack of courage, lack of statesmanship, and principally too much idealistic, 'woolly' and muddled-headed thinking. They have good intentions, but unfortunately are somewhat deficient in good common sense!

Welby campaigned on a platform of taxation reform, reduction in the cost of living, more housing, better food and an end to nationalisation. He wanted to see the Iron and Steel Act repealed and coal, gas, electricity and transport decentralised. He also argued that British rearmament was 'a vital necessity', indeed the top priority:

> With Russian Imperialistic Communism capturing by arms or Fifth Column one third of the world, and still on the march, Labour has resembled an ostrich with its head in the sand, and six sad years have been wasted. We will not avoid war by appeasement, but through strength.

Welby portrayed himself to electors as 'a Member of the Church of England, and an all-round Sportsman'.[16] He also played the family card by persuading his mother to campaign with him.[17] Behind the scenes, however, Conservative party officials were pessimistic. They felt Welby was 'not particularly well suited' to a constituency like Coventry East and that his chances of

---

15 Gavin Welby candidate's form, 6 March 1945, Bodleian Library, Conservative Party Archives [CPA], CCO 220/3/69/5.
16 Gavin Welby campaign leaflet, election addresses (1951), CPA, PUB 229/10/3, p. 29.
17 'Candidate's Rosette Returned', *Coventry Evening Telegraph*, 23 October 1951, p. 7; 'Mr Welby's Hecklers Subdued', *Coventry Evening Telegraph*, 25 October 1951, p. 3.

victory were 'not very bright'.[18] His campaign team blundered by deliberately misquoting Crossman in one of their leaflets, so Crossman threatened to sue for libel, just three days before the election. Welby was forced to make humble apology in the *Coventry Evening Telegraph*, the day before the polls opened, blaming his agent.[19] He seemed less concerned about his reputation in Coventry than in London, where he feared, as his solicitor put it, that even 'a farthing damages' would harm his prospects socially and politically, as well as in business.[20] Crossman's libel suit was withdrawn, but Welby was trounced in the polls.

Undeterred, Welby continued to build connections amongst the political and cultural elite, and his wealth opened doors. He owned a thoroughbred racehorse called *Gay Green*. He claimed to have travelled to 30 countries. Amongst his gentlemen's clubs in London, he numbered the Carlton Club (closely associated with the Conservative Party), Buck's Club, the Bath Club, the Royal Automobile Club, the International Sportsmen's Club, the Hurlingham Club and the Lansdowne Club; as well as the Travellers Club on the Champs-Elysées in Paris, and the Muthaiga Country Club in Nairobi. He was fluent in French and professed to be an accomplished athlete who enjoyed golf, tennis, polo, skiing, hunting, squash and fencing.[21] This life of leisure was punctuated by brief romances. In 1952 Welby and the young socialite Patricia Kennedy (daughter of Joseph Kennedy, former American ambassador to Britain) were said to be 'intoxicated about each other'.[22]

18   Memorandum by Colonel R. Ledingham (Conservative party agent for the West Midlands), 11 January 1951, CPA, CCO 1/8/299.
19   Penman, Johnson and Ewins (solicitors) to Gavin Welby, 22 October 1951, CPA, CCO 1/9/299; 'Mr Crossman Complains of Tory Pamphlet', *Coventry Evening Telegraph*, 22 October 1951, p. 5; Gavin Welby, 'Public Notice', *Coventry Evening Telegraph*, 24 October 1951, p. 7.
20   R.A. Rotheram and Co. (solicitors) to A.H. Watson (Conservative Central Office), 24 and 29 October 1951, CPA, CCO 1/9/299.
21   Gavin Welby candidate's forms, 6 March 1945, 3 May and 21 December 1955, CPA, CCO 220/3/69/5.
22   'Walter Winchell of New York: Man About Town', *Washington Post*, 17 March 1952, section B, p. 9.

He also introduced Patricia's older brother, Senator John F. Kennedy, to 21-year-old Swedish aristocrat Gunilla von Post on the French Riviera in August 1953. Kennedy and von Post became lovers. The future president told her that Welby 'looks like a playboy, but he's conservative underneath'.[23] In a love-letter he wrote in some amusement about 'our friend – the cold, frozen Mr Gavin Welby'.[24] In March 1955 Welby sold his two whiskey companies to Hiram Walker and Sons, the distillery empire. He became a 'name' at Lloyd's, the London insurance market, and at the age of 44 never needed to work again.

Welby whisked Jane Portal off her feet, after his letter of introduction from Piers Dixon. She agreed to go out with him, fell quickly for his charms, and 'before she knew what had happened' found herself engaged to be married within a few weeks of meeting. Perhaps for Welby romance and political ambition were intertwined since his bride happened to be both the Prime Minister's secretary and the Chancellor of the Exchequer's niece. Jane was willing to overlook the fact that Gavin had been married before, but she never discovered the identity of his first wife. 'I used to try and question him', she remembered, 'but it would end in such terrible arguments, that I very feebly used to give up.' She hoped for a wedding in Kensington, but he insisted they must go to America so that he could finalise his divorce. So they simply 'did a bunk'. Jane walked out on her job with Churchill, and eloped to Baltimore, Maryland, without telling her parents.[25] There she and Gavin were married at Govans Presbyterian Church on 4 April 1955 by a local minister, though the wedding was not recorded in the church register, and there were no friends or family so two strangers were brought in off the street to act

23 Gunilla von Post, *Love, Jack* (New York: Crown Publishers, 1997), pp. 19–33.
24 John F. Kennedy to Gunilla von Post, 25 June 1955, at 'Love Letters from the Prince of Camelot' (19 August 2001), www.getkempt.com. These letters were sold to an anonymous bidder at auction in 2010.
25 Interview with Lady Williams, 13 January 2014.

as witnesses.[26] After three or four days the couple returned to London, though Gavin was initially too embarrassed to tell his French housekeeper, Miss Jeangrand, about the new arrangement so he put Jane up in the Rembrandt Hotel for a night before she was allowed to move into his flat at 17 Onslow Square. When Jane's father heard about these goings-on, he simply asked, 'Why do you have to behave like Bonnie and Clyde?' A wedding reception was held at 11 Downing Street, courtesy of Rab Butler, but Jane quickly realised that she had 'made the most terrible mistake'.[27]

Gavin Welby still hoped for a career in parliament, and did not shy away from mentioning his new wife's political connections in his Conservative party application. His candidacy was supported by prominent Tory politicians and diplomats like Sir Ronald Cross (Governor of Tasmania), John Foster, Sir Wavell Wakefield and Sir Edward Boyle. As his specialisms, he listed foreign policy (especially Anglo-American relations), economics, export trade and farming.[28] He was unexpectedly given a second opportunity to contest a seat in the general election of May 1955 at Goole in Yorkshire. The Conservative candidate pulled out at short notice, ostensibly 'for business reasons', though in reality because of an 'unexpected five years old skeleton in his cupboard'. It was 'a most embarrassing situation' for the local party, and they scrambled to find a substitute.[29] Welby was drafted in at the last minute. The chairman of the Goole Conservative association, the Earl of Rosse, told party headquarters: 'His qualifications were so outstandingly good that we felt justified in making the decision ourselves, in view of the shortage of time. I think that we are extraordinarily lucky, in fact, to be

26   *Times*, 26 April 1955, p. 14; Maryland State Archives, marriage licence for Gavin B. Welby and Jane Portal, 4 April 1955, certificate number 9898.
27   Interview with Lady Williams, 13 January 2014.
28   Gavin Welby candidate's forms, 6 March 1945, 3 May and 21 December 1955, CPA, CCO 220/3/69/5.
29   Earl of Rosse to John Hare, 15 February 1955, CPA, CCO 1/11/195.

able to secure a man of such calibre.'[30] Yet Welby's prospects of winning were non-existent, with only a month to campaign in a constituency where he was a complete stranger. He threw together some rough campaign leaflets, announcing 'We can't afford any more Socialism, so make sure it's Welby', but was easily defeated by the established Labour MP, George Jeger.[31] It marked the end of Gavin Welby's political ambitions.

A Broken Home

Justin Portal Welby was a honeymoon baby. He was born at Queen Charlotte's Hospital in Hammersmith on 6 January 1956, almost exactly nine months to the day after his parents' wedding. He was baptised at Holy Trinity, off the Brompton Road, a society church in Kensington with a broad evangelical tradition. His godparents were Susan Batten (his aunt), Adam Butler (his mother's cousin, later a Tory MP and Permanent Private Secretary to Margaret Thatcher), and two members of the minor aristocracy, Robin Vanden-Bempde-Johnstone (a foreign office diplomat, later Baron Derwent) and Flora Fraser (later Lady Saltoun).[32] Major Bill Batt, a Norfolk landowner and passionate evangelist, also committed privately to pray for the boy every week.

It was soon apparent, however, that the Welbys' relationship was in turmoil and within three years their marriage had collapsed. By the autumn of 1958 Jane had packed her bags and retreated to her parents' home at Blakeney on the north Norfolk coast, along with two-year-old Justin and his Swiss

---

30 Earl of Rosse to John Hare, 20 April 1955, CPA, CCO 1/11/195.
31 Gavin Welby's campaign leaflet, election addresses (1955), CPA, PUB 229/11/12, p. 61.
32 *Times*, 14 April 1956, p. 8.

nanny.[33] They tried to keep their relationship difficulties out of the public gaze and at first denied it, but the tabloid press soon sniffed out the story, even sending a reporter from London to Blakeney. The *Daily Mail* broke the news in its gossip columns, and Jane complained: 'It makes me feel absolutely sick, but there is nothing to be done & now everybody knows, so there we are.'[34] They were divorced in February 1959.

Gavin insisted on taking charge of his son, whom he adored, as Jane recalled: 'There was no question that he wouldn't fight me to the last ditch to keep hold of Justin.'[35] She was at a disadvantage, unable to afford proper legal advice, and acceded to Gavin's demand that he should have custody, a decision she came to regret. He promised to pay for Justin's education, though childcare was divided equally. Jane found a small flat on Kensington Church Street and joined a typing pool to make ends meet. So Justin spent his early years shuttling between his father and mother in London and his grandparents in Norfolk as they all took turns to look after him. Adam Butler was made his legal guardian in case of Gavin's death.[36] The arrangements were generally amicable, but sometimes strained and Gavin liked to communicate via lawyer's letter.

Before long Gavin was again engaged to be married, this time to Vanessa Redgrave, a 23-year-old budding actress, less than half his age. She was on the cusp of stardom following in the footsteps of her parents, Sir Michael and Lady Redgrave, as a celebrity of stage and screen. In June 1960 the Welbys, father and son, spent a weekend at The George Hotel in Odiham, Hampshire, so that Gavin could court Vanessa at the Redgraves' home nearby. Vanessa, according to her mother,

---

33 Iris Portal to Rab Butler, 6 October 1958, Cambridge, Trinity College Archives, Rab Butler Papers, RAB A3, letter 109.

34 Jane Welby to Rab Butler, 14 October 1958, Rab Butler Papers, RAB A57, letter 3; 'Rab's Niece Sues', *Daily Mail*, 14 October 1958, p. 12.

35 Interview with Lady Williams, 13 January 2014.

36 Codicil (26 May 1966) to the will of Gavin Welby (13 October 1964), proved at London, 20 July 1977.

was 'completely infatuated', 'absolutely *radiant*, over the moon with joy'.[37] She told her parents of her determination to wed this 'sweet darling man ... I love Gavin very much and am so happy!'[38] At first Lady Redgrave was not sure what to make of Welby: 'Gavin looks 40 [actually he was 49], kind of mysterious, attractive. He has money & doesn't work.'[39] But within a few days, intrigue had been replaced by alarm, as she wrote in distress to her husband: 'But he is a real horror. ... He strikes everyone as a no-good type with God knows what sort of background. You know I'd not mind about class, money, *anything* if he wasn't patently a pretty rotten piece of work.'[40] She admitted that Welby was 'very attractive physically', albeit that he adored his own bronzed body, but it was difficult 'to pierce the façade' of small talk.[41] Vanessa's younger sister agreed, declaring that their marriage would be 'wrong and disastrous ... though he is attractive he is not the sort of person anyone could live with for more than a month or two'.[42] A family friend gave a similarly damning verdict, telling Michael Redgrave that Welby

> strikes me as quite a pleasant casual drinking acquaintance whom one might encounter in the South of France amongst the idle gad-abouts. But as soon as you go beyond the casual drink you find him very self-opinionated and hard with albeit the occasional softer touches that are temporarily endearing. He is *not* of Vanessa's world & I can't see how, at his age, he could ever become part of it. I cannot see how their marriage could ever be successful & it could only be detrimental to her career. He is physically attractive & she is completely bowled over by him ... I only hope she will see him in his true perspective in time.[43]

37 Rachel Redgrave to Michael Redgrave, 2 June 1960 and no date [6 June 1960], V&A Museum Archives, Theatre and Performance Collections, Sir Michael Redgrave Papers, THM/31/3/6/15/2 and THM/31/3/6/15/4.
38 Vanessa Redgrave to Michael Redgrave, 2 June 1960, THM/31/3/6/45/2.
39 Rachel Redgrave to Michael Redgrave, 2 June 1960, THM/31/3/6/15/2.
40 Rachel Redgrave to Michael Redgrave, no date [6 June 1960], THM/31/3/6/15/4.
41 Rachel Redgrave to Michael Redgrave, 7 June 1960, THM/31/3/6/15/3.
42 Lynn Redgrave to Michael Redgrave, no date [June 1960], THM/31/3/6/35/1.
43 Nicholas [?] to Michael Redgrave, no date [6 June 1960], THM/31/3/6/15/4.

The Redgraves were especially concerned that marriage to Welby might put an end to Vanessa's acting career, and that he was looking not only for a new wife but also a new stay-at-home mother for Justin, attracted both by Vanessa's beauty and her 'maternal sweetness'. Her mother urged: 'I only pray we can prevent marriage. I'd give it a few months *if* that, once her eyes are opened after the first flush is over.'[44] Vanessa was not besotted for long and called off the engagement 'for many many reasons'.[45] To her parents it brought 'great relief' and they were glad to see the back of Gavin Welby.[46] Unlike his father, however, young Justin left a good impression on the Redgrave clan: 'His child is angelic. We all loved him.'[47]

During the 1960s Gavin Welby declined into alcoholism. His son recalled: 'It wasn't an easy upbringing. ... He was very affectionate, brilliant intellectually but quite demanding. ... I lived with him but I didn't know him very well.'[48] Elsewhere he described it as 'a very dysfunctional home ... it was pretty rough stuff for many years'.[49] This home environment inevitably took an emotional toll. In an article in December 2000 on the redemption of painful memories, Justin wrote: 'Christmas comes with lots of memories. My recent ones have been very happy, since I was married and part of a family. My childhood ones were the reverse.'[50] One Christmas, for example, Gavin refused to get out of bed, so Justin spent the day by himself looking out of the window and searching for food in an empty fridge.[51] By contrast, the long periods he spent with his Portal grandparents at Blakeney were 'a haven of calm', often in company with his Batten cousins.

---

44   Rachel Redgrave to Michael Redgrave, no date [6 June 1960], THM/31/3/6/15/4.
45   Vanessa Redgrave to Michael Redgrave, no date, THM/31/3/6/45/4.
46   Rachel Redgrave to Michael Redgrave, no date, THM/31/3/6/15/5.
47   Rachel Redgrave to Michael Redgrave, 7 June 1960, THM/31/3/6/15/3.
48   Lewis, 'New Archbishop', p. 1.
49   New Wine London and South East Summer Conference (Justin Welby interviewed by Mark Melluish), 29 July 2013.
50   Justin Welby, 'Thought for the Month', *Southam Parish Church News* [hereafter *SPCN*] (December 2000).
51   *Private Passions* (Justin Welby interviewed by Michael Berkeley), BBC Radio 3, 22 December 2013.

The Portals had a large walled garden, a child's idyll, and a French housekeeper, Malvina, renowned for superb cooking. It was on the Norfolk coast that Justin learned to sail. His grandmother, Iris Portal, was an especially significant early influence. She was a daughter of the Raj, wife of a Lieutenant-Colonel in the Indian Army, younger sister of Rab Butler, a biographer in her later years and lived until the grand age of 97 in 2002.[52] She instilled in Justin a love of politics and history, and was 'merciless about the obligation to serve', priorities which shaped his outlook on life.[53] Amongst his earliest memories, when he was about five years old, was being forced to watch the Budget on television and taken to tea with Winston Churchill. 'There's politics in the blood', he said.[54]

Eton College

Justin Welby's early education was at Gibbs pre-preparatory school in Kensington. In 1964, at the age of eight, he was sent away to boarding school, to St Peter's, an Edwardian preparatory school for boys in Seaford on the Sussex coast. He left little impression upon the school record, apart from a star performance as Nerissa, the waiting-maid in Shakespeare's *Merchant of Venice*, in his final year.[55] Next he moved in 1969 to Eton College near Windsor, England's premier public school. The school was at a low ebb, with a dip in numbers, and the controversial headmaster Anthony Chenevix-Trench was dismissed in July 1970 amidst allegations of administrative incompetence, heavy drinking and a *Private Eye* exposé of his

---

52   'Obituaries: Iris Portal', *Daily Telegraph*, 22 November 2002, p. 29.
53   Interview at New Wine Conference, 29 July 2013.
54   Sam Macrory, 'Archbishop's Move', *Total Politics* (August 2013), p. 62.
55   'Theatricals', *St Peter's, Seaford: The School Magazine* no. 105 (1968), pp. 27–9.

pleasure at beating the boys.[56] He was replaced by Michael McCrum (later Master of Corpus Christi College, Cambridge) who set about restoring Eton's reputation and raising its academic standards. Welby boarded in South Lawn (one of 25 houses at Eton), with about 50 other boys. Many of his housemates were wealthy and went on to careers as investment bankers, stockbrokers, property developers, scientists, surgeons, and army officers. They included minor nobility and members of the Rothschild and Hambro banking dynasties.[57] 'I know I didn't have much money', Welby observed, 'but I don't ever remember thinking everyone else has got so much more. It was clear other people were wealthier than we were. I probably was at the bottom end. But you know, school is school, you just get on with life.'[58] He had no fond memories of Eton, but only of 'the loneliness of being in a crowded boarding school, where you had to be very self-sufficient'.[59] His extracurricular interests were amateur dramatics, including directing plays, the Combined Cadet Force, sailing and rowing, though with typical self-deprecation, he recalled: 'At school I was so obviously average that competitiveness (except in my imagination) was pointless.'[60] His housemaster, Francis Gardner, remembered him as 'a model boy, though not one of great distinction'.[61]

At Eton daily chapel was obligatory, 15 minutes every morning at the start of the working day, either in Lower Chapel (for younger boys) or College Chapel (for senior boys). This involved a Bible reading, prayers and a short hymn, though the majority of pupils merely endured it and

56 Tim Card, *Eton Renewed: A History from 1860 to the Present Day* (London: John Murray, 1994); Mark Peel, *The Land of Lost Content: The Biography of Anthony Chenevix-Trench* (Edinburgh: Pentland, 1996).
57 'Eton Classmates Form a Who's Who of the Great and the Good', *Sunday Telegraph*, 11 November 2012, p. 21.
58 Lewis, 'A Master of Reinvention', p. 6.
59 *Private Passions*, 22 December 2013.
60 Justin Welby, 'Thought for the Month', *SPCN* (July 1996).
61 Cole Moreton, '"You Have No Future in the Church": Justin Welby Was Once Rejected for Ordination, Now He's the Next Archbishop of Canterbury', *Sunday Telegraph*, 11 November 2012, p. 20.

the masters (known in the Eton lexicon as *beaks*) were usually more concerned with checking attendance than with spiritual edification. David Jones, the *conduct* (senior chaplain) in the early 1970s, acknowledged that these morning chapels played little, if any, part in the religious experience of most boys, and with the agreement of the headmaster he instituted an alternative assembly for sixth-formers in the School Hall where they could consider life's big questions more seriously.[62] Chapel was also obligatory at the weekends – 'congregational practice' on Saturdays (hymn-singing, led by the precentor), and a full choral service on Sundays with a visiting preacher (often a bishop or other Anglican dignitary). Welby viewed Eton religion unfavourably. He remembered chapel as a good place to finish schoolwork, like learning French irregular verbs, and the only interesting event he could recall was the day the headmaster fell out of the pulpit. He was, though, fixated by a sermon from the anti-apartheid campaigner Trevor Huddleston (Bishop of Stepney), a man for whom 'the power and the conviction in life came from something beyond anything I knew – he was absolutely mesmeric'.[63]

About 100 Eton boys were confirmed each year, either by the Bishop of Oxford (as diocesan bishop) or the Bishop of Lincoln (as college visitor), and Welby chose to take part. He was prepared by David Jones who remembered him as 'a very quiet and a very modest boy'.[64] Thus Welby stood publicly to confess Christian faith according to the liturgy of the Church of England, though he looked back on this experience as mere religiosity. He 'vaguely assumed there was a God. But I didn't *believe*.'[65] Outside school he seldom attended church, even at

62   Interview with David Jones, 22 January 2014.
63   *Travellers' Tales* (Justin Welby interviewed by Patrick Forbes), Premier Christian Radio, 31 March 2013.
64   Interview with David Jones, 22 January 2014.
65   Charles Moore, 'I Was Embarrassed. It Was Like Getting Measles', *Daily Telegraph*, 13 July 2013, p. 19.

Christmas.[66] As archbishop, writing an imaginary letter to his 14-year-old self, he penned the lines:

> Dear Justin, You are rarely good at anything, a fact you know well and worry about. But don't worry – it does not measure who you are. Keep on dreaming of great things, but learn to live in the present, so that you take steps to accomplish them. Above all, more important than anything, don't wait until you are older to find out about Jesus Christ and his love for you. He is not just a name at Chapel, but a person you can know. Christmas is not a fairy story, but the compelling opening of the greatest drama in history, with you as one of millions of players. Life will often be tough, but you will find more love than you can imagine now.[67]

In April 1973, during his final year of school, Welby and his mother attended a party at the home of a stockbroker friend and Old Etonian, George Nissen, on Chiswick Mall overlooking the River Thames, to watch the annual Oxford and Cambridge boat race. There they met another Old Etonian, Simon Barrington-Ward, an Anglican evangelical clergyman responsible for training missionaries for the Church Missionary Society (CMS) as Principal of Crowther Hall, Birmingham. As the Welbys talked with Barrington-Ward about Justin's uncertain future, it was proposed that the teenager should enrol for a 'gap year' in Kenya with the Youth Service Abroad scheme run by CMS. When Gavin Welby was told of the plans, he strongly resisted the idea – partly fearing for his son's safety in famine-struck East Africa, partly perhaps believing that a Christian mission placement was a waste of time if his son was to get on in the world. Gavin refused to fund the trip, but Jane forced the issue by selling a diamond ring she had inherited from her godmother to enable Justin to travel.[68]

66   Justin Welby, 'How I Came to Christ at Cambridge', *The StAG MAG* (magazine of St Andrew the Great, Cambridge) (January / February 2013).

67   'What Would You Tell Your 14-Year-Old Self?: A *Spectator* Christmas Survey', *Spectator*, 14-28 December 2013, p. 24.

68   Interview with Lady Williams, 13 January 2014.

During his latter teenage years Welby bore a heavier burden for caring for his alcohol-dependent father. Gavin's behavior was increasingly erratic and he could be volatile, irrational, dishonest and prone to shouting. 'It was all very complicated', Justin explained. 'You never knew what was going to happen. The experience of living with a parent who had a drink problem is ... very shaping as to one's views of what human beings are like.'[69] Gavin's wealth had evaporated and he moved from flat to flat in London. On one occasion father and son had to pack their suitcases quickly and do 'a moonlight flit' probably because Gavin had run out of money to pay the rent or was trying to dodge his creditors.[70] Justin discovered later that his father had defaulted on the last two years of his Eton fees. His A level examinations in early summer 1973 coincided with a particularly stressful meltdown in their relationship and as a result he fared badly in his three subjects – History (grade C), English (grade D), and French (grade E). This seemed likely to halt his ambition to study at Cambridge University, though he stayed on at school for an extra term to sit the Cambridge entrance examination in December 1973 and to everyone's surprise was offered a place at Trinity College. His great-uncle, Rab Butler, was by now Master of Trinity, so the college was doubly careful to scrutinise his papers lest there be even a hint of nepotism.

As Welby bid Eton farewell, his housemaster wrote to his grandmother in Norfolk reflecting upon his school career and strength of character:

> I need scarcely say that Justin's success at Trinity has given me a very great deal of pleasure. Throughout his five years at Eton he has shown a brave and conscientious determination, and for much of the time my worry has been that his ambition was outstripping what really appeared to be within his powers. His previous exam results were never very distinguished, and his

---

69   Dominic Lawson, 'So Many Crosses to Bear', *Sunday Times Magazine*, 17 March 2013, p. 25.
70   Moore, 'I Was Embarrassed', p. 19; Interview at New Wine Conference, 29 July 2013.

performance in his A levels was rather modest by the standard of most Cambridge candidates; so I did not really expect him to stand much more than an outside chance of coming up to Trinity's requirements. That he did is thus all the more gratifying. One thing I am sure you realise: it is an achievement for which he has worked very, very hard; not only in the last six months but really throughout his time at Eton (and, dutifully and uncomplainingly, during much of his school holidays).

While I have admired the tenacity with which he has worked, I think more remarkable is the way he has coped with his 'family problems'. In the earlier days at Eton he was almost unaware of the complications in the background of his life; but in the last two years or so they have become ever more acute. I hope it may have been some help to him that he has felt able to talk quite freely about them to me; but I have never felt able to give him much in the way of advice because he has always seemed to know for himself what to do. Indeed, I have been most impressed by his understanding and tact. He has derived encouragement too from David Jones, our chaplain who originally prepared him for Confirmation, and I know David has taken a most deep and sincere interest in all the problems with which Justin has been faced.

I am glad to say that he has always seemed happy at school and he has always had plenty of friends among his contemporaries in my House. I have often wondered, on the other hand, how happy his holidays have been. Obviously he has always enjoyed enormously his visits to Blakeney, and his sailing has been an outstanding joy and a relief from the more serious issues of his life; but his father has never been able to provide for him in London the entertainment and facilities that many boys of his age have been able to enjoy, and even the occasional trips to France have lacked the glamour and companionship that he would have liked. Or so I suspect; but Justin has been much too loyal ever to complain or even to show any dissatisfaction, and for this I greatly respect him. His assignment in Kenya will be his first real moment of freedom, and he ought to be daunted by the prospect of being so far from friendly faces and at tackling a job for which he has had virtually no training; but he has tremendous inner resources, and I have no doubt he will cope with it efficiently and to his own, as well as everyone else's, satisfaction. It will give him the confidence to assert the independence which, now eighteen, he certainly deserves and which by his level-headed commonsense he has undoubtedly earned. Many a boy would have been driven off the rails completely by the problems which Justin has had to face, and I admire enormously the patience and wisdom he has shown in dealing with them.[71]

Soon he was on an aeroplane bound for Africa, his first introduction to a continent he would grow to love.

71   Francis P. E. Gardner to Iris Portal, 27 December 1973, Lady Williams' papers.

Chapter 2

⊸∞⊷

Kenya

Kiburu is a small trading station at a dusty road junction in central Kenya, close to Mount Kenya National Park, about 80 miles north of Nairobi. The settlement was little more than a couple of shops and a few dwellings, but the Anglican Church established a *harambee* school there, a community secondary school for pupils who did not make the grade to enter the better government schools. It taught up to school certificate (equivalent to O level) though many of the pupils were in their early twenties. Although numbers fluctuated considerably during the year, there were typically 160 pupils in four forms, many of whom lived in dormitories on the school compound, and three Kenyan teachers including the headmaster and his deputy. The Church Missionary Society regularly sent volunteer teachers to Kiburu on their Youth Service Abroad scheme, usually in a pair. One of the YSAs placed there during the academic year 1972–73 was David Runcorn, later a prominent Anglican evangelical theologian and author.

Justin Welby flew to Kenya on 6 January 1974, his eighteenth birthday. His fellow YSA at Kiburu, Phil Kelly, had already been there a term and was three years Welby's senior, having just graduated in Latin from Leeds University. They were the only two Europeans in the immediate area and shared a small house on the school compound, built from timber with a *mabati* (corrugated iron) roof. The house had been constructed by a Scandinavian married couple, so there was only one bedroom, and the dining room, sitting room and kitchen were open plan. There was a communal long-drop *choo* (toilet) outside. This was a far cry from the luxuries of Eton College, though the two young men bought a plastic bathtub to improve their comfort.[1] They employed a cook, Mahinda, who also looked after their cleaning and laundry. Welby was responsible for teaching mathematics (even though he had failed his own elementary maths O level at the first attempt) and ran a French club. However, with youthful impatience, he found it difficult to adjust to the administrative disorganisation and lessons which did not keep to schedule, as Kelly reported to his parents: 'somehow the African idea of time is very different from the European. It irritates me, but sends Justin hopping mad.'[2]

Welby made the most of his sojourn in East Africa to explore the region as a tourist. He climbed Mount Kenya, for example, though he felt violently sick at the summit,[3] and visited the Menengai Crater in the Great Rift Valley.[4] His major trek during the Easter Vacation was in the direction of Victoria Falls, on the Zambezi River between Zambia and Rhodesia, though he never reached his goal. With a friend, Ian Harrison, he hitchhiked and bussed across Tanzania, via Arusha, Dodoma, Iringa and Mbeya, but they turned back at the Zambian border at Tunduma because it was too expensive to enter the country.[5] As a consolation, Welby made an impromptu visit to Uganda to the shores of Lake Victoria, through Jinja (where he viewed Owen Falls Dam and the reputed source of the Nile River) to Kampala.[6] During these months, though only a teenager, he also enjoyed meeting some of the British political establishment in Kenya. He was invited to lunch at the Residency in Nairobi by the British High Commissioner, Sir Antony Duff (later Director-General of the security service, MI5, under Margaret Thatcher). There

1   Phil Kelly to Paul and Alison Kelly (his parents), 1 February 1974, Phil Kelly papers.
2   Phil Kelly to Paul and Alison Kelly, 29 March 1974.
3   Justin Welby to Jane Welby, 27 February 1974, Lady Williams' papers.
4   Phil Kelly to Paul and Alison Kelly, 10 May 1974.
5   Justin Welby to Jane Welby, 25 April 1974.
6   Justin Welby to Jane Welby, 2 May 1974.

he also met Sir Anthony Nutting, a former British Minister of State for Foreign Affairs who had famously resigned from the government in 1956 in protest at Anthony Eden's handling of the Suez crisis; and Keith Oakeshott from the Foreign and Commonwealth Office who was on an inspection tour of Saint Helena, Tristan da Cunha and Ascension Island. Welby wrote home that Duff and Nutting 'spent most of Lunch talking about Suez, and being fairly derogatory about Eden, and quite funny about Rab'. He enjoyed travelling in the High Commissioner's chauffeur-driven Daimler Vanden Plas limousine, the largest car in Kenya, even bigger than President Jomo Kenyatta's Mercedes.[7] Kelly commented: 'usefully connected is our man from Blakeney!'[8]

Most significantly, during his months at Kiburu school Welby began to think more deeply about the Christian faith. In later years, when asked to narrate his spiritual history he always looked back to a particular night in Cambridge in October 1975 as his conversion moment, suggesting that in Kenya he had not been a true Christian. Yet Kiburu was a period of spiritual awakening and even of profound Christian dedication, which mirrored his later conversion. The Church Missionary Society discovered that sending young YSAs to Africa could have a major impact on their religious beliefs, though it was a risky strategy. Some English teenagers were impressed by the vibrancy of African Christianity and strengthened in their faith; others experienced such culture shock and isolation from their support networks at home that they abandoned their faith altogether. Kelly was alert to the dangers: 'it is disorientating enough to come out here but to lose one's faith in God, however small, can be a shattering blow. It really is make or break for many of us here.'[9]

There was an Anglican church in the Kiburu school compound which Welby and Kelly dutifully attended most

7   Justin Welby to Jane Welby, 21 February 1974.
8   Phil Kelly to Paul and Alison Kelly, 8 February 1974.
9   Phil Kelly to Paul and Alison Kelly, 10 May 1974.

Sundays, though the liturgy and preaching was in Kikuyu so they understood almost nothing. The traditional services appeared far from vibrant. To the English visitors they seemed long and dull, led by a catechist in robes, reading from the *Book of Common Prayer* in Kikuyu, with men and women separated on different sides of the church.[10] Welby had a better experience visiting Nairobi Cathedral where the service was in English: 'The congregation was large, and multiracial, which was pleasant to see. Although the sermon was not exactly inspiring, the service was very enjoyable.'[11] On another occasion he and Kelly were guests of honour at the laying of a foundation stone for a new church at Karimaini.[12] It was not so much African Christianity which made an impact upon Welby, however, but the experience of sharing a small house with his fellow YSA. He was 'very impressed' by Kelly and found 'his quality of life very striking'.[13] Kelly himself was a new Christian, having been converted as an undergraduate through the ministry of St Matthias, Burley, in Leeds, a charismatic Anglican church. Kelly began each morning with half an hour of 'quiet time' to pray and read his Bible, and for this he colonised the bedroom, so Welby was forced to spend the time quietly in the living room. Amongst the books on the shelf were a Bible, a few Christian paperbacks including Dennis Bennett's *The Holy Spirit and You* (1971), some old *National Geographics* and a copy of Walter Bagehot's *The English Constitution* (1867).[14] Welby showed no interest in the Christian literature and instead whiled away the hours with Bagehot, assuming it would be 'less boring than the Bible', but after reading the tome a couple of times he picked up the Bible.[15]

10   Interview with Phil Kelly, 23 January 2014.
11   Justin Welby to Jane Welby, 2 May 1974.
12   Justin Welby to Jane Welby, 21 March 1974.
13   HTB Leadership Conference (Justin Welby interviewed by Nicky Gumbel), 13 May 2013.
14   Interview with Phil Kelly, 23 January 2014.
15   HTB Leadership Conference, 13 May 2013.

In later years Welby described this emerging interest in Christianity in different ways. He said he 'sensed there was a God and that he was somewhere around', but was unsure what to do about it.[16] He recalled: 'everyone around me clearly knew this Jesus person in a way that I didn't. That's my earliest recollection of something impinging on my consciousness.'[17] Nevertheless Kiburu also gave Welby the opportunity to reflect on his family relationships and the future direction of his life. Although he had escaped from his father's orbit, the letters from home were often abrasive and upsetting. In Kelly's words, Gavin Welby was 'a fairly highly strung man' and after a spate of 'frantic letters' from Kensington, Justin had to resort to telling his father that he would not reply if they continued.[18] Amidst this emotional duress from home, there was trauma at school. On Sunday afternoon, 2 June 1974, the two YSA volunteers received a report that a student in Form I, Bosco Karumba, who had only joined that term, had committed suicide by hanging himself in the woods within the school compound. They were the only teachers on site, so, despite their youthful inexperience, were forced to take charge. As they cut down the body they tried to keep up their courage with gallows humour by singing the Eton boating song, with its lines 'Swing swing together, with your bodies between your knees'.[19] Kelly explained to his parents:

> Justin and I, since I was on duty, had the melancholy task of dealing with the affair. The police came at about six, found no conclusive evidence for a motive, took his belongings, statements etc, and when the photography unit failed to turn up they took his body to Kerugoya hospital mortuary at about 10 p.m. All the while the students followed the actions of myself, Justin and the police from a safe distance, mortally horrified at the whole thing. Well, I can't say that I slept too

16 'An Evening with Justin and Caroline Welby' (interview with John Mumford), Trent Vineyard, Nottingham, 27 January 2013, www.vineyardchurches.org.uk.
17 Travellers' Tales, 31 March 2013.
18 Phil Kelly to Paul and Alison Kelly, 29 March and 10 May 1974.
19 Interview with Phil Kelly, 23 January 2014.

well myself during this past week. Sospeter [the headmaster] and I had to go and identify the body at the mortuary the next day ...[20]

Perhaps this disturbing ordeal led Welby to dwell more deeply on eternal questions. A fortnight later he recommitted his life to Christ, as Kelly reported:

> Justin is trying to write a letter to his Dad, a rather special letter in which he is hoping to put things right between them – relations have never been very good. A rather strange and heart warming story comes out. Justin says that for the last eleven months or so his Christian faith has been in decline so much so that a fortnight ago he reckons that he was more agnostic than Christian. But he felt that I had got something which he hadn't so he began praying again in his morning quiet times and a couple of days ago re-dedicated his life and accepted Christ as Lord, since when he has felt much better and also had the growing feeling to write to his Dad about their mutual relations. This is all a little overwhelming for me. I have certainly not felt as if I had the Spirit of love and joy bubbling over within me recently, but evidently I *have* been used in a most unexpected way to bring Justin to a deeper commitment. So I rejoice and feel slightly, no, very small at the same time – I have such little faith yet here am I being used by the Almighty for His work. I had practically forgotten what it was like.[21]

That week the two YSAs tried to start a Christian Union at the school, though there was a lack of interest amongst the students. Welby's moment of Christian rededication at Kiburu slipped from his memory in later years. In August 1974 he flew home to England and to the absorbing entertainments of undergraduate life, pushing questions of faith far from his mind. It was to be his conversion in Cambridge, not in Kenya, which formed the dominant narrative, with Kiburu remembered only as a staging post on the journey to full faith.

---

20   Phil Kelly to Paul and Alison Kelly, 7 June 1974.
21   Phil Kelly to Paul and Alison Kelly, 21 June 1974.

Chapter 3

---⊗⊗⊗---

Cambridge

Trinity College was the largest and wealthiest college within the University of Cambridge, boasting royal connections and a fistful of Noble Prize winners. Prince Charles was a student there until 1970 and the vast majority of the student body was drawn from public schools. Of the 206 undergraduates admitted in Michaelmas Term 1974, 14 were from Eton.[1] Like many other colleges it remained a male-only preserve, admitting women undergraduates for the first time in 1978. For Justin Welby, Trinity was an obvious choice because his great-uncle, Baron Butler, had been elected as Master in 1965 when he retired from the House of Commons. Welby wanted to be a barrister so he began a degree in law, though perhaps it was more his father's ambition than his own. He enjoyed constitutional and international law, which both had political dimensions, but found the more technical disciplines like torts and contracts boring, and achieved only a third class in the examinations at the end of both his first and second years. Therefore he switched to modern history, with an emphasis on economics, which meant staying in Cambridge for a fourth year and led ultimately to the award of an upper-second-class degree.[2] Beyond academics, however, it was a period of life changing decisions. At Cambridge Welby formed several life-long friendships and met his future wife. He also came clearly and decisively to Christian faith and was pushed forward into Christian leadership.

---

1   I am grateful to Jonathan Smith (Trinity College archivist) for these figures.
2   *The Historical Register of the University of Cambridge, Supplement 1976–80* (Cambridge: Cambridge University Press, 1984), p. 502.

Student Evangelism

Student Christianity in Cambridge was vibrant. The largest of all the student societies was the Cambridge Inter-Collegiate Christian Union (CICCU), an evangelical movement which connected Christian groups in all the colleges and was affiliated to the Inter-Varsity Fellowship. The CICCU celebrated its centenary in 1977 and its official history is the tale of enthusiastic student witness in the face of secularism and the threat of liberal theology.[3] During the fundamentalist controversies of the 1910s, the CICCU seceded from the Student Christian Movement and its evangelical doctrinal basis continued to affirm the supreme authority and infallibility of Scripture, the wrath of God at human sinfulness, the sacrificial and substitutionary death of Christ, the work of the Holy Spirit in granting repentance and faith, and the expectation of Christ's 'personal return'. Within each of the colleges there were Bible study groups, prayer meetings and evangelistic events. Each weekend the CICCU invited one of Britain's leading evangelical preachers to deliver a Bible exposition on Saturday evening in the Union Society debating chamber, followed by an evangelistic address on Sunday evening at Holy Trinity church. In the mid-1970s these were typically attended by 400 students each Saturday and 200–300 each Sunday.

In the months before Welby's arrival in Cambridge there was a flurry of Christian conversions amongst the undergraduates. When David Watson (vicar of St Michael-le-Belfrey in York) preached in November 1973 two dozen professed faith in a single day. Particularly significant was the CICCU mission week in February 1974, called 'Christ Alive', led by David MacInnes, an Anglican clergyman and evangelist. Among the new converts at Trinity College were two Old Etonians a year ahead of Welby – Nicky Lee and Nicky Gumbel, best friends

---

3   Oliver Barclay, *Whatever Happened to the Jesus Lane Lot?* (Leicester: Inter-Varsity Press, 1977). See further, David Goodhew, 'The Rise of the Cambridge Inter-Collegiate Christian Union, 1910–1971', *Journal of Ecclesiastical History* vol. 54 (January 2003), pp. 62–88.

and room-mates. Lee and his girlfriend, Sila Callander, were deeply struck by MacInnes' address on the cross of Christ, as she later testified:

> It was a revelation to me. I kept saying to myself, 'Why did nobody ever tell me before *why* Jesus died on the cross?' It was as if everything I had ever known fitted together, not just intellectually, but also emotionally and spiritually. Everything made sense when the cross was explained.[4]

When they informed Gumbel they had become Christians he was horrified, though he did agree to meet over lunch the next day with MacInnes who spoke of the transforming power of 'a personal relationship with Jesus'.[5] Gumbel began to read through the New Testament in his old school Bible:

> I was completely gripped by what I read. I had read it before and it had meant virtually nothing to me. This time it came alive and I could not put it down. It had a ring of truth about it. I knew as I read it that I had to respond because it spoke so powerfully to me. Very shortly afterwards I came to put my faith in Jesus Christ.[6]

Lee and Gumbel were two of the so-called 'five Nickys' amongst the zealous young Christians within the CICCU, also including Nicky Campbell, Nicky Hills and Nicky Wells. Four of the five had been at Eton together. Another new believer in this wide circle of friends was Ken Costa from Johannesburg, a graduate student at Queens' College. The new converts had a passionate desire to bring others to faith in Christ. Charles Moore, another Old Etonian at Trinity College and later editor of *The Spectator* and the *Daily Telegraph*, recalled that 'Two of the Nickys used to invite me to hearty and delicious teas (evangelicals love buns and crumpets) and talk to me about Jesus, sometimes playing me tapes of sermons by prominent

4   Nicky and Sila Lee, *The Marriage Book* (London: Alpha International, 2000), p. 7.
5   Jonathan Aitken, *Heroes and Contemporaries* (London: Continuum, 2006), p. 226.
6   Nicky Gumbel, *Questions of Life* (Eastbourne: Kingsway, 1993), p. 70.

preachers.'[7] Gumbel carried pockets full of evangelistic tracts to distribute to all and sundry.[8]

Into this environment Welby arrived fresh from Kenya in October 1974, and amongst his new friends were several in the Christian Union. During his first year he remained apparently unmoved by their attempts at evangelism. He attended college chapel occasionally, but only for the music. When John Hamilton, an Anglican ordinand at Ridley Hall theological college and Trinity graduate, challenged Welby to think more deeply about the implications of following Jesus Christ, Welby beat a hasty retreat.[9] He was far more attracted to rowing, as cox of the Trinity first boat, which absorbed most of his energies, as described by one of his crew members:

> He was an expert cox and was in the last four for Boat Race selection. He had nerves of steel, which he used to lure a chasing boat in the Bumps into the bank by deliberately cornering at the last possible moment and not affording the chasing boat enough time to correct its path. He drove the crew hard, as was necessary, but drove himself hard too: while we ate large muscle-building meals together in the evenings, he, as cox, had to sit with us (team building!) but make do with the odd lettuce leaf. In addition, he was sent on runs in high summer wearing a waterproof jacket in order to sweat off as much further weight as possible.[10]

The start of Welby's second year was a crucial turning point. On the first Sunday evening of term, 12 October 1975, he agreed to go with Nicky Hills to the CICCU evangelistic address at Holy Trinity church. The sermon was on the question 'Who is Jesus?' by John Gladwin (Tutor at St John's College, Durham, and later Bishop of Chelmsford), though

7   Charles Moore, 'Why It Needs an Alpha Male to Save the Church of England', *Daily Telegraph*, 10 November 2012, p. 28.
8   Aitken, *Heroes and Contemporaries*, p. 227.
9   *Travellers' Tales*, 31 March 2013.
10   Letter from Charlie Arbuthnot, 11 December 2013.

Welby was unmoved.[11] In fact he was 'bored out of my mind. It was probably very good but didn't hit the button with me.'[12] They returned to Hills' rooms at Trinity (K2, New Court) to talk further about the Christian faith, as Welby remembered:

> I was convinced that if I became a Christian all the things I enjoyed doing I'd have to stop doing. He showed me that the heart of Christian faith is nothing to do with rules and regulations, it is all about a person called Jesus who died for me on the cross so that all my sins could be forgiven and the barrier between me and God could be broken down.[13]

> He explained it to me, what Jesus did for me on the cross, this was out of love for me, it was because of me – and everyone else, but me. And I suddenly saw the grace, the freedom, the free giving of God, which meant that to follow him would not be constraining but would be the most ultimately liberating thing I could ever do. That's where the cross led me.[14]

Hills read some words of Jesus from the Bible, 'Behold, I stand at the door and knock; if anyone hears my voice and opens the door, I will come in to him and eat with him, and he with me' (Revelation 3:20), and then asked, 'So what now?' Welby replied, 'I think I need to pray.' It was about ten minutes to midnight. The archbishop recalled:

> I opened my life to Jesus, and was aware of something changing completely ... There was someone there. When I said, 'Come into my life, be in charge of my life', clearly something happened. God answered. It wasn't very emotional – I didn't burst into tears, or fall over or anything. It was just I was very clear that something had changed.[15]

---

11   For details of the CICCU preachers in Michaelmas Term 1975, see CICCU Executive Minutes, 6 June and 6–11 September 1975, Cambridge University Library, MS Add 8722 A2/9.
12   *Travellers' Tales*, 31 March 2013.
13   HTB Home Focus (Justin and Caroline Welby interviewed by Nicky Gumbel), 27 July 2013.
14   *Songs of Praise* (Justin Welby interviewed by Bill Turnbull), BBC 1, 24 March 2013.
15   *Travellers' Tales*, 31 March 2013.

Elsewhere he testified: 'There was a long run-up to it, but the surrender to God was a moment ... like the world changing, like someone I'd never known coming into the room and being there. It was a world in which there was a presence and a purpose I had never known'.[16] Hills felt that Welby was 'crying out to be convinced' and that even before their conversation that night he was already 'almost converted', 'fruit ripe for the picking'.[17] Through this conversion experience the cross of Christ was fixed as central in Welby's own spiritual narrative as the focal point of the Christian life, and was a theme on which he often dwelt and spoke passionately in later years. He wrote, for example:

> The cross is the moment of deepest encounter and most radical change. God is crucified – my Friend died – in some way, for me. Merely writing or reading these words together in one sentence is overwhelming. A person caught by the implications of the cross will be a person who has found the fullness of the life which is the gift of God.[18]

A couple of weeks after his conversation with Hills, Welby was by himself in his room reading chapter three of John's Gospel. When he reached verse 16 ('for God so loved the world that he gave his only Son that all those who believe in him should not perish but have eternal life') he had an 'overwhelming sense' that he was 'personally, individually loved by God'.[19] Spontaneously, he began to speak in 'tongues'. He had no idea what to make of this supernatural prayer language but David Watson was in Cambridge a few days later and explained more to him about its significance for the Christian life.

---

16   Lawson, 'So Many Crosses to Bear', p. 27.
17   Interview with Nick Hills, 23 January 2014.
18   Justin Welby, 'Foreword', in Graham Tomlin, *Looking Through the Cross: The Archbishop of Canterbury's Lent Book 2014* (London: Bloomsbury, 2013), p. viii.
19   'Facing the Canon: J. John in Conversation with Archbishop Justin Welby' (video recording), 13 March 2014.

Bash Camps

As a young Christian, Welby was connected into a vast evangelical network. With many of his Trinity friends he attended the Round church in Cambridge where the vicar, Mark Ruston, a bachelor in his early sixties, had a particular ministry to students. Ruston was described by his friend, Maurice Wood (Bishop of Norwich), as 'the Charles Simeon of our generation'.[20] The Prayer Book services deliberately imitated the style of a public school chapel, a familiar environment for most students, and the Sunday morning preacher at the Round was usually the same man invited by the CICCU that weekend. Jonathan Fletcher, Ruston's curate 1972–76, also invested much of his time in 'personal work' with students. For example, after Gumbel's conversion Fletcher met with him at least every week for a year, then every fortnight in the second year and every month in the third.[21]

Much of Welby's early grounding in Christian doctrine was gained through the 'Bash camp' network. E. J. H. Nash, affectionately known as 'Bash', was an Anglican clergyman appointed by Scripture Union in 1932 to work especially with public school boys.[22] His strategy was to evangelise the social elite because he knew a high proportion of Britain's future leaders would be educated at those schools. A regular pattern of summer camps (or houseparties) was established at Clayesmore School in the small Dorset village of Iwerne Minster for boys from the top 30 schools in the country; with additional camps at Lymington in Hampshire for boys from the 'second tier' of public schools, and at Rushmore in Dorset for girls. They adopted a military terminology once popular in the early twentieth century – Bash was known as

---

20   Christopher Ash, Mary Davis and Bob White (eds), *Persistently Preaching Christ: Fifty Years of Bible Ministry in a Cambridge Church* (Fearn, Ross-shire: Mentor, 2012), p. 152.

21   Ash, Davis and White, *Persistently Preaching Christ*, p. 155; *Dear Friends: Selected Writings of Jonathan Fletcher* (London: Lost Coin, 2013), p. 14.

22   John Eddison (ed.), *Bash: A Study in Spiritual Power* (Basingstoke: Marshall, Morgan and Scott, 1983).

'commandant', his deputy as 'adjutant', and the leaders as 'officers'. The camps instilled a disciplined approach to the Christian life, with a particular emphasis on sound doctrine and daily personal devotions (a 'quiet time' for Bible reading and prayer). Bash's teaching focused on the simplicity of the gospel, which he summarised as ABC – Admit your need as a sinner, Believe that Christ died on the cross in your place, Come to Christ in repentance and faith.[23] He retired from overall leadership in 1968, replaced by David Fletcher (older brother of Jonathan Fletcher), but remained involved at Iwerne until the late 1970s.

The Bash camp ministry extended to undergraduates, especially at Cambridge and Oxford, where new converts like Nicky Gumbel and Justin Welby were mentored. As Old Etonians they were invited to Iwerne initially as 'senior campers', a category invented for those who were no longer schoolboys but not yet equipped to be 'officers'. Senior campers were responsible for menial chores like serving at tables, washing dishes, cleaning bathrooms and lavatories and sweeping corridors, alongside which they received Bible teaching. David Watson described his own experience as a senior camper, peeling potatoes and scrubbing pots and pans, as a vital early lesson that humble service was the basis of all Christian ministry.[24] At its peak in 1977, there were 285 boys at camp and 139 senior campers. By the early 1980s over 7,000 boys had passed through Iwerne camps alone.[25] Many of the leading Anglican evangelical ministers in the second half of the twentieth century were Bash campers, including John Stott, Dick Lucas, Timothy Dudley-Smith, Michael Green, David MacInnes, David Sheppard, Maurice Wood, Henry Chadwick, Mark Ruston, Julian Charley, John Collins, Hugh Palmer, Mark Ashton, Paul Perkin, John Coles, William

---

23   Dick Knight, 'The Speaker', in Eddison, *Bash*, pp. 50–1.
24   David Watson, *You Are My God: An Autobiography* (London: Hodder and Stoughton, 1983), pp. 33–4.
25   Richard Rhodes-James, 'The Pioneer', in Eddison, *Bash*, pp. 24–5, 27.

Taylor and numerous others. One diocesan bishop went so far as to say that Bash had 'done more to change the face of the Church of England than anyone else this century'.[26] Parts of Gumbel's Alpha Course had their roots in the basic gospel foundations provided by Iwerne. Welby was involved in the camps as an undergraduate and again as a businessman and theological college student in the 1980s and early 1990s. They laid particular emphasis on training young leaders, giving them confidence to teach the Bible and lead others to faith in Jesus Christ.

During Welby's first months as a Christian he was discipled by Nicky Hills, also a Bash camper, who met with him every week to study the Bible together. He also formed a close bond with Charlie Arbuthnot, another Old Etonian and stroke of the Trinity first boat, who had been converted shortly before going up to Cambridge. These young friends were eager evangelists. For example, Welby and Arbuthnot spent many hours talking with James Behrens, also an Old Etonian and a nominal Jew, and invited him to the CICCU evangelistic addresses on Sunday evenings in Michaelmas Term 1975, in the weeks immediately after Welby's own conversion. The address on 30 November was by Gervais Angel (lecturer at Trinity College, Bristol) who gave ten reasons why he believed in the resurrection of Jesus, which left Behrens still sceptical. Nevertheless, the following morning before lectures Welby visited Behrens who asked him a few questions and then announced he was ready to become a Christian, so Welby led him in a prayer of commitment. Welby and Arbuthnot cautioned Behrens that his new evangelical faith might be undermined by the Trinity College chaplains, so they introduced him instead to the Round church and Bash camps.[27] Likewise in February 1977, Welby and Arbuthnot invited Michael Reiss, another member of the Trinity first boat, to the CICCU mission addresses by John Stott. Reiss had been

26   Quoted in Ian Dobbie, 'The Leader', in Eddison, *Bash*, p. 69.
27   Interview with James Behrens, 24 February 2014.

raised in a secular family but found that Stott's expositions of the Christian gospel made sense and he put his faith in Christ.[28]

Holy Trinity Brompton

During the vacations, when home in Kensington, Welby began to attend Holy Trinity Brompton (HTB), where he had been baptised as a baby. He was particularly attracted by the ministry of Sandy Millar, curate from 1976, a former barrister and a pioneer of the emerging charismatic movement. Several of his Cambridge friends, like Gumbel and Costa, joined the church after they graduated and moved to jobs in the City of London as barristers or businessmen. But the conservative evangelical leadership at the Round church and Bash camps was cautious about charismatic theology, indeed sometimes vocally hostile. Therefore in 1977, in common with several of his student friends, Welby migrated from the Round to St Matthew's church on the outskirts of Cambridge where the vicar, Sidney Sims, was more sympathetic.[29]

It was through HTB that Welby met his future wife. At the start of his third year as a student, in the autumn of 1976, he was introduced to Caroline Eaton, aged 18, who was just beginning a classics degree at Newnham College in Cambridge. She was the daughter of a stockbroker and, like Welby, was raised in Kensington, at Langham Mansions, Earls Court. Caroline's older sister, Mary Eaton, had become a Christian in August 1973 at a convention called SPRE-E (short for 'Spiritual Re-Emphasis'), a training week in evangelism and the arts organised by the Billy Graham Evangelistic Association and Campus Crusade for Christ, attended by 11,600 delegates, 70 per cent of whom were under the age of 21. Each evening

28   Interview with Michael Reiss, 11 January 2013.
29   Aitken, *Heroes and Contemporaries*, p. 228.

thousands more young people from across London were invited to 'Jesus is the King' rallies at Earls Court, where Billy Graham issued a call to Christian commitment, and Mary Eaton was one of many who responded.[30] Caroline recalled the impact of her sister's new faith:

> I saw a huge change in her, and that was very attractive. What I understood from what I saw was that Jesus was her friend. As I came to the point of going to University I was just very nervous, and I wanted to know that I had somebody who was going to be with me whatever, through big decisions and little decisions. And I knew I had to ask Jesus into my life.[31]

Mary took Caroline to a new Bible study group at HTB, run by Sandy Millar and his wife Annette in their home in Onslow Square, and there Caroline committed her life to Christ in September 1976. The Millars asked Welby to look after her in Cambridge so he invited her to one of his regular Sunday evening supper parties at his rooms in Trinity College before the CICCU evangelistic address. Their first meeting was thus a meal with 11 other young men. A few months later Justin and Caroline began dating.

There were other significant changes in Welby's family relationships at the same period. In March 1975 his mother was remarried at Kensington registry office to Charles Williams, an investment banker and managing director of Barings, who in 1985 was raised to the peerage as Baron Williams of Elvel. Williams' father, N. P. Williams, was a noted Anglican theologian in the early twentieth century and Lady Margaret Professor of Divinity at Oxford 1927–43.[32] Welby and Williams hit it off immediately, and Williams was impressed by the young man's 'ruthless streak' which he thought could do much good if directed in the right way.[33] Meanwhile, in March 1977, Welby's complex and difficult

30   David Coomes, *SPRE-E '73* (London: Coverdale House, 1973).
31   HTB Home Focus, 27 July 2013.
32   Eric Kemp, *N. P. Williams* (London: SPCK, 1954).
33   Interview with Lady Williams, 13 January 2014.

relationship with his alcoholic father suddenly ended. Gavin Welby was found dead in his Kensington flat after suffering a heart attack, aged 66. Justin's first reaction was 'relief ... liberation', and then guilt for feeling that way.[34] He reflected: 'It took me a long time after he died to ... think back over my time with him with any equanimity. It had just been all so painful. It was about twenty years before I could go through his scrapbooks without just finding it intolerably painful and for reasons I probably can't analyse.'[35] Gavin's funeral at HTB was taken by Andy Arbuthnot, Charlie's father. Justin was the sole beneficiary of the estate, valued at £102,000.[36]

One of HTB's mission partners was Jackie Pullinger, a young Christian who had been working since 1966 in the notorious Walled City of Kowloon, a contested tract of land between Hong Kong and China. Her story was told in *Chasing the Dragon* (1980), a charismatic classic and international bestseller. It recounts Pullinger's ministry among triad gangs and heroin addicts, gambling and opium dens, prisoners and child prostitutes. She laid particular emphasis upon the gifts of the Holy Spirit, such as prophecy, 'words of knowledge', miraculous healings and especially 'speaking in tongues'. She had witnessed many addicts withdraw pain-free from heroin, without medication, when they were converted to Christ and began to 'pray in the Spirit'. In February 1978 Pullinger visited England and Ken Costa arranged for her to spend a weekend in Cambridge amongst the undergraduates. Costa asked Welby and Arbuthnot to organise it, and they soon roped in Michael Stockwood (Gonville and Caius College) and Nick James (Sidney Sussex College). These four young men committed to praying together every evening at 10 p.m. for six weeks before Pullinger's visit. They did not advertise their prayer meeting but news spread by word of mouth and

34   Justin Welby and Caroline Welby, 'Grief', New Wine seminar 2006, audio recording.
35   Lawson, 'So Many Crosses to Bear', p. 25.
36   Will of Gavin Welby (13 October 1964), proved at London, 20 July 1977.

before long there were 40 people praying regularly, 10 or 12 each night.[37] Arbuthnot explained:

> All we knew about Jackie was that she was fluent in all the gifts of the Spirit and all we knew about ourselves was that we weren't. So the weekend was likely to be unnerving unless we learnt fast. ... So we met daily and agreed on two ground rules: (1) no one would lead except the Holy Spirit and (2) if anyone felt led to use any spiritual gift, they must do so – we needed to learn. Over the next few weeks, the meeting grew to around a dozen people and there was a flow of prophecy, tongues with interpretations, pictures etc. – all suggesting that God would pour out his Spirit in abundance over the weekend.[38]

Pullinger spoke at various events at Trinity College, Caius College, Newnham College (at Caroline Eaton's invitation), St Matthew's church and at a main meeting with 120 students in an upper room of the Henry Martyn Hall, attached to Holy Trinity church. Her portrayal of the Spirit-filled life had a profound effect upon Welby. 'Countless people were filled with the Holy Spirit and started speaking in tongues', Arbuthnot recalled, 'a number of people were healed and a handful converted. The prophetic pictures had certainly been accurate and we wondered for a while if Cambridge was on the brink of revival.'[39] The Pentecost symbolism of 120 people in an upper room praying in tongues, much like the New Testament church (Acts 1–2), was not lost on the participants. Pullinger concluded: 'I was thrilled that the students in a missionary hall received the power of the Spirit to preach good news to the poor.'[40]

Although Welby no longer attended the Round church, he lodged for his final year in Cambridge with Mark Ruston at the Round church vicarage, 37 Jesus Lane. Decades later the archbishop reflected upon the 'extraordinary privilege' of his year with Ruston and its impact on his young Christian life:

37   Information from Michael Stockwood, 10 April 2014.
38   Letter from Charlie Arbuthnot, 11 December 2013.
39   Letter from Charlie Arbuthnot, 11 December 2013.
40   Letter from Jackie Pullinger, 20 February 2014.

Mark was someone whose personal holiness shone out in every aspect of his life. ... We prayed together regularly, talked together a great deal, and I was continually inspired by him to seek to follow Christ more closely. He had a profound consciousness of his own fallibility and sinfulness combined with a deep assurance of the grace of Christ, and the two together gave one a real sense of what it was for someone to live with their life consumed with love for Jesus and for those around. ... He was not quick to take against people but, on the contrary, sought to hear and see the best even in those with whom he disagreed profoundly. He was above all a person whose spiritual life in the study of scripture and in personal prayer flowed from an intimate walk with Jesus Christ.

Welby explained that his years in Cambridge were of foundational significance in his life, because he came to faith, was grounded in 'a clear and simple understanding of the Gospel', and was exhorted to lifelong faithfulness to Christ.[41]

41   Welby, 'How I Came to Christ at Cambridge'.

Chapter 4

Career and Calling

The possibility of ordination in the Church of England was Welby's first instinct for life after university. Within a few months of his conversion he sensed a call to Christian ministry. With three friends – Charlie Arbuthnot, James Behrens and Chris McGowan – he hiked in July 1976 for 17 days across the Highlands of Scotland from Kyle of Lochalsh to Montrose. One morning after breakfast and a time of prayer in the mountains, Arbuthnot asked what God had been saying, to which Welby replied, 'God's told me I'm going to be a Bible teacher.'[1] The following December 1976 Welby and Behrens attended the 'Islington Week', organised by the Church Pastoral Aid Society, designed to give evangelical students from Cambridge and Oxford a brief taste of parish life in inner-city north London. They were taught about vocation to ordained ministry, given an opportunity to preach, and lodged with local clergy to experience vicarage life at first hand. Behrens was sent to St Stephen's, Canonbury Road.[2] Welby and Graham Kings (an undergraduate at Hertford College, Oxford) stayed in the chilly vicarage at St Mary Magdalene's, Holloway Road, but Welby left Islington convinced that he was not suited to be a clergyman.[3]

1   Interview with Charlie Arbuthnot, 13 December 2012.
2   Interview with James Behrens, 24 February 2014.
3   Welby, 'How I Came to Christ at Cambridge'; information from Graham Kings, 24 March 2013. For an earlier description of the Islington Week, see 'On the Hard Pavements of Islington', *Church of England Newspaper*, 16 December 1966, p. 7.

Elf Aquitaine

Unsure where to turn, Welby initially considered the diplomatic service, but soon abandoned the idea. His stepfather had business contacts in Paris, so he was offered an interview with Société Nationale Elf Aquitaine, a large state-owned French oil company. The opportunity 'just seemed too good to miss'.[4] Elf Aquitaine, Welby explained, had

> a major row with their English subsidiary and decided they wanted to employ a Brit. I think there were two reasons for this – firstly they wanted to study the species and try to understand it, and secondly, they wanted to train someone up to think like a Frenchman and go back to the UK and be useful rather than troublemaking.[5]

So with no knowledge of finance, and no French beyond A level, Welby found himself in central Paris from September 1978, living in an apartment on Rue Pierre Lescot and beginning intensive language study. It was meant to be an 18-month placement but turned into five years, securing finance for Elf's international projects. He described his first boss, Kjell Skjevesland, as 'a larger than life character. He had a flair for his job, but was rather chaotic. There was no administration, and little communication. It was enjoyable to work for him although not efficient, and there was a steady stream of crises.'[6] The Elf finance department were nicknamed 'sharks' and Welby was quickly given significant levels of responsibility, for example in finding $2 billion in May 1980 for the hostile acquisition of Kerr-McGee, an American oil and uranium giant (stopped at the last minute by United States government intervention). His colleague, Thomas Knutsen, described the ethos of the department: 'It was very challenging but we were young and the sky was the limit. I

---

4   *Travellers' Tales*, 31 March 2013.
5   'Meet the Dean Designate', *Liverpool Cathedral Life* [hereafter *LCL*] no. 47 (June 2007), p. 3.
6   Justin Welby, 'Hope Springs Eternal', *Chilvers Coton Pew Sheet* (13 September 1992).

don't think I've been more impressed with a brain than I was with Justin's.'[7] Elf had a stake, with other international oil companies, in the Bonny LNG project, a multi-billion-dollar scheme to liquefy natural gas from the oil and gas fields in the Niger Delta, strategically based at a plant on Bonny Island near Port Harcourt. As an alternate member on the finance committee for the project, Welby flew frequently to Nigeria, though the meetings took place in Lagos and he did not visit the Niger Delta in person until 20 years later. The Bonny LNG project collapsed following the military coup in 1983 before ground was broken or contracts signed.

Welby's employment by Elf coincided, it was later revealed, with a period of bribery, embezzlement and intimidation by company officials as they tried to protect their financial interests across Africa and elsewhere. When the scale of malpractice surfaced in the 1990s it led to one of the longest corruption investigations in France's history. Elf executives were accused of paying bribes to foreign governments and siphoning off at least £200 million from the company coffers to fund their own lavish lifestyles. Of the 37 defendants, 31 were convicted, and a dozen were jailed.[8] André Tarallo, the senior director in charge of African operations during Welby's time with the organisation, was sentenced to four years in prison. When Welby was appointed as Archbishop of Canterbury, the *Mail on Sunday* tried unsuccessfully to link him to the Elf scandal, hinting that his later work in Nigeria promoting reconciliation was 'a form of atonement for the sins of Elf and the other major oil companies'. But Welby robustly refuted the allegations, stating that it was 'absurd given my youth and lack of seniority' to think he was responsible for Elf's strategy or knew anything about its dubious practices.[9] Elsewhere he explained: 'Obviously I read with some fascination later about

7   George Arbuthnott, 'The Archbishop and the Oil Sharks', *Mail on Sunday*, 10 March 2013, pp. 32–3.
8   'Elf Oil Chiefs Jailed in £200m Fraud Scandal', *Times*, 13 November 2003, p. 18.
9   Arbuthnott, 'The Archbishop and the Oil Sharks'.

Elf's corruption ... but when you were part of the international finance team you didn't know anything about that. That was all handled by people high up who were doing this stuff. I knew nothing about it.'[10]

Nationwide Festival of Light

In June 1979 Welby proposed to Caroline Eaton, after her final examinations at Cambridge. She spent their few months of engagement, between graduation and wedding, working as a typist for the Nationwide Festival of Light (NFOL), a campaign organisation which sought to defend Britain's Judeo-Christian moral heritage.[11] Launched in 1971, the movement's purpose was summarised by Eddy Stride (rector of Christ Church, Spitalfields and chairman of the executive committee) as 'to actively promote the values of human dignity expressed in the Biblical view of family life'.[12] NFOL campaigned on a wide range of issues, and the bulletin which announced Eaton's wedding to Welby was dominated by articles on pornography, obscenity, family breakdown, prostitution, abortion, homosexuality, the cinema and television.[13] The director, Raymond Johnston, was an Anglican evangelical layman and a former lecturer in education at the University of Newcastle upon Tyne, who brought to NFOL what its first

---

10　Lawson, 'So Many Crosses to Bear', p. 27.

11　On the NFOL, see John Capon, *And There Was Light: The Story of the Nationwide Festival of Light* (London: Lutterworth, 1972); Flo Dobbie, *Land Aflame!* (London: Hodder and Stoughton, 1972); Amy Whipple, 'Speaking for Whom? The 1971 Festival of Light and the Search for the "Silent Majority"', *Contemporary British History* vol. 24 (2010), pp. 319–39; Matthew Grimley, 'Anglican Evangelicals and Anti-Permissiveness: The Nationwide Festival of Light 1971–1983', in Andrew Atherstone and John Maiden (eds), *Evangelicalism and the Church of England in the Twentieth Century: Reform, Resistance and Renewal* (Woodbridge: Boydell, 2014), pp. 183–205.

12　NFOL Executive Committee Minutes, 21 December 1976 (in possession of Penny Howell).

13　*Nationwide Festival of Light Bulletin* no. 7 (January 1980), p. 48. I am grateful to Matthew Grimley for this reference.

historian called 'some much-needed intellectual muscle'.[14] His analysis of family breakdown in modern Britain, *Who Needs the Family?* (1979), was welcomed by the *Church Times* as 'a clarion call ... to do spiritual battle for the conversion of England'.[15] Johnston lectured at Holy Trinity Brompton on the topic 'Must Britain Rot?', arguing that the nation was under divine judgement for forsaking the Bible.[16] He looked with admiration to the United States of America where the Moral Majority helped to sweep Ronald Reagan into the White House, hoping that their example would encourage more British Christians 'to gird up our loins'.[17]

The clashes between NFOL and campaigners for gay rights were especially notorious. Its launch event in Westminster Central Hall was infiltrated by the Gay Liberation Front dressed as bogus nuns who set off stink-bombs and attempted to storm the platform. In October 1977 a NFOL rally at All Souls, Langham Place, was disrupted by members of the Gay Christian Movement who sat amongst the congregation with badges which read, 'Yes, I too am a homosexual'. John Stott, the usually unflustered rector emeritus, wrestled with demonstrators who tried to grab the microphone until the police ejected them from the church, including two gay clergymen.[18] Caroline Eaton's brief spell with NFOL, as its most junior member of staff, coincided with the publication by the Church of England in October 1979 of *Homosexual Relationships* (the Gloucester Report) which argued that same-sex couples legitimately enjoyed 'a companionship and

14   John Capon, 'Festival Flashback', NFOL broadsheet (1979), CARE Trust Archives, London.
15   Margaret Daniel, 'Stopping the Rot', *Church Times*, 13 July 1979, p. 6. See further, Andrew Atherstone, 'Christian Family, Christian Nation: Raymond Johnston and the Nationwide Festival of Light in Defence of the Family', in John Doran, Charlotte Methuen and Alexandra Walsham (eds), *Religion and the Household* (Woodbridge: Boydell, 2014), pp. 456–68.
16   Ken Stewart, 'Must Britain Rot?', *The Brompton Magazine* (November 1981), p. 4.
17   Raymond Johnston, 'Now is the Time for Pressure', *Church of England Newspaper*, 16 January 1981, p. 5.
18   Gordon Fyles, 'Sinner Saving, Not Sinner Bashing', *Church of England Newspaper*, 21 October 1977, pp. 1, 3.

physical expression of sexual love similar to that which is to be found in marriage', though not equivalent to marriage. It admitted that the Bible condemned homosexual acts, but proposed that advances in scientific knowledge meant such relationships could be welcomed by modern Christians as 'genuine expressions of love'.[19] Shocked by these sentiments, Johnston declaimed on behalf of NFOL the 'moral treachery in our churches', lamenting that even clergy were now publicly teaching that Anglican ministry was compatible with a homosexual lifestyle.[20] He believed the bishops and clergy of the Church of England had abdicated their responsibilities for moral leadership.[21]

On 15 December 1979 Welby and Eaton were married at Holy Trinity Brompton by Sandy Millar, with Charlie Arbuthnot as best man. At the reception, Ken Costa was master of ceremonies. The young couple honeymooned in Jerusalem, though perhaps they looked suspicious to the Israeli authorities because they were searched for about an hour at the airport before being allowed to enter the country. Back in Paris, they moved into an apartment in the 16th arrondissement, one of France's wealthiest districts, near the Trocadéro Gardens and the Eiffel Tower. Caroline trained to teach English (TEFL) to French students, while Justin continued his international travels.

---

19   *Homosexual Relationships: A Contribution to Discussion* (London: CIO, 1979), pp. 36, 52.
20   Raymond Johnston, 'Homosexual Relationships', *Reformed Anglican* vol. 5 (January 1980), p. 25.
21   Raymond Johnston, 'Christian Morality and the Church of England', in Anthony Kilmister (ed.), *When Will Ye Be Wise? The State of the Church of England* (London: Blond and Briggs, 1983), pp. 99–122; Raymond Johnston, 'The Moral State of the Church of England', in David Samuel (ed.), *Concern for the Church of England* (London: Church Society, 1985), pp. 7–12.

Bible Smuggling

With a particular concern for persecuted believers on the other side of the Iron Curtain, the Welbys signed up during the summer holidays with the Eastern European Bible Mission (EEBM). Founded by a Dutch Christian, Hendrik Vogelaar (under the pseudonym 'Hank Paulson'), the EEBM had been smuggling Bibles and other Christian literature into the Communist bloc since 1971.[22] It was closely associated with Open Doors, the Bible-smuggling operation launched in the 1950s by another Dutchman, 'Brother Andrew', as told in his best-selling autobiography, *God's Smuggler* (1967). Each summer the EEBM recruited 40 or 50 young adults from western Europe and North America as short-term missionaries, who were sent out in small groups to different regions of Eastern Europe, posing as tourists. They had to pass suspicious border guards, and dodge informers and secret police, to rendezvous with underground churches. Several young Christians from Holy Trinity Brompton went on these mission trips, including Arbuthnot who travelled to Hungary in 1978 and East Germany in 1979, and he recruited Welby who enjoyed the sense of adventure. EEBM's secret headquarters were a farm at Dinteloord near Roosendaal in Holland, where Welby spent ten days of manual labour in May 1979 helping to demolish a barn. It was a significant week because it was there, while spending long evenings in prayer and Bible reading, that he decided to propose to Caroline. He also committed himself to travelling to Eastern Europe the following summer.

EEBM had a fleet of five Renault camper vans, custom-built to carry between 800 and 1,200 Bibles or books in hidden compartments, each van registered in a different country to avoid attracting attention to their Dutch origins.

---

22   For the EEBM story, see Hank Paulson, *Beyond the Wall: The People Communism Can't Conquer* (Ventura, California: Regal Books, 1982). Further details from Hank Paulson, 24 February 2014.

They also used Russian Ladas and Czech Skodas for research trips. Volunteers were trained by a former intelligence officer from the United States military in how to recognise different interrogation techniques, to memorise maps and code words, and the importance of burning any incriminating materials before reaching the border, as well as how to appeal to ambassadors if arrested. They were not told their destination until shortly before departure and were not allowed to inform their families where they were going because secrecy was essential. In 1980 the Welbys, on their first holiday after honeymoon, journeyed with Arbuthnot to Czechoslovakia, as Arbuthnot recalled:

> The border was marked as usual with guns, dogs and watchtowers but Hank, very wisely, had given us so much to do that we couldn't focus too much on worrying. We were required to report back on all the techniques used at the border – how many guards? what questions were asked? were mirrors used under the cars? what languages did they speak? This was all part of Hank's thorough collection of data allowing the Dutch base to learn which crossing points were easier and which harder and thus direct teams to the easiest points. Caroline opted to make some sandwiches as we crossed, with suitably sticky honey and at a table conveniently located over the switch that released the secret panels providing access to the Bibles. Our hope was that the guards would not want to interfere with her lunch preparation – and particularly the honey – and would miss their moment. ... God's peace flooded through us and the sense that mere men at the border were trying to outwit God's children was wonderful.[23]

The three friends delivered their contraband to several Czech contacts in the network of underground churches, sometimes with the coded message, 'Hank sends greetings from Holland'. On one occasion they turned up a forest track in order to pack the Bibles into bags for swift delivery, but the van got stuck and they had to flag down a lorry to pull them out.

---

23   Letter from Charlie Arbuthnot, 11 December 2013.

They then noticed that they had punctured the oil sump so went to a local garage for repair, praying intensely because the mechanics might easily discover the secret compartments. They returned later to find the mechanics had raised the van to head height and were gazing at its undercarriage without noticing anything suspicious.

In June 1981 the Welbys travelled alone to Romania, then in the iron grip of Nicolae Ceauşescu. At one road block they were flagged down and a Securitate officer (a member of the Romanian secret police) came to the window, but instead of ordering them to get out he asked for a lift into the local town. He sat in the front seat of the van, between the Welbys and directly over some of the smuggled Bibles, as they tried to remain calm and chatted in French. The officer took them to his flat, offered them Albanian wine, and showed them around the town. They had memorised an address where they were meant to deliver some of their literature, but had no idea where it was, until by coincidence the Securitate officer pointed out the exact street, which the Welbys interpreted as an explicit answer to prayer. They also rendezvoused in a wood with members of an underground church and met a pastor who had been imprisoned several times by the authorities. The whole experience was 'hugely formative for us', Caroline observed, because it taught them to trust God and brought them into contact for the first time with people for whom following Christ was a serious risk.[24] By the summer of 1982 Caroline was pregnant with Johanna (born in November) and they called a halt to their Eastern European escapades. Nevertheless the Welbys stayed in touch with the EEBM for several years through Hank Paulson and his wife, Mona, who in 1986 named their only son Michael Justin Vogelaar because they were so impressed with Justin Welby's Christian commitment.

24   HTB Home Focus, 27 July 2013.

In Paris the Welbys were members of St Michael's church, an Anglican evangelical congregation just a hundred yards from the British embassy and formerly known as 'the Embassy Church'. It was a diverse and transient community, with a particular ministry to business people on secondment in Paris from London or New York, British au pairs, bilingual secretaries, students at the Sorbonne or the Alliance Française, and embassy staff. In his first year Welby was a leader of the 'Wednesday Club', a mid-week discussion group for students, and from 1980 he and Caroline ran 'Pathfinders', a small youth group for 11- to 14-year-olds.[25] He was elected to the church council and served as the council's secretary.[26] Particularly memorable was the visit the Welbys helped to host of Jackie Pullinger for a week in March 1981, during her European speaking tour, with a focus upon mission to the poor. At the main Sunday morning service she told the St Michael's congregation that she had a message for them from God, but it was delivered in the unusual form of a 'tongue' which she sang. The chaplain, Peter Sertin, began to feel perspiration run down his back as he worried about what the British attachés and other diplomatic staff would think. After a long silence, Welby stood up and gave an interpretation of the tongue, which Pullinger then expounded at length without notes. Marilyn Sertin, the chaplain's wife, recalled: 'you could have heard a pin drop, it was absolutely incredible ... nobody moved, it was just mesmerizing, it appeared just to flow from her.'[27] Pullinger called the Sertins and the Welbys to the front of church to pray for anyone who wished to receive the gift of tongues. It was a significant few days in the life of the church which saw some brought to Christian faith, delivered from the occult, strengthened in Christian discipleship or called to public Christian ministry.

25   'Justin Welby', *St Michael's News* (May – June 1980), p. 10.
26   St Michael's, Paris, Church Council Minutes. Welby was elected to the council on 12 May 1980, was elected secretary on 4 May 1981, re-elected secretary on 3 May 1982 and attended his last meeting on 7 March 1983.
27   Interview with Marilyn Perry (formerly Sertin), 19 December 2013.

Tragedy

In May 1983 Welby was posted by Elf Aquitaine back to London to run the treasury for its subsidiary, Elf UK, focused upon the oil fields in the North Sea. On the day they returned to England from France, Monday 30 May, tragedy struck. The furniture van went ahead, followed by Caroline and seven-month-old Johanna in the car, accompanied by a young family friend who was driving, while Justin remained in Paris. Travelling on the autoroute towards Amiens the car swerved down an embankment and crashed. No other vehicle was involved. Johanna was strapped into her carrycot on the back seat, but both carrycot and infant were thrown from the car and she suffered a fatal head injury. As she lay in intensive care in Amiens hospital, there were prayer meetings in Paris and London for miraculous recovery, but she died four days after the accident, on 3 June.

In later years the Welbys reflected publicly on this deep bereavement, 'the most utter agony'.[28] It was a period of paradoxical emotions. Justin described it as 'a very dark time ... but in a strange way it actually brought us closer to God'.[29] They felt 'the intensity of God's presence ... an enormous sense that amidst it all God is faithful, that the anchor holds'.[30] In particular, he recalled the days of prayer during Johanna's critical illness:

> That was prayer at its rawest, because it's the prayer of just 'Oh God, help! Oh God, where are you? What's going on? Are you going to do something or aren't you?' ... That was prayer at its most profound, and getting exactly the answer we didn't want most of all in all the world, and yet sensing that God was at the centre of this.[31]

28   Lawson, 'So Many Crosses to Bear', p. 27.
29   Neil McKay, 'Path to Durham Marked by Tragedy', *The Newcastle Journal*, 3 June 2011, p. 7.
30   HTB Home Focus, 27 July 2013.
31   *Songs of Praise*, 24 March 2013.

The home groups at St Michael's church all met on Thursday evenings, so on 2 June they spent the time praying for Johanna and her parents. Three or four of the groups had the same Bible verse brought to mind, 'suffer the little children to come unto me, and forbid them not, for of such is the kingdom of God' (Mark 10:14). This became a particularly significant verse for the Welbys as they gave the outcome to God and entrusted their injured infant daughter into his eternal care. She died on the Friday morning. Justin later wrote: 'our children belong to God, as do we, and both our future and theirs is in His hands'.[32] In the context of this deep grief, he took strength from the cross of Christ:

> God is aware of our suffering, of the suffering of this very broken world, and our suffering was as nothing compared to many people. And he is at work even in the darkest places. ... The cross is the great pointer where the suffering, and sorrow, and torture, and trial, and sin, and yuck of the world ends up on God's shoulders, out of love for us.[33]

He reflected: 'we learnt the fallibility and the brokenness of the world in a completely new way'.[34]

Caroline explained that the days between the accident and Johanna's death were 'full of God-incidents. God answered every prayer – not always as we would have liked. And so for me in many ways it was a very rich time of spiritual discovery ... a number of truths became heart-knowledge', especially about God's sovereignty, faithfulness and presence. She continued: 'I have never felt God as close as I did that week. And in a very odd way it makes those memories bitter-sweet. It was the worst time, and yet for me it was a time of extreme closeness to God in that pain.' Sitting at the roadside waiting for the ambulance to arrive, she had 'one of the most powerful experiences of God that I have ever had'. Her immediate reaction after the crash was that maybe somehow she was

32   Justin Welby, 'Thought for the Month', *SPCN* (July 1996).
33   *Travellers' Tales*, 31 March 2013.
34   Interview at New Wine Conference, 29 July 2013.

at fault for not praying hard enough before the journey, but she felt God speak directly to her of his sovereign care and control, no matter what the circumstances or the length of her prayers. Caroline testified to their personal experience of the truth of the New Testament promise that 'all things work together for the good of those who love God, who are called according to his purpose' (Romans 8:28). She said, 'Although what happened to us was dreadful ... God can bring good things even out of the worst circumstances.' For example, a friend to whom she had been witnessing about Christ for three years became a Christian at Johanna's funeral at St Michael's on 9 June.[35] Sandy Millar led the service and Peter Sertin gave the address on the Bible verse, 'You will grieve, but your grief will be turned into joy' (John 16:20).[36]

Back in London, the Welbys lived in Chiswick, but they re-joined Holy Trinity Brompton, where the church family was a particular source of strength in their bereavement. They already had many friends in the congregation and Caroline's sister, Mary Eaton, was the vicar's secretary.[37] Three months after the accident, they journeyed with a group led by Millar to the Vineyard Christian Fellowship in Anaheim, California, where they were particularly helped by Penny and Bob Fulton (John Wimber's brother-in-law). The Fultons prayed for the Welbys 'to be released so that we could express our pain freely to God ... a very liberating experience'.[38] Each year on Johanna's birthday the Welbys went out for a family meal, bought a family present and celebrated her life. 'Speaking from our own family experience of a very painful and sudden loss,' Justin noted, 'if you do not take hold of the anniversary it will take hold of you.'[39] One of Caroline's favourite Bible verses was 'You keep my tears in a bottle' (Psalm 56:8), a sign of God's intimate knowledge and care, and that no tear is

35   Welby and Welby, 'Grief'.
36   Typescript of Peter Sertin's funeral address, 9 June 1983, Lady Williams' papers.
37   *The Brompton Magazine* (October 1982).
38   Welby and Welby, 'Grief'.
39   Justin Welby, 'A Bitter Anniversary', *The Treasurer* (September 2002), p. 17.

wasted. More than 20 years after the tragedy, she concluded that 'our experiences have directly contributed to where we are now', both in pastoral ministry and Justin's calling to work amongst grieving communities in conflict situations.[40]

Enterprise Oil

Welby did not remain long with Elf UK. After only a year he was head-hunted by Enterprise Oil, a new company created by the privatisation of British Gas's offshore oil fields in the North Sea. The denationalisation of Britain's public assets was accelerated during the 1980s by Margaret Thatcher's Conservative government. Large parts of British Telecom, British Airways, Jaguar and Rover (parts of British Leyland), British Aerospace, British Petroleum and British Gas were sold into private hands. Enterprise Oil was floated on the London stock market in June 1984 and raised £392 million for government coffers.[41] The company began life with five oil wells, £90 million in cash, no debt, but hardly any employees. As Welby put it, 'Enterprise sprang fully formed from the womb.'[42]

The Enterprise Oil team was rapidly recruited from other oil companies and accountancy firms, and there were 90 on the payroll by Christmas 1984. Welby was one of the early arrivals, the thirty-first employee,[43] chosen as the new group treasurer to run all the long-term and short-term finance and insurance deals. It was a boom time for the company, with exponential growth. In 1985 Enterprise Oil acquired Saxon

---

40   Welby and Welby, 'Grief'.
41   On the background, see Stephanie M. Hoopes, *Oil Privatization, Public Choice and International Forces* (Basingstoke: Macmillan, 1997), pp. 37–56.
42   Gary Humphreys, 'How to Stir in the Oil', *Euromoney* (June 1986), p. 37.
43   Justin Welby, *Can Companies Sin? 'Whether', 'How' and 'Who' in Company Accountability* (Nottingham: Grove Books, 1992), p. 17.

Oil for £130 million, which gave it significant new acreage in the North Sea. The following year it absorbed ICI's oil and gas interests, providing a stake in Indonesia and Egypt, and staff numbers increased to 158. Expansion was temporarily slowed by the volatility of the oil price, which collapsed at one point from $28 a barrel in January 1986 to just $9 a barrel in July. The following autumn witnessed 'Black Monday', the worldwide stock-market crash of 19 October 1987. Welby remembered:

> The events of October 1987 are often referred to as the melt-down of the markets. My clear memory is of the whole executive board of directors standing in my office gazing in awe at a Topic Screen (showing FTSE prices) as waves of red chased across the screen. The use of nuclear metaphors was apt. A system that seemed safe had assumed a life of its own.[44]

But the markets quickly recovered. By March 1988 Enterprise Oil was valued at £1,029 million and was included for the first time on the FTSE 100 Index (the largest 100 companies listed on the London stock exchange). The next year it acquired the exploration and production interests of Texas Eastern for £442 million, which doubled its daily production rate and increased its reserves by a third. By the end of 1989 the company had a presence in France, the Netherlands, Denmark, Gabon, the Seychelles and Laos, with offices in Rome, Jakarta, Ho Chi Minh City and Stavanger (Norway). During 1984 Enterprise Oil produced 31,000 barrels of oil and gas a day. Five years later it was producing 125,000 barrels, with reserves of 924 million barrels. It recorded a turnover in 1989 of £337 million and pre-tax profits of £149 million. Since its flotation, its market value had increased by over 700 per cent, to just under £3,000 million. From humble beginnings, Enterprise Oil was now firmly established as one of the largest exploration and

---

44   Justin Welby, 'The Ethics of Derivatives and Risk Management', *Ethical Perspectives* vol. 4 (July 1997), p. 92.

production companies in the world, ranked amongst the United Kingdom's largest 30 businesses.[45]

In this environment, Welby continued to develop his leadership and management gifts, which he later brought to the Church of England. He highlighted two themes in particular – the need for clear decision-making, and for collegiality: 'Treasury teaches you to be decisive. Markets don't allow you to hang about and vacillate. And treasury teaches you about teamwork and working collaboratively.'[46] One of his responsibilities as group treasurer was to watch prices 'like a hawk',[47] since they made such a difference day to day, and *Euromoney* praised his 'nimble portfolio management strategy'. An example of the need for decisive action was Enterprise Oil's issue of a £50 million Eurobond in April 1986, the timing of which was all important. Welby recalled that when the practicalities were arranged they 'just waited for the day that seemed right and jumped'. When the moment came, 'I looked at the screen. Everybody screwed up their courage and I said, "All right; we'll do it."'[48]

Welby particularly enjoyed the opportunity to shape the company's infrastructure and culture from the beginning, an 'unforgettable' experience. He believed that the creation of an Enterprise Oil 'ethos' was key to its early success, with an emphasis on the 'right way of doing things' which affected policies on safety and personnel. This ethos was instilled in practical ways like a staff canteen where everyone ate, regardless of rank or department, which fostered deeper relationships. He reflected: 'There was little obvious hierarchy; someone pouring coffee in a meeting would as likely be a Director as a secretary. Loyalty to staff was high. Power was delegated to the lowest possible level. Ideas and criticism from all employees were generally welcome.' This 'good ethos'

---

45   See further Enterprise Oil annual report and accounts, 1983–89.
46   Peter Williams, 'Of Secular and Sacred', *The Treasurer* (July – August 2011), p. 43.
47   Justin Welby, 'When the Bubble Bursts …', *The Treasurer* (December 2009 – January 2010), p. 45.
48   Humphreys, 'How to Stir in the Oil', pp. 37–8.

was 'both taught and caught' and inevitably influenced the workforce. Welby remembered: 'At oil industry parties it was amusing to guess someone's employer before being told, on the basis of the stamp of corporate ethos on their character.'[49]

During his years at Enterprise Oil, Welby was provoked to think more deeply about the intrinsic ethics of finance by a question from one of the curates at Holy Trinity Brompton, Paul Perkin: 'What is an ethical treasurer?'[50] He gave 'the normal banal answer: someone who doesn't fiddle their expenses and sleep with their secretary', but Perkin retorted that that was simply a decent human being, and Welby had no reply.[51] He was forced to develop a more holistic theology of corporate ethics and responsibility, on which he lectured and wrote frequently in later years. His chosen profession of money and oil focused the issues in a particularly sharp way, as he explained in 2011:

> Serious, sensible Christianity is holistic. It should incorporate and transform every aspect of life. It is dangerous to start artificially to separate the secular and sacred because you end up with a privatised approach to faith which has no impact on life. … The ethics came out of working in an extractive industry often in developing countries where ethical questions were very frequent. During my time there I came to realise there was a gap between what I thought, believed and felt was right in my non-work life and what went on at work.[52]

During Welby's penultimate year at Enterprise Oil, the industry was rocked by the Piper Alpha disaster on the night of 6 July 1988. The Piper Alpha platform in the North Sea, operated by Occidental Petroleum, was destroyed by two gas explosions and a colossal fire, with the loss of 167 lives. Occidental's parent company admitted responsibility, after a catalogue of management and safety errors. Welby later pondered the

49   Welby, *Can Companies Sin?*, pp. 17, 21.
50   Welby, 'The Ethics of Derivatives and Risk Management', p. 92.
51   Giles Fraser, 'The Saturday Interview: Bankers Beware! Bankers Beware!', *Guardian*, 21 July 2012, p. 37.
52   Williams, 'Of Secular and Sacred', p. 45.

tragedy in his booklet, *Can Companies Sin?* (1992), which argued that companies were moral agents which should be held ethically accountable. Although acknowledging the importance of individual responsibility, he emphasised social obligation. He insisted that a biblical account of justice must include the idea of 'corporate accountability', pointing for example to God's judgement on the builders of the Tower of Babel (Genesis 11) as 'a corporate punishment of a corporate sin'.[53]

After leaving the oil industry, Welby continued to write about business ethics in the light of his early career experience. In an article in *Third Way* magazine in 1996 on multinational corporations, entitled 'Taming the Beasts', he observed that 'Evil and sin permeate all human structures, from the monastery to the multinational'. He was especially critical of giant companies which gobbled up vast resources and took huge financial risks:

> if we put them in the dock, the charge sheet is long. Political interference (especially in the Sixties) and non-interference (especially today). The debt crisis caused, or abetted, by the major banks. The exploitation of non-renewable resources, with little or no return to the countries they come from. The sophisticated marketing of harmful products. The list goes on.

Although he admitted that the world was 'stuck with the beasts', such as Shell and ICI, he maintained that it was the responsibility of richer nations to control them through regulation and public pressure.[54] Commenting later on multi-billion-dollar mergers in the financial and business world, and the forthcoming launch of the Euro currency in 1999, Welby returned again to the image of the Tower of Babel. He wrote:

> The Christian response is to say that however big the structures built by human beings, God is greater. ... The empires of finance and power built in today's paper will be the case studies of

53   Welby, *Can Companies Sin?*, p. 19.
54   Justin Welby, 'Taming the Beasts', *Third Way* vol. 19 (September 1996), pp. 22–3.

failure in 20 years, or perhaps a hundred. But God will be the same, not selfish but giving and open.[55]

Welby continued to read widely on economics and financial ethics, which enabled him to speak authoritatively on these topics with technical knowledge as well as theological insight. As a clergyman and bishop his daily newspaper of choice remained the *Financial Times*.

Call to Ordination

Holy Trinity Brompton, where the Welbys were members of the congregation, went through a period of significant change and growth during the 1980s. When Sandy Millar arrived as curate in 1976 the main Sunday morning service was sung mattins with robed choir, and the congregation was predominantly elderly. With the blessing of his vicar, Raymond Turvey, Millar began gently to encourage charismatic renewal, which persuaded young Cambridge converts like Gumbel, Costa and Welby to join the church in the late 1970s. Turvey was succeeded in 1980 by John Collins, a leading figure within the Anglican charismatic movement who had trained both David Watson and David MacInnes as his curates in a previous parish. Church life at HTB was transformed over the next decade as Collins and Millar worked hand in hand as vicar and senior curate (they swapped roles after five years), with a growing and talented team of lay people. To encourage the congregation in evangelism Collins frequently took small groups with him to other parishes in England on short missions. HTB's distinctive principles were freedom in worship, intimacy with God, ministry with all the gifts of the Holy Spirit, and church growth. They learnt much on

55   Justin Welby, 'Thought for the Month', *SPCN* (June 1998).

all these themes from John Wimber (leader of the Vineyard Movement) who first visited HTB from California in 1982 and became a firm friend and trusted advisor.[56] Wimber led many conferences in Britain during the 1980s and was widely known for his books *Power Evangelism: Signs and Wonders Today* (1985) and *Power Healing* (1986), and for his many aphorisms such as 'Faith is spelt RISK'. His impact upon the theology and future direction of the Anglican charismatic movement was considerable.

A key Vineyard emphasis was church planting. Wimber's friend and colleague in the church growth department at Fuller Theological Seminary in Pasadena, Professor C. Peter Wagner, famously asserted: 'Planting new churches is the most effective evangelistic methodology known under heaven.'[57] Some Anglicans were beginning to advocate church planting across parish boundaries, notably David Pytches (vicar of St Andrew's, Chorleywood, from 1977) who also learnt a great deal from Wimber. Pytches had witnessed the remarkable success of church planting as a missionary and Anglican bishop in South America during the 1960s and 1970s.[58] The leadership at HTB decided to follow suit, attempting to reverse the numerical decline of the Church of England, which in Sandy Millar's words was 'geared to maintenance not mission'. The American textbooks on church planting suggested beginning with a disused cinema, or an empty warehouse with a parking lot, and needed translation into a Kensington context. What central London did possess, unlike California, was dozens of old Victorian churches which had fallen into a state of disrepair with dwindling congregations, or had shut altogether. The first idea was to plant a church

---

56   Sandy Millar, 'A Friend's Recollections', in David Pytches (ed.), *John Wimber: His Influence and Legacy* (Guildford: Eagle, 1998), pp. 269–87.
57   C. Peter Wagner, *Strategies for Church Growth: Tools for Effective Mission and Evangelism* (Ventura, California: Regal Books, 1987), pp. 168–9.
58   David Pytches and Brian Skinner, *New Wineskins: Defining New Structures for Worship and Growth Beyond Existing Parish Boundaries* (Guildford: Eagle, 1991); David Pytches, *Living at the Edge: Recollections and Reflections of a Lifetime* (Bath: Arcadia, 2002).

south of the river, in Southwark diocese, because many of the HTB congregation lived in the area around Balham and Clapham. They identified St Mark's, Battersea Rise, as a possible location but the Bishop of Kingston resisted the idea and all the Battersea clergy voted against it (except one, who abstained, because he thought 'God might be in it'). Therefore the first plant, in 1985, was in London diocese at St Barnabas, Kensington, with the blessing of the Bishop of Kensington, Mark Santer. There was already a tiny existing congregation, perhaps 15 people and 'on its last legs', but HTB sent 100 people and one of their curates, John Irvine. Two years later the plant to St Mark's, Battersea Rise, did go ahead, with 50 people from HTB and another of their curates, Paul Perkin.[59] These were the first of many plants sent out from HTB over the next 25 years to help revive struggling congregations, recognised as one of the reasons that London diocese bucked the trend of church decline.[60]

In this context Justin Welby learned many of the key lessons he would bring to his later ministry as a rector, cathedral dean and bishop. He enjoyed the excitement of being part of a thriving and innovative congregation, and saw that 'it is natural for churches to grow'. He was also impressed by the leadership style of Collins and Millar, in particular 'the toughness with which they led, but a toughness wrapped in love'.[61] Welby was encouraged at HTB in his role as a lay Christian leader, despite his demanding job at Enterprise Oil. He preached occasionally at main Sunday services, served on the parochial church council and the executive committee, and had spiritual oversight of one of HTB's 'pastorates' (a cluster of four or five small Bible study groups). Many from

---

59   Interviews with John Collins and Sandy Millar, December 2012. For further reflections, see Sandy Millar, 'Perspectives on Church Planting', in Roger Ellis and Roger Mitchell, *Radical Church Planting* (Cambridge: Crossway, 1992), pp. 201–10.

60   John Wolffe and Bob Jackson, 'Anglican Resurgence: The Church of England in London', in David Goodhew (ed.), *Church Growth in Britain: 1980 to the Present* (Farnham: Ashgate, 2012), p. 35.

61   HTB Leadership Conference, 13 May 2013.

Welby's pastorate joined the first church plant to St Barnabas in 1985, though he remained at HTB. He also saw a number of his close friends leave their secular professions and become Anglican clergymen. For example, Nicky Gumbel gave up his work as a barrister in 1983 to train for ordination at Wycliffe Hall, Oxford, before re-joining HTB as curate in 1986. Nicky Lee also joined the staff as curate in 1985, after several years as a teacher.

Welby's own thoughts of ordination had faded in the years since Cambridge. He explained: 'I had a stimulating job in a good company with people I liked, and I got hooked into it.'[62] But this calling was reignited at an evening service at HTB in 1987 while listening to a visiting preacher, John McClure, senior pastor of the Vineyard Christian Fellowship in Newport Beach, California, and a close friend of John Wimber. McClure spoke of his own call to Christian ministry in 1970 despite the competing attraction of an excellent job offer in Los Angeles from the research division of Kobe, a major pumping-equipment company, a subsidary of Baker Oil Tools.[63] Welby felt 'an extraordinary, powerful, almost audible, inner resonance' and sensed God saying, 'That's the choice I want you to make.'[64] On the way home he raised the question with Caroline, who recalled: 'It came as a complete shock. We had two children, we were very nicely settled and we knew enough vicars and their wives to have lost our romantic ideas about how nice it would be. It just seemed like a huge upheaval.' They made a list of pros and cons and prayed for guidance. 'There were so many cons, so many things we'd miss: home, friends, family, money, security. And the only pro was that if this was what God wanted us to do, all those

62   Serena Allott, 'For Better, For Worse', *Telegraph Magazine*, 8 December 2001, p. 53.
63   Information from John McClure, 2 February 2014.
64   *Private Passions*, 22 December 2013; 'Justin Welby', *Alpha Journal* (October 2013), www.alpha.org/journal.

things would be meaningless.'[65] It was 'an inescapable sense of call'.[66]

The path to ordination was far from straightforward, as the diocese put obstacles in Welby's way. He had no incentive to leave the oil industry: 'I was reluctant, I must admit – kicking and screaming, really! The Church of England process for assessing vocation is very slow, quite wisely, I think, and I went through an increasingly bumpy series of interviews.'[67] The new Bishop of Kensington from August 1987 was John Hughes (former warden of St Michael's College, Llandaff), a catholic opponent of the ordination of women whose appointment by Bishop Graham Leonard of London was seen as a political move.[68] He was suspicious of HTB and did not warm to Welby whom he assumed had led a sheltered life at Eton, Cambridge and Kensington. The bishop had previously worked for the Advisory Council for the Church's Ministry (ACCM) and bluntly told Welby, 'I've interviewed more than a thousand candidates for ordination and you don't come in the top thousand. I can tell you, you have no future in the Church of England.'[69]

Welby was sent for an initial interview to the vicar of St Mary Abbots on Kensington High Street and a panel of three lay women. It did not go well. They asked what he would do in the imaginary scenario of visiting female parishioners who needed help with blocked drainpipes. He answered that he would send Caroline up a ladder to clear them (because she was better at DIY). Next they enquired whether he could adapt from the wealthy world of Enterprise Oil to the impecunious lifestyle of a clergyman in the Church of England. He looked around the plush surroundings of St Mary Abbots and barely resisted the temptation to say that

65   Allott, 'For Better, For Worse', p. 53
66   'Unveiling a New Bishop of Durham' (video produced by Aegies on behalf of Durham diocese, July 2011), www.youtube.com.
67   'Meet the Dean Designate', p. 3.
68   'New Bishop Chosen for Kensington', *Church Times*, 14 August 1987, pp. 1, 16.
69   'Facing the Canon', 13 March 2014.

he thought he could adapt really quite quickly! Impatience with pomposity and a mischievous sense of humour, especially irony, were characteristic of Welby's approach. The longer the discernment process was drawn out, the less he wanted to be ordained. Meanwhile his work at Enterprise Oil was going exceptionally well: 'I had a time where I couldn't put a foot wrong in terms of calling the markets. During that period we were doing some very complex deals and everything worked and I was thinking I'm really good at this.'[70]

Millar pushed Bishop Hughes to allow Welby to go to the next stage of discernment, a national Church of England 'selection conference'. Eventually he was dispatched in early summer 1988 for three days of interviews at the Derby diocesan retreat house. In the final interview with David Smith (Bishop of Maidstone) he was asked why he wanted to be ordained. Welby replied, 'Well I don't, really, because I'm enjoying what I'm doing now.' The bishop looked rather nonplussed and asked why then he was there, to which Welby explained that 'I had this overwhelming feeling (shared by Caroline) that it was the right thing to do – it was a call from God'. When Smith asked what Welby would do if he was rejected by the Church of England, he replied: 'I'll go back to London and take my wife out for the most expensive meal I can afford, to celebrate.'[71] He was duly recommended, though it was too late to give notice to his employers in time to begin ordination training that autumn, so the process was delayed another year.

Ordination meant a massive drop in salary. In the business sector Welby commanded an annual income of over £100,000, but the average stipend for Church of England clergy in 1989 was just £9,500 (plus tied accommodation). One hesitation in pursuing ordination was the knowledge that they would be unable to educate their children privately.[72] At the Enterprise Oil leaving party, Welby's boss quipped that his transfer to the

70   Williams, 'Of Secular and Sacred', p. 44.
71   'Meet the Dean Designate', pp. 3–4.
72   Allott, 'For Better, For Worse', p. 53.

Church of England was 'the only known case of a rat joining a sinking ship'.[73] His career prospects would have been very different had he remained with the company. He was replaced as group treasurer by his deputy, Andrew Shilston, who in 1993 was promoted again as Enterprise Oil's finance director, and later became finance director of Rolls Royce. Yet as Welby and his family headed to theological college in Durham, he told *The Times* that his new ambition was 'to work at an inner city church'.[74]

73   Justin Welby, 'Thought for the Month', *SPCN* (March 1997).
74   'Calling for Welby', *Times*, 9 June 1989, p. 25.

Chapter 5

Growing Churches

Cranmer Hall, where Justin Welby began as a theological student in September 1989, was one of a dozen residential theological colleges in the Church of England, part of St John's College within the University of Durham.[1] It was noted in the 1960s for being the first Anglican college to pioneer the ministerial training of women and men together. During the 1980s and 1990s it enjoyed a broad Anglican evangelical ethos, encompassing a wide spectrum of spiritualities from Calvinist to catholic. There was a greater emphasis on liturgy than in most evangelical colleges and an optional daily eucharist. The inauguration in 1988 of the Wesley Study Centre added an ecumenical dimension, bringing Methodists and Anglicans together. During Welby's years as an ordinand, the Principal of St John's College was Anthony Thiselton (a renowned biblical scholar) and the staff included three future diocesan bishops, Ian Cundy (Warden of Cranmer Hall), Peter Forster and John Pritchard.

Welby's decision to train in the north-east of England was a deliberate move away from the establishment centres of power and wealth in London and the south-east. Sandy Millar had trained at Cranmer Hall in the mid-1970s, as had two recent HTB curates, Nicky Lee and Tom Gillum. It was also Nicky Gumbel's first choice before he was diverted to Wycliffe Hall in Oxford.[2] The Welbys arrived in Durham with a growing family, after the births of Timothy (June 1984),

---

1   T. E. Yates, *A College Remembered: St John's College, Durham 1909–2000* (second edition, Spennymoor: Macdonald Press, 2001); Amabel Craig (ed.), *Fides Nostra Victoria: A Portrait of St John's College, Durham* (London: Third Millennium, 2008).
2   Aitken, *Heroes and Contemporaries*, p. 233.

Katharine (May 1986) and Peter (November 1988). In an interview for the *Telegraph Magazine*, Caroline recounted her initial panic when the Enterprise Oil salary stopped, during which 'I counted every penny and we lived on chicken livers', but they soon embraced the new pattern of life:

> I enjoyed it, but there were pressures. I had to get used to Justin being at home during the day, he battled with feeling de-skilled, and these things carried on into his curacy. He found it very hard never knowing whether he was doing a good job, and we both realised we had totally underestimated how hard the work – much of it dealing with life and death issues – would be.[3]

Welby did not enjoy the college experience. The loss of career was painful and the de-skilling was stark.[4] Although he continued with some consultancy work in London, sitting on a panel to arbitrate on financial disputes concerning the construction of the Second Severn Crossing, the life of a theological student was a clear break with the past. Having been responsible for securing huge financial deals in the City and for moving oil-tankers around the world, he now found himself being asked to reconcile the student milk bill and to negotiate with a photocopying firm about their punitive contract with the junior common room (an injustice he helped to expose by a television appearance on *Watchdog*).[5]

Since he was over 30, Welby would normally have spent only two years at theological college, but ACCM agreed to pay for him to study for a third year because they saw him as a future leader. In his first two years he gained a bachelor's degree in theology (upper-second class), followed in his third year by a diploma in ministry, though he was renowned for sitting at the back of lectures and falling asleep. He began to put his mind especially to the connections between Christian theology and finance, and his booklet, *Can Companies Sin?*

3   Allott, 'For Better, For Worse', p. 53.
4   *Travellers' Tales*, 31 March 2013.
5   [Justin Welby], '£3,000 Each', *St John's College Record* (1992), pp. 17–18.

(1992), began life as a college dissertation. These years in Durham were in many ways a broadening experience. The Welbys lived on The Avenue near the city centre and attended their local parish church, St John's, Neville's Cross, an eclectic mix of catholic, evangelical and charismatic spiritualities – more varied theologically than St Michael's, Paris, or HTB. Just before their arrival the rector left the Church of England for Roman Catholicism. Welby's three pastoral placements were likewise mixed: at Dryburn Hospital in Durham, shadowing the chaplain; at St James the Great in Darlington, with Ian Grieves, a traditional Anglo-Catholic parish; and at Holy Trinity, Parr Mount in St Helens, with Christopher ('Kik') Woods, a charismatic evangelical vicar in a deprived Urban Priority Area. He also spent a summer placement in 1990 at the Vineyard Christian Fellowship in Newport Beach reconnecting with John McClure. Welby demonstrated a catholicity of approach, a desire to learn from contrasting perspectives, and an ability to straddle different ecclesiastical worlds in an eirenic manner. His college contemporaries found it impossible to pigeon-hole him.

Chilvers Coton

The Welbys naturally assumed that after Durham they would return to London for curacy, but there were no openings. Instead they were put in touch with Coventry diocese by a friend at St John's College, Chris Russell (later a member of Welby's team at Lambeth Palace), son of the Archdeacon of Coventry. Welby was ordained at Coventry Cathedral in June 1992 by Bishop Simon Barrington-Ward, who almost 20 years before had been the means by which he went to Kenya as a teenager with the Church Missionary Society. His title parish was Chilvers Coton, with a population of

13,000 people, a working-class suburb of Nuneaton in the West Midlands and a former coal-mining district with high levels of unemployment. The Hill Top estate, in a corner of the parish, was an Urban Priority Area and there was a large Muslim population. Nuneaton's major hospital, the George Eliot Hospital, was also in the parish (Chilvers Coton's claim to fame was that Eliot had been baptised there in 1819). It was a far cry from the world of barristers and stockbrokers in Kensington. 'You've always been with people who do things', Barrington-Ward told the Welbys, 'it's time you lived in a place where people have things done to them.'[6]

Even in the early days of his ordained ministry, Welby had a high view of the authority of the bishop to direct and deploy the clergy as he saw fit. In subsequent years he never treated the Church of England as an open job market, with freedom of choice and independent movement, but ministered in the places he was sent. As Archbishop of Canterbury, he told a group of ordinands in Kensington: 'If you're offering yourself for ordination, you're offering yourself to Jesus to go wherever he takes you', and the call to a specific location was 'as often as not, discerned and recognized by the church'. Ordinands, therefore, must 'be disposable, in every sense of the word – be at the disposal of God, be at the disposal of the church, and be ready to be disposed of. That's taking up our cross. And if you're not ready for that, don't get ordained.' Indeed the Welbys worked in various towns and cities in the post-industrial Midlands and north of England that they would never have chosen for themselves 'in a million years', but they 'sensed what God was saying through our church leaders, who we trusted to be spiritual people. ... Get out there. The fields are white for harvest all over the country. So say yes to God, and you'll normally hear him through your bishop!'[7]

6   *Travellers' Tales*, 31 March 2013.
7   St Mellitus College, London (Justin Welby interviewed by Graham Tomlin), 2 December 2013.

Chilvers Coton parish church had an electoral roll of 205, with an evangelical ministry sympathetic to charismatic renewal. The mission budget was directed towards organisations such as the Church Missionary Society, the Bible Society, Youth for Christ, Scripture Union and the Church Army.[8] It was also a socially conservative church. When parliament voted in February 1994 to lower the age of consent for gay sex from 21 to 18, Welby's vicar, John Philpott, told the congregation that every concession to sinful human nature – such as easy divorce, abortion, contraception for unmarried couples, and the promotion of gay clergy – was 'a compromise with Christian virtues of fidelity and chastity'. Philpott declared:

> The biological and social pressures not to conform to God's highest standards are simply enormous but no church should deliberately aim at lower standards in order to court popularity. ... The standard the young people in this church are being set for age of consent is marriage. It may not be P.C. (Politically Correct) but it is B.C. (Biblically Correct). As the nation moves further away from the biblical norms Christians should be able to present an alternative lifestyle which others will find demanding but attractive just as they did in the second century.[9]

In sharp contrast to Chilvers Coton's urban context, the vicar and curate also had oversight of the picturesque parish of Astley, a small neighbouring village. Surrounded by farmland, it had historic links with Lady Jane Grey who lived at Astley Castle, and the medieval church was included in *England's Thousand Best Churches* (1999), by Simon Jenkins, as one of Warwickshire's gems.[10] The Astley congregation was 'faithful and few', mostly elderly, with an electoral roll of just 26 and only 14 Easter communicants.[11] There were serious proposals

8   *Chilvers Coton Annual Report* [hereafter CCAR] (1994).
9   John Philpott, 'The Age of Consent', *Chilvers Coton Pew Sheet* [hereafter CCPS] (6 February 1994).
10   Simon Jenkins, *England's Thousand Best Churches* (London: Allen Lane, 1999), p. 707.
11   John Philpott, 'Astley Preface', CCAR (1992).

in 1992 that the church be made redundant, but they decided 'to soldier on in faith'.[12]

Welby reported back to his friends at Cranmer Hall: 'we are hard worked, challenged, and confident that we are in the right place'. Philpott gave him 'a lot of rope' to pursue new initiatives.[13] Although the curate quipped, 'we have L-plates on, and may be hazardous to other users of the church', he made an immediate impact.[14] His first focus was reviving the children's and youth work, which led to the appointment in October 1993 of Simon Betteridge as the parish's first youth minister. Welby pushed the idea through the parochial church council (PCC) and masterminded the necessary finances, including securing an annual gift of £5,000 from Enterprise Oil.[15] He also launched holiday clubs for primary school children, led for three summers in a row by Bernie and Jean French of 'Lantern Ministries', whom Welby had met when on placement at Holy Trinity, Parr Mount. 'What, more Holiday Club?', he mischievously asked, 'That curate has a one track mind.'[16] Caroline was closely involved with Justin's parish work, as she later explained: 'We see his ministry as a joint thing. He does all the upfront stuff but we pray together, discuss issues, balance views, think through our vision.'[17] She co-ordinated the children's work, including the Junior Church.[18] One of the Welbys' skills as a couple was in nurturing local leadership by helping members of the congregation to identify their spiritual gifts and giving them the confidence to minister to others. The music group was reborn, including Caroline on guitar, to play at the monthly Family Service.[19] Justin led the

---

12   John Philpott, 'Astley Preface', CCAR (1993).
13   *Cranmer Hall: Ember List 1993*.
14   Justin and Caroline Welby, 'A Very Warm Welcome', CCPS (5 July 1992).
15   Chilvers Coton PCC Minutes, 26 April and 11 October 1993; Justin Welby, 'A New Appointment', CCPS (19 September 1993).
16   Justin Welby, 'Holiday Club (Again)!', CCPS (1 August 1993).
17   Allott, 'For Better, For Worse', p. 53.
18   Caroline Welby, 'Junior Church', CCAR (1993); Caroline Welby, 'Fun with the Children', CCPS (29 May 1994); Caroline Welby, 'Junior Church', CCAR (1994).
19   Robert Berry, 'Music Group', CCAR (1994).

healing ministry team, which offered prayer for healing and spiritual renewal.[20]

Alongside children's and youth work, Welby's second major focus was evangelism, especially the 'Alpha Course'. This ten-week programme was familiar at HTB in the 1980s as a regular course in Christian basics for the church members, but it was rolled out as a national initiative for the first time in 1993 seeking to reach non-believers, and its influence grew exponentially. There were 200 Alpha Courses running in the United Kingdom in 1993, rising to 2,500 by 1995, and 10,500 by 1998. Within its first decade it was reckoned that 3 million people had been through the course worldwide, in over 75 countries.[21] Welby was an early adopter and Alpha became his preferred evangelistic tool throughout his later ministry. He attended the first Alpha Conference at HTB in May 1993 and was selected as one of Alpha's 28 regional advisers, covering Warwickshire, known locally in the diocese as 'Mr Alpha'.[22] He ran the course three times at Chilvers Coton during 1994, attended by between 65 and 70 people in total, mostly regular church members though a dozen were on the fringe and there was some modest church growth as a result. Philpott agreed that the course had 'a major impact on raising spiritual awareness and expectations'.[23] It formed part of Welby's wider strategy to engage the whole congregation in evangelism: 'We may not be Billy Grahams, but we all need to be witnesses to our own experience of a living and loving God.'[24] He and Betteridge approached the Warwickshire prison service to explore the possibility of using Alpha amongst

20   Justin Welby, 'Healing Ministry', CCAR (1992); Justin Welby, 'Healing Ministry', CCAR (1993).
21   For statistics and critique, see Stephen Hunt, The Alpha Enterprise: Evangelism in a Post-Christian Era (Aldershot: Ashgate, 2004); Andrew Brookes (ed.), The Alpha Phenomenon: Theology, Praxis and Challenges for Mission and Church Today (London: Churches Together in Britain and Ireland, 2007).
22   Chilvers Coton PCC Minutes, 19 July 1993; Justin Welby, 'The Alpha Course', CCPS (17 October 1993); 'Alpha Regional Advisers', Alpha News (April 1995), p. 14.
23   John Philpott, 'Mission and Worship Committee', CCAR (1994).
24   Justin Welby, 'Alpha', CCAR (1994).

offenders, long before 'Alpha for Prisons' became popular.[25] He also travelled to Uganda in November 1994 with a team led by Christopher Woods to train Alpha leaders at Makerere University, Kampala. It was Welby's first mission trip to Africa since his CMS placement 20 years before, and he was left with two overwhelming impressions:

> First, we are one church. The passion for Christ was what united us to the Christians there. Many of their problems are different. Most are worse than ours. But they know Jesus, and welcome others who do the same. Secondly, contact across cultures pays dividends on a huge scale.[26]

The Welbys continued to borrow ideas from across the evangelical spectrum. Justin attended preaching conferences for younger ministers run by the conservative evangelical Proclamation Trust. He also praised HTB's church-planting initiatives as a model for other parishes and began to develop his thesis that faithful churches were growing churches: 'Where God is worshipped, listened to and obeyed, whatever happens decay is not likely to feature.'[27] Conversely, 'A church that doesn't worship is a social club, but a church that worships badly sooner or later ceases to exist.'[28] As a family the Welbys attended New Wine, a popular Christian holiday week under canvas at the Royal Bath and West Showground near Shepton Mallet, in Somerset. New Wine was launched in 1989 by Bishop David Pytches, drawing together crowds of charismatic Christians by its emphasis on the gifts of the Holy Spirit. The Welbys went for many years throughout the 1990s and early 2000s (until they switched in 2008 to 'Home Focus', the HTB summer teaching holiday at Pakefield in Suffolk) and they called New Wine 'our lifeline, spiritually'.[29]

25   Interview with Simon Betteridge, November 2012.
26   Justin Welby, 'Out of Africa', CCPS (27 November 1994).
27   Justin Welby, 'Resuscitated Churches', CCPS (16 January 1994).
28   Justin Welby, 'All Together', CCPS (11 October 1992).
29   Justin Welby, sermon at New Wine London and South East Summer Conference, 29 July 2013, www.archbishopofcanterbury.org. See also Justin Welby, 'Thought for the Month', SPCN (September 1998).

In 1994 a strange phenomenon, the 'Toronto Blessing', swept through the charismatic world. It came to birth at Toronto Airport Vineyard church where members of the congregation were overcome by uncontrollable laughter, shaking, weeping, falling down, and making animal noises. Over 2,000 British churches followed suit, including HTB, with the encouragement of Sandy Millar and Nicky Gumbel. The dramatic events made front-page headlines in the national newspapers.[30] The head of communications at HTB, Mark Elsdon-Dew, called it 'a press officer's nightmare. Instead of doing my job of promoting a growing church run by respectable, godly people I was dealing with the spectre of the same respectable people rolling around on the church floor.' When one Anglican archdeacon arrived for a meeting with Gumbel he was told, 'I'm afraid you'll have to wait. Nicky is crawling around on his hands and knees. He's having a Holy Spirit experience and he can't get off the floor.'[31] The Toronto Blessing also reached Nuneaton. In July 1994 the Chilvers Coton youth club attended Soul Survivor (the youth arm of New Wine) and were impressed by what they encountered, hoping for more of the same in their local church. The youth reported back:

> Last year's conference had some pretty strange goings on ... but was nothing compared with this year's!! It was strange to see respectable adults 'roaring' like lions with others shaking and screaming; laughing, crying and collapsing. You name it ... they did it! ... A number of people from Coton experienced an intense filling of the Holy Spirit. Through this their lives have been transformed and they have come to know Jesus as their Saviour and their friend. Indeed, we seem to have brought back with us a 'helping' of the Holy Spirit ... The question is: 'Do we want the Holy Spirit's ministry at Coton as a regular part of each service?'[32]

30 For history and analysis, see especially David Hilborn (ed.), *'Toronto' in Perspective: Papers on the New Charismatic Wave of the Mid-1990s* (Carlisle: Acute, 2001).
31 Aitken, *Heroes and Contemporaries*, pp. 239–40.
32 Alan Berry, 'The Soul Survivor Experience', *CCPS* (4 September 1994).

Two months later Caroline Welby and Simon Betteridge were despatched to Toronto on a fact-finding trip, with friends from St Barnabas, Kensington, and St Paul's, Onslow Square (HTB church plants in London). They returned to Chilvers Coton having witnessed 'some amazing things'.[33] Betteridge reported that they 'experienced God moving in a very powerful way', including physical healings.[34]

During his curacy Justin Welby revealed by his brief articles in the Sunday pew-sheet a particular interest in repentance, forgiveness and church discipline. For example, there was a media frenzy in June 1994 when Peter Irwin-Clark, evangelical vicar of Shirley parish, Southampton, banned a couple from his church for living in adultery.[35] He was rebuked in the press for his lack of compassion for sinners.[36] Reflecting on the controversy, Welby argued that the Christian gospel of forgiveness for sins could not be isolated from repentance and restitution:

> God cares about both justice and forgiveness. That is why Jesus took our deserved punishment on the cross, opening the way to knowing God's love. The church is about forgiveness, but in the same way, recognising that if it is to be genuine there must be a sense of justice in the way that wrongs are dealt with.[37]

Three months later there was more scandal when the *News of the World* revealed that the newly elected Bishop of Durham, Michael Turnbull, had been convicted in 1968 of an act of gross indecency committed with a Yorkshire farmer in a public toilet in Hull.[38] He faced pressure to resign but he denied he was gay and at his enthronement publicly repented his

33   *CCPS* (25 September 1994).
34   Chilvers Coton PCC Minutes, 10 October 1994.
35   'Adultery Row Vicar Defiant', *Times*, 15 June 1994, p. 5.
36   Nerissa Jones, 'Dear Peter Irwin-Clark: Didn't Jesus Say We Had To Be Without Sin To Throw Stones?', *Independent*, 16 June 1994, p. 21.
37   Justin Welby, 'Crime and Punishment', *CCPS* (19 June 1994).
38   'Bishop of Durham in Gay Sex Scandal', 'Shame at Heart of the C of E', and '"Homosexuality is Incompatible with the Ministry"', *News of the World*, 25 September 1994, pp. 1, 6–7. For further press comment, see 'Bishop Shrugs off Indecency Revelation', *Times*, 27 September 1994, p. 2.

former misdemeanour. Gay-rights campaigner, Peter Tatchell, was arrested as he tried to confront the bishop at Durham Cathedral, and afterwards wrote to the *Church Times*:

> Where is the ethical consistency, when senior clergy who have furtive casual sex in public toilets are forgiven and promoted, while parish priests in open, honest, loving homosexual relationships are damned and cast out? For how much longer can the Church sustain such moral acrobatics?

Tatchell claimed at least eight bishops were 'living a lie' by supporting the Church of England's condemnation of homosexuality while they themselves were, or had been, in homosexual relationships.[39] In Chilvers Coton, Welby again observed that the public criticism of Turnbull was a result of the world's incomprehension of forgiveness, 'the central Christian virtue. ... We must pray for Christians in public positions, and especially pray that their own experience of God's forgiveness is lived out in their daily lives with others.'[40] The same month Jonathan Dimbleby's candid biography of Prince Charles, serialised in the *Sunday Times*, revealed the heir to the throne's miserable childhood and loveless marriage, which led Welby to reflect on the importance of reconciliation and fresh starts.[41] This gospel of forgiveness was rooted in his understanding of the cross of Christ:

> The church is human. Thus it fails, falters and sins. Its leaders are foolish, sometimes. Its members deny by their lives the truth they proclaim by their presence at church. ... Good Friday reminds us of the consequences of that. Jesus took all our sin, lived with all our potential of failure, overcame it and died on the cross for us.[42]

Welby's years in Chilvers Coton were brief, but his vicar applauded his 'creative energy' and proclaimed: 'Justin's

39   Letter from Peter Tatchell, *Church Times*, 4 November 1994, p. 11.
40   Justin Welby, 'Fitting In When We Should Stand Out', *CCPS* (16 October 1994).
41   Justin Welby, 'Starting Over Again', *CCPS* (23 and 30 October 1994).
42   Justin Welby, 'Inescapably Human, Hopefully Glorious', *CCPS* (16 April 1995).

capacity for work and readiness to take initiatives is remarkable'.[43] He was champing at the bit to lead a parish himself, and was soon sent by Bishop Barrington-Ward to a new field of ministry.

Southam

In September 1995 Welby was instituted as rector of St James church, Southam, an attractive market town in rural Warwickshire, still in Coventry diocese. With a population of 6,000 people, it was large enough to boast two or three hotels, four schools, four churches (Anglican, Roman Catholic, Congregational, and a Community Church), its own mayor and council offices, and a good range of leisure and community facilities. Although the town included industrial estates on its outskirts, it was surrounded by farms, riding stables and a polo club. This was a far cry from the City of London, but nor was it the 'inner city' to which Welby had once felt called. He joked that he could see cows from his bedroom window.[44] After a year he was also handed responsibility for St Michael and All Angels church in Ufton, a neighbouring village with little more than a church, a pub and 200 residents.

Southam's previous Anglican incumbent, Ralph Werrell, had retired at Christmas 1994, aged 65, after a dozen years in the parish. He was a traditional evangelical who loved the *Book of Common Prayer* and spent his retirement writing a doctoral thesis on the theology of William Tyndale.[45] When the Welbys arrived it was the first time there had been children living at the rectory for a generation or more. They were now

43   *CCPS* (27 June 1993) and *CCPS* (17 September 1995).
44   Justin Welby, sermon at St John's College, Durham (17 May 2011), www.ustream.tv/channel/codec-vidiblog.
45   Ralph S. Werrell, *The Theology of William Tyndale* (Cambridge: James Clarke, 2006).

a family of seven, after the births of Eleanor (February 1992) and Hannah (July 1995), and their busy home was noted as a place of relaxed hospitality and welcome. During their first year they focused on building relationships and 'entertained like lunatics'.[46] With a full diary and growing responsibilities, Welby developed a very practical form of spirituality, praying for his new parish as he did the family ironing – a sign of devotion both to his family and his parishioners, and typically efficient in redeeming the time. He later described his ministry in Nuneaton and Southam as 'fairly bog standard',[47] but in Southam he demonstrated that a typical Anglican parish could be reorientated from decline to growth.

One of Welby's first priorities was to put the medieval church building in good working order. Werrell's last prayer before departing was that his congregation might see 'the end of the long tunnel of financial worries' because of repairs to the church.[48] There had been no major refurbishment since the 1870s and the building was in a poor state with leaky roof and crumbling masonry. As Welby dryly observed, 'Bits keep falling off and they are very expensive to replace.' The 700th anniversary of Southam church was in 1996, a good opportunity to celebrate the past and catch a vision for a renewed future. Fundraising efforts included special concerts, an art and design competition, a flower festival, and a sponsored parachute jump by the rector over Hinton-in-the-Hedges airfield.[49] Soon Welby brought forward an ambitious plan for restoration and development with the aim 'to make the building fit to serve a twenty-first-century Southam, not a nineteenth-century one.'[50] This meant substantial changes. As well as vital repairs to the roof, windows and stonework, there was to be new heating, a new sound system, and proper

---

46   Justin Welby, 'Reconciliation and Forgiveness', part 2, New Wine seminar 2003 (with Court Clarkson), audio recording.
47   Williams, 'Of Secular and Sacred', p. 44.
48   Letter from Ralph S. Werrell, *SPCN* (January 1995).
49   Justin Welby, 'Thought for the Month', *SPCN* (September 1996).
50   Justin Welby, 'Thought for the Month', *SPCN* (May 1998).

toilet and catering facilities. A raised platform was to be built at the front of the nave for worship, concerts and plays, with the organ and choir stalls moved to the back of church. More radically, it was suggested that the chancel be turned into a separate meeting room, and that the Victorian pews be replaced by chairs.[51] Welby turned to liturgical history to persuade his parishioners to embrace the changes, writing in his parish magazine in May 1998:

> Pews were an eighteenth century invention. Organs came in during the last century, replacing small music groups. This year in the morning we have replaced the organ by a small music group. What goes round comes round. Any living building must change to suit the community. The building is the servant, not the master of those who use it. God does not demand pews or organs, and can be worshipped as well in a school or community hall, or under a tree.[52]

The aim was for a more flexible and modern building, which would not only be used by Christians on a Sunday, but become 'a focal point for the community' all week round. The full package of structural restoration and reform was costed at £425,000, and was a constant theme throughout Welby's incumbency, with a rolling programme of development.[53] He saw through many of the changes, though some took place only after the Welbys left Southam in 2002 (the pews were removed in 2004), and others were abandoned for lack of money.

   Despite this major focus on redevelopment, the rector was keen to emphasise that the church was not its fabric but its people, 'not heritage but communities of believers, and not institutions but vibrancy of faith and reality of encounter with God through Christ'. Therefore it would not matter, ultimately, if St James became 'picturesque ruins' and the congregation had to meet on the Southam recreation ground,

51   'Church Plans', *SPCN* (March 2001).
52   Justin Welby, 'Thought for the Month', *SPCN* (May 1998).
53   Justin Welby, 'Thought for the Month', *SPCN* (April 2000).

provided Christian life in the town remained strong.[54] In January 2001 arsonists set fire to some screens in the church, which threatened a major blaze and the fire brigade rushed out to douse the flames. Welby maintained: 'even if it had all burned, the church in its real sense would still be there. The people are the church, not the building. ... God's church, those people who try to follow what he says, and know Him, are not destroyed by such things.'[55] Years later, as Archbishop of Canterbury, he reflected further on the 'complex dance' in the local church between the past and the present, between its precious heritage and its contemporary mission. He argued that church buildings

> make a wonderful servant, but a very bad master. When the buildings dominate our agenda, when the issues of minor change or normal maintenance are the waking thought and regular nightmare of clergy and people, then the building has become an idol which must be dethroned, and put back in its place.

He asserted: 'God has not retired! ... Empty and cold churches, evidently struggling to keep going, do not proclaim "God is with us"; they may suggest that "God was with us". God has not fossilized!'[56]

The renewal of the buildings in Southam allowed greater freedom and flexibility in public worship. On arriving in the parish, Welby inherited a traditional congregation where the typical pattern of Sunday services was 8 a.m. holy communion, 10 a.m. sung mattins with robed choir, and 6.30 p.m. evensong, mostly from the *Book of Common Prayer*, with occasional variation towards the *Alternative Service Book (1980)*. He allowed this to continue for a year, and then brokered a new deal, with the agreement of the PCC. The services at 8 a.m. and 6.30 p.m. remained 'very traditional', but at 10 a.m. there

---

54   Justin Welby, 'Thought for the Month', *SPCN* (October 1996).
55   Justin Welby, 'Thought for the Month', *SPCN* (February 2001).
56   Justin Welby, sermon at Westminster Abbey, 28 November 2013, National Churches Trust diamond jubilee, www.archbishopofcanterbury.org.

was greater informality and modern music led by a worship band (often with Caroline on the keyboard), deliberately seeking to appeal to families and those outside traditional Anglicanism. The purpose of Sunday services at St James, Welby taught, was 'to meet God and know Him, not just sit in uncomfortable seats listening to unfamiliar music'.[57] By 1999 he could write: 'Many people want to know God, but aren't too keen on what they remember of the formal church; but what they remember may not be what is happening today!'[58] Nonetheless, style remained unimportant:

> But all that is irrelevant to the real issue of Christian faith, which is not whether we worship in a traditional or radically different way (one is as good or bad as the other) but whether we worship God with commitment and passion that opens our lives to His power to change and renew us. ... Churches may be more or less traditional, but God is beyond all that. Knowing Him is neither traditional nor modern – but it is essential.[59]

Elsewhere he wrote: 'Packaging is not the problem. I do not believe that the outward appearance of a service is likely to be decisive in attracting people to faith in Christ as much as the reality of God being met in the service.'[60] When asked years later, as Bishop of Durham, how to reconcile modern and traditional forms of worship, Welby replied: 'Why does it have to be one or the other? They're both doing immensely valuable work, and different people are encountering God in each service. Wonderful! Praise God – let's get on with it!'[61]

Another key part of Welby's church growth strategy in Southam, as in Chilvers Coton, was the revival of the children's and youth work. Before his arrival the Sunday School met for 35 minutes in church, between the two morning services. In October 1996 it was rebranded as SALT (for under 10s) and

57   Justin Welby, 'Thought for the Month', *SPCN* (June 1999).
58   Justin Welby, 'Thought for the Month', *SPCN* (September 1999).
59   Justin Welby, 'Thought for the Month', *SPCN* (January 1999).
60   Justin Welby, 'Thought for the Month', *SPCN* (March 1997).
61   'Unveiling a New Bishop of Durham'.

LAZER (for 10–14s), led by Caroline in the rectory during the 10 a.m. service – with their five children as the core of the group. At the same time Claire Bulman, the first in a long line of 'gap year' students on Welby's staff team, was recruited to re-launch the youth work. IMAGE (for 11–16s) met at the rectory on Sunday evenings with a regular membership of a dozen and the Youth Alpha course was amongst its early activities. This ministry to young people flourished and helped to attract families to the church. Within three years IMAGE had doubled in size and moved to the Roman Catholic church hall. ID, a Friday evening group for 15–18s was started in 2001. The children's work also outgrew the rectory. In June 2000 it was rebranded again as 'The Adventure Zone', now meeting in St James Primary School, with music, drama, Bible stories, crafts, puppets and games. A few months later 'The Activity Zone' (for under 4s) was begun during the main morning service. Alongside these weekly activities, the Welbys instituted a children's holiday club in the summer, run by all four Southam churches. Repeating the Chilvers Coton formula, the first three in 1997–99 were led by Bernie and Jean French, but afterwards by a lay team from the local churches.[62] The holiday club of 2002 catered for 181 children (almost a third of the primary school children in the town) and involved over 80 helpers.[63]

Evangelism was a top priority. 'The New Testament is clear,' Welby wrote in an early letter to the congregation, '*every Christian is always a missionary!*'[64] He admitted that they were weak in fulfilling the Great Commission: 'Here is an area in which we struggle. It is so unanglican apart from anything. True, but it is Christian. It does not usually mean banging on doors. But it does usually mean that each of us can explain why being Christian matters.'[65] To give the congregation greater

62   *St James Southam Annual Reports*, 1997–2002.
63   SPCN (September 2002).
64   Justin Welby to members of St James, Southam, 11 August 1996 (filed with Southam PCC Minutes).
65   Justin Welby, 'Rector's Report', *St James Southam Annual Report 2000*.

confidence in sharing their faith with others, they undertook
a six-week training course from the Church Pastoral Aid
Society called *Lost for Words*. Seeking to reach adults with
the gospel, Welby focused especially on a rolling programme
of Alpha Courses, mostly in the rectory or in people's homes
and on one occasion in the Southam Sports and Social Club.[66]
He explained in his parish magazine that 'The aim of any
church is to introduce people to God, and to do so in such a
way that they can develop their own faith as a result.' Alpha
fitted the bill because it gave opportunity to discuss the claims
of Christianity in a non-pressured environment, with plenty
of hospitality, 'principally creamy cakes'.[67] He described the
course as 'Entertaining, sociable, unthreatening ... and often
life-changing!', and testified to conversions such as a Southam
woman who through Alpha was 'met by Christ' in a dramatic
way, experiencing healing and forgiveness 'in an instant'.[68]
In 1999 Welby persuaded Churches Together in Southam to
host a town-wide Alpha, explaining: 'As churches we disagree
on some things but unite on the most important facts of the
Christian faith, which is what Alpha is about', though this
ecumenical experiment was not repeated.[69] He also invited a
couple of visiting teams to Southam for parish missions, one
led by his old friend John Irvine from St Barnabas, Kensington.
Another key dimension of church growth which Welby had
imbibed during his years at Holy Trinity Brompton, was the
importance of small groups for Christian nurture. By 1999 St
James had nine mid-week groups, with 75 people meeting in
homes around the town for Bible study, prayer and mutual
encouragement.[70]

Learning lessons from the global church was also
significant, as Welby exhorted his congregation to look

---

66   *SPCN* (October 2000).
67   Justin Welby, 'Thought for the Month', *SPCN* (March 1997).
68   *SPCN* (September 2001); Justin Welby, 'Thought for the Month', *SPCN* (January
      2002). See also, Justin Welby, 'Thought for the Month', *SPCN* (October 1998).
69   Justin Welby, 'Thought for the Month', *SPCN* (December 1998).
70   Justin Welby, 'Thought for the Month', *SPCN* (September 1999).

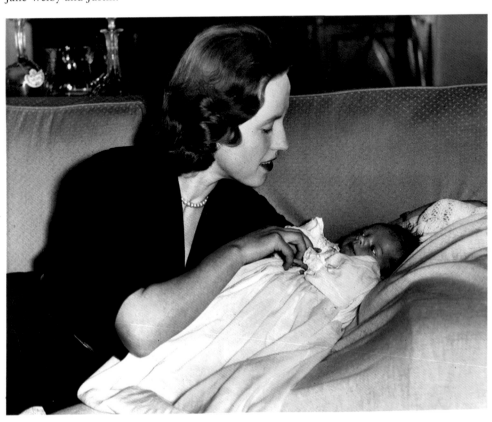

The archbishop's father, Gavin Welby, formerly Gavin Weiler, as a child.

Gavin Welby's campaign leaflet in the 1951 General Election.
[© Conservative Party Archives, Bodleian Library, Oxford]

Jane Welby and Justin.

Justin Welby, aged four.

At St Peter's preparatory school,
in Seaford on the Sussex coast.

Engagement to Caroline Eaton,
June 1979.

Wedding at Holy Trinity Brompton,
December 1979.

With his conservative evangelical mentor, E. J. H. Nash (centre),
and a Cambridge friend, Nick James (right).

Caroline Welby and Charlie
Arbuthnot posing as tourists in
Prague during their Bible-smuggling
expedition in 1980.
Justin is behind the camera.

Group Treasurer of Enterprise Oil, aged 30. [*Euromoney*, October 1986 © Bodleian Library, Oxford]

Monitoring the stock market in Barclays De Zoete Wedd's
trading room in the City of London.
[Enterprise Oil Annual Report and Accounts 1988, © Bodleian Library, Oxford]

Ordinands and tutors at Cranmer Hall, Durham in 1991. Justin Welby is at the centre of the back row. [© Cranmer Hall, Durham]

Ordination as priest at Coventry Cathedral, July 1993. With the family are Welby's mother and stepfather, Lord and Lady Williams of Elvel.

The rector of Southam.

beyond their parochial concerns. During his years in Southam he led two teams to East Africa under the auspices of Sharing of Ministries Abroad (SOMA), an Anglican mission agency which emphasised ministry in the power of the Holy Spirit. In January 1997 his team went to Iringa, in Ruaha diocese in central Tanzania, at the invitation of the diocesan bishop, Donald Mtetemela (primate of Tanzania from 1998). There they worked intensively for five days with the Maasai, training local church leaders in the Alpha Course, although they mistakenly left behind the Alpha manuals specially translated into Swahili on the carousel at Dar-es-Salaam airport.[71] Welby noted that some parts of the Alpha ethos, like small group discussion, did not transfer well from Kensington to Tanzania, while Alpha talks on topics like the existence of the demonic could be taken for granted and were unnecessary.[72] For three weeks in March and April 2000 he led another team, including four members of the Southam congregation, to Luweero diocese, Uganda, where they ran a conference for Anglican clergy, workshops for lay readers and school assemblies. The trip was overshadowed by the horrors at Kanungu a few days earlier, where hundreds of members of the millennial cult, the Movement for the Restoration of the Ten Commandments of God, were burned alive in a locked church, either group suicide or murder. Their leaders had claimed to receive visions from the Virgin Mary about the imminent end of the world. Hundreds of bodies were discovered in mass graves at other sites belonging to the cult across southern Uganda, poisoned or stabbed.[73] As news of these atrocities dominated the headlines, the SOMA team taught on true Christianity from the Book of Acts. 'Faced with the recent cult murders, and clergy who appeared deeply demoralised,' Welby explained,

---

71   Don Brewin, *It Will Emerge: The Joys and Heartaches of Over 15 Years of Short-Term Mission* (second edition, Milton Keynes: Lulu, 2014), p. 69.

72   Justin Welby, 'Tanzania: Diocese of Ruaha', *Sharing* (SOMA newsletter) (June 1997), p. 2.

73   Richard Vokes, *Ghosts of Kanungu: Fertility, Secrecy and Exchange in the Great Lakes of East Africa* (Woodbridge: James Currey, 2009).

'we focused on the Real Church and the Real Jesus. The emphasis on practical, applied, biblical teaching struck a powerful chord.'[74] For the English visitors the experience was 'an eye opener', especially noticing the Ugandan approach to holistic mission which encompassed education, health care, agriculture and finance, not only erecting new church buildings. Welby reflected: 'whatever the difference in circumstances, we found a deep common unity of faith ... Christ brought unity of heart and Spirit in worship to God'.[75] Global perspectives, especially African, were to become increasingly important in his later ministry.

The recruitment of a strong staff team, and the nurturing of leadership gifts amongst the congregation, was another key dimension of Welby's church growth strategy. Soon after arriving in the parish he began to shape his team. In early 1996 he was joined by Trevor Rogers, a non-stipendiary minister and former mayor of Southam. That autumn St James' 'gap year' youth worker arrived, the first of many. In July 1999 Fiona Newton, a lay chaplain at Rugby school, was ordained as full-time curate for Southam, an indication of diocesan confidence in Welby's abilities as a trainer and of his commitment to the ordination of women. A few months later Alison Toulmin was commissioned by the Archdeacon of Warwick as area youth worker, to work for three years in Southam and the surrounding villages under Welby's oversight. He resisted any ideas of the rector as a one-man-band and was especially eager to deploy lay leaders. During his final months in Southam, he established a Ministry Leadership Team of ten people responsible for the church's worship, pastoral care and outreach, emphasising that the laity were now taking on roles previously reserved for the clergy: 'The Rector is not the boss', an indication of his collaborative instinct.[76]

74   Justin Welby, 'Diocese of Luweero', *Sharing* (June 2000), p. 2. See also Justin Welby, 'Report on SOMA Visit to Luweero Diocese, Church of Uganda', SOMA Archives (in possession of Don Brewin).
75   Justin Welby, 'Thought for the Month', *SPCN* (May 2000).
76   Justin Welby, 'Thought for the Month', *SPCN* (August 2002).

The many new strategies which Welby initiated in a few short years were not all smooth going, as the congregation struggled to adapt to some of his ideas. He bluntly told the PCC that they 'must accept changes', though he apologised for his lack of communication.[77] There were evident tensions in integrating newcomers with established members at St James. 'The church is growing and growth is often very hard to cope with,' he acknowledged. 'But the alternative is oblivion.'[78] There was also concern when he introduced adult baptism by immersion; and when the PCC conducted a SWOT analysis (Strengths, Weaknesses, Opportunities, Threats) they placed home groups under Threats as well as Strengths.[79] The Ministry Leadership Team was a particular bone of contention because it appeared to undermine the authority of the PCC, though Welby reassured them it was not about power or control.[80] Money was always short and the church regularly struggled to pay its annual 'parish share' to the diocese. When there was a surplus in 2002, for the first time, the PCC celebrated the news as 'a real answer to prayer and a miracle!'[81] Welby was not unaffected by the criticisms, although according to his curate, Fiona Newton, he had 'courage to be radical, to be revolutionary'. He decided on the basis of strong analytical skills what was needed, and then brought root and branch change. Whilst being a strategic thinker, he was 'a man on his knees in prayer, first and foremost', and was able to carry people with him not by force but because they admired the quality of his life.[82]

Welby's various attempts to stimulate local church growth had demonstrable effect. The Southam service register reveals a steady, if unspectacular, increase in the regular Sunday

77   Southam PCC Minutes, 25 November 1997.
78   Justin Welby, 'Report of the Rector', *St James Southam Annual Report 1997*.
79   Southam PCC Minutes, 27 May and 25 November 1998.
80   Southam PCC Minutes, 3 February and 24 November 1999; 14 February, 13 June and 18 July 2001.
81   Southam PCC Minutes, 20 February 2002.
82   Interview with Fiona Newton, 14 November 2013.

congregation. The traditional services remained fairly static across the period, attracting on average 21 people in the morning and 37 in the evening. But the informal morning service flourished, more than doubling in size from an average of just 34 in 1996, to 74 adults by 1999 and 80 by 2002.[83] Welby was particularly absorbed in collecting church growth data, laid out in his annual reports, sometimes complete with bar-graphs and scatter-graphs recording monthly attendance. By his own calculations, the normal adult Sunday attendance across all services had risen from 80 in 1995 to 128 in 2001, with perhaps 200 in the church overall, though this was only 3 per cent of the population in the parish. He believed they were on 'the cusp' of moving from being a small church to a large church.[84] Nevertheless, Welby was careful to emphasise that 'Christian faith is not about numbers at church, but living with God, day in and day out, and finding the difference He makes.'[85]

The Welby family remained in Southam for seven years, their most stable period in one location and nearly twice as long as Justin spent in any other post in the Church of England before reaching Canterbury. Nevertheless, he was a man in perpetual motion, and even in Southam was soon looking on to the next thing. In February 2000, after only four and a half years in the parish, he advised the PCC to begin formulating their criteria for their next rector. Although he stressed that he was not planning to leave yet, he wanted them to be prepared.[86] In the event, he remained until October 2002. On his departure, one of his congregation reflected: 'Justin is a man of many abilities. One might say he has been a New Broom, and the

83   St James Southam, Register of Services (1992–2008), Southam Parish Archives. Calculations based on the six month period from January to June for 1996, 1999 and 2002, excluding Easter Sunday, Mothering Sunday, Civic or Churches Together services, and Baptism services.
84   *St James Southam Annual Report 2001.*
85   Justin Welby, 'Thought for the Month', *SPCN* (March 1997).
86   Southam PCC Minutes, 17 February 2000.

dust from his sweeping has made some of us splutter a bit, but he has encouraged us to take some deep breaths of fresh air.'[87]

Teaching the Faith

As rector Welby contributed over 70 articles to his parish magazine, *Southam Parish Church News*, in the form of a 'Thought for the Month'. The genre is necessarily brief and broad-brush, written partly to build connections with a non-Christian readership in the town, and does not allow for the exposition of detailed or nuanced theology. Nevertheless these articles provide a snapshot into some of Welby's central concerns and opinions as a parish minister, and therefore are worth sampling here.

One dominant motif was Welby's desire to call his parishioners to faith in Christ. His articles were peppered with evangelistic challenge, beginning with his very first letter in which he laid out his stall:

> The church is there to remind people that God exists, and call all of us to faith in Jesus Christ, who lived, died and rose from the dead so that we can know God as the centre of our lives, in reality and experience. The church is not a home for saints; Christians do not claim to be better than other folk, but they do claim that God has touched their lives and given new meaning to them.[88]

Welby could write from experience that God 'provides the still centre of life in turmoil, and the fiery excitement of life in tedium'.[89] He frequently spoke of the forgiveness, acceptance and peace found in Jesus Christ. Christ, he affirmed, lived and died and rose again 'to break all the barriers that separate us

---

87   Irene Cardall, 'Some Notable Rectors', *SPCN* (October 2002).
88   'Letter from the Welbys', *SPCN* (August 1995).
89   Justin Welby, 'Thought for the Month', *SPCN* (July 2002).

from God, to give us a chance to know Him, and to give us the promise of heaven, if we belong to Him'.[90] In a nutshell, the rector declared, 'The Christian claim is simply that through Jesus we meet God.'[91]

Welby's emphasis was both Christ-centred and explicitly cross-centred, serious about human sin and its divine remedy through the crucifixion. In the context of the 1995 murder trials of O. J. Simpson in Los Angeles and serial killer Rosemary West in Gloucester, Welby wrote:

> the authentic Christian message is grimly realistic about the world. Jesus Christ died on the Cross so that we can be put right with God, and experience His love. If the world was not so bad God would not have needed to do anything. It is exactly because of all the evil that He provided a way of giving us hope.[92]

Sometimes he explained the death of Christ in moral terms, as 'the greatest example of love and commitment that there is'.[93] At other times Welby emphasised the penal and substitutionary dimensions of the atonement, that on the cross Jesus 'took the punishment for all the sin we have ever or will ever commit. ... He was cut off from His Father ... Jesus faced the full weight of wickedness, and its full cost in our place, so that we can find the way to God.'[94] This remained a theme of his teaching and he wrote in later years that when Jesus was crucified, 'the full force of God's justice burst on Him and not us'.[95] Welby was explicit that Christ died 'so that those who believe in him might go to heaven'.[96] Equally significant in his doctrinal framework was the bodily resurrection of Christ and he was willing to stake all on the historicity of the Gospel accounts:

90   Justin Welby, 'Thought for the Month', *SPCN* (April 2001).
91   Justin Welby, 'Thought for the Month', *SPCN* (July 1998).
92   Justin Welby, 'Thought for the Month', *SPCN* (November 1995).
93   Justin Welby, 'Thought for the Month', *SPCN* (March 1996).
94   Justin Welby, 'Thought for the Month', *SPCN* (April 1998).
95   Justin Welby, 'The Book of Lamentations: Five Addresses for Holy Week', Coventry Cathedral 2006, p. 11.
96   Justin Welby, 'Thought for the Month', *SPCN* (March 1996).

If Jesus did not rise from the dead, the Christian faith is untrue. If His bones were found, I (and I hope all other clergy) would quit. The parish church, the Roman Catholic church and the chapel would simply be museums to a discarded superstition. That is why it all matters. If it is true, then all other Christian claims follow. There is life after death in heaven, and death has been defeated, which is the best news that there could be.[97]

Welby not only announced the gospel message but urged his readers to respond. For example, when the Church of England's doctrine commission published *The Mystery of Salvation* (1995), which attracted wide press coverage for its advocacy of annihilationism (defining hell as 'total non-being' rather than 'eternal torment'), Welby took the opportunity to present the stark choice between heaven and hell. Rather than criticise the report's theology, he bluntly challenged his parishioners: 'God holds us responsible for our choices about Him. ... The choice that aims us for heaven is to believe Him, trust Him and centre our lives on Him. The choice that directs us to hell is to deny Him, disobey Him and ignore Him.'[98] Later he reiterated: 'Christians believe that God gives us choices. To believe or not. To obey Him or not. Also, that the choice we make has consequences, for ever.'[99] The call of Jesus demanded 'more than a token nod, and a quid in the plate', but to make him 'the central focus of our lives'.[100]

Another dominant motif in Welby's magazine articles was his call for the Christian church to be socially and politically engaged. For example, during the 1996 BSE crisis which saw exports of British beef banned by the European Union, with a major impact upon local Warwickshire farms, the rector insisted that it was wrong to blame the farmers. Instead pressure should be put upon the government to promote agricultural methods which upheld the Bible's teaching to care

97   Justin Welby, 'Thought for the Month', *SPCN* (April 1996).
98   Justin Welby, 'Thought for the Month', *SPCN* (February 1996).
99   Justin Welby, 'Thought for the Month', *SPCN* (November 1999).
100   Justin Welby, 'Thought for the Month', *SPCN* (March 1996).

for the natural world instead of exploiting it.[101] Two years later Welby weighed into the saga over the Millennium Dome, suggesting that the vast sums of public money would have been much better spent on relieving poverty and suffering: 'I'm not sure if Jesus would have been very keen on domes. Especially multi-million pound domes. I often think that he would not have been very keen on big buildings at all.'[102] In May 1997, in advance of the general election, Welby's usual 'Thought for the Month' was replaced by contributions from the local Conservative, Labour and Liberal Democrat candidates on the question, 'What is a good vote?'[103] He urged his parishioners to abandon cynicism about national politics and use their influence wisely:

> Christians believe there is a God who not only governs events but holds us each responsible for the part we play, however small ... we will answer to God for what our vote (or abstention) stands for. ... No party has a monopoly of truth or right, but we each need to vote as if ours was the only vote, or the decisive one.[104]

Likewise at the 2001 general election he reiterated that no political party had 'a monopoly on morality, or for that matter on Christian truth', though it would be wrong for Christians to vote for anyone who 'overtly and consciously set out to pass laws that were unethical', like the racist policies of the National Front. He maintained: 'Christians believe that God is active in the world and that in the end all government is under His control. In the bible, nations are seen as getting the government they deserve.'[105]

Cardinal Hume and the Roman Catholic episcopate were especially commended by the rector of Southam for their public statements on economic and moral issues. Indeed

101   Justin Welby, 'Thought for the Month', *SPCN* (June 1996).
102   Justin Welby, 'Thought for the Month', *SPCN* (February 1998).
103   *SPCN* (May 1997).
104   Justin Welby, 'Thought for the Month', *SPCN* (April 1997).
105   Justin Welby, 'Thought for the Month', *SPCN* (June 2001).

he praised Hume as one of Britain's two or three greatest spiritual leaders of the twentieth century.[106] Welby made clear his own opposition to moral relativism by which ethics were considered a private concern rather than a public truth, as he wrote in his magazine:

> By all means do what you like, but if you ignore what God says is right then you will be judged by Him. So the church says that it has a duty to proclaim what it believes to be right and attempt to persuade others. People may ignore it, but they will have been warned. No individual or church can force people to behave in a certain way. The Inquisition is long gone! However, I hope that the church will not be cowed into silence on matters of economic justice or morality just because saying them may be unpopular.[107]

In a speech in the House of Lords in July 1996 on Britain's moral and spiritual well-being, Archbishop George Carey addressed the need to 'strengthen the moral fibre of our nation' by re-instilling rules for society based upon the Judeo-Christian tradition, principally the Ten Commandments and the example and teaching of Jesus.[108] Carey's comments attracted considerable press attention and Welby noted that it was difficult for the church to speak out about public morals because

> it gives the impression that morality and Christianity are the same thing. They are not. You can be a morally upright atheist, or Buddhist or whatever. To be a Christian is to know and love God and to have experienced His love and forgiveness. That experience should lead to a desire to lead a good life; but the experience of God's love comes first.[109]

He observed that Jesus laid down few rules, and indeed broke some, because Jesus' concern for individuals always came before 'an impersonal application of a rule'. Nevertheless,

---

106 Justin Welby, 'Thought for the Month', *SPCN* (August 1999).
107 Justin Welby, 'Thought for the Month', *SPCN* (February 1997).
108 Hansard, House of Lords, 5 July 1996, columns 1691–5.
109 Justin Welby, 'Thought for the Month', *SPCN* (August 1996).

Jesus was also 'very strong on morality. ... He was not soft in any way at all, but He was loving.' It was a sad irony, Welby wryly remarked, that when bishops talked about social injustice they were told to stick to morals, and when they talked about morals they were called hypocrites. He asked:

> So is it worth it? Should anyone try to talk about morals? I think the answer is strongly yes! We need reminding that there are absolute standards ... Equally, if the church is to talk about morals it should be in the context of faith in Jesus Christ who both has the highest standards and forgives those who are truly sorry and come to Him seeking to start again. Simple exhortations to be better ... are valueless by themselves.[110]

This desire to hold together both the demands of biblical morality and the offer of forgiveness was demonstrated by Welby's attitude to homosexuality. In 1999 the Children's Society, an Anglican charity working with vulnerable children and young people, decided to place children with gay and lesbian couples for fostering and adoption. At Welby's urging, the Southam PCC wrote to the Children's Society expressing their concern and warning that future financial support from the parish was in doubt unless there was a rethink.[111] In *Southam Parish Church News* the rector explained the reasons for their protest:

> Of course morality matters, sexual morality included, although not the most of all, and for someone who claims to be a Christian ... the standards of expected sexual morality are clear. Throughout the bible it is clear that the right place for sex is only within a committed, heterosexual marriage. Interestingly, all recent research also shows that the children of such a relationship are likely (not always but often) to be happier and more stable. Also, that relationships based on Christian standards of morality (no sex outside marriage) tend (not invariably) to last longer. However, the bible is also clear, and all our experience says, that few – if any – of us always

---

110   Justin Welby, 'Thought for the Month', *SPCN* (August 1996).
111   Southam PCC Minutes, 22 September 1999.

keep to the standards. Whether it's past or present affairs, homosexual or heterosexual, or in many other ways, our sexuality is one of the most powerful forces within us – and it often leads us astray.

Yet he also wanted his parishioners to be assured that the Christian gospel offered forgiveness for sexual sins when they were repented: 'past mistakes, or failings, or actions do not condemn forever. ... All of us need the chance to start again.' Welby reiterated that although God made moral rules he 'also makes ways for forgiveness' through Jesus Christ, the only sinless person.[112] The Southam protest made no impact upon the Children's Society's policy and 14 years later, as Archbishop of Canterbury, Welby accepted the invitation to become the society's president.

A theology of grace governed Welby's response to other stories in the press. When Lawrence Dallaglio was forced to resign as England rugby captain in May 1999 after a drugs scandal exposed by the *News of the World*, Welby spoke both against press hypocrisy and of the power of the Christian gospel to bring redemption to sinners. He declared:

> All human beings are fallible. We all have considerable weaknesses to drinking, lying, jealousy, anger, foolishness, deceit, sexual misconduct, drugs – the list is endless. It does not matter who you are, or what you do. The bible calls it sin, and says that we all tend towards it.

Yet Jesus offered forgiveness to anyone who admitted they had done wrong and gave Him control of their lives:

> That is why Christianity is good news. It is real about the disease, and real about the cure for the disease. It's only the News of the World and the other tabloids that live in a dream world where they expect *anyone* to be perfect and provide no answer when we find they are not, except simple, unforgiving, condemnation.[113]

112   Justin Welby, 'Thought for the Month', *SPCN* (December 1999).
113   Justin Welby, 'Thought for the Month', *SPCN* (July 1999).

Welby was likewise critical of the tabloid frenzy in January 2002 when Prince Harry was found to have been sent, aged 16, to a drugs rehabilitation centre by Prince Charles. He wrote sarcastically: 'What a surprise, a teenager has too much to drink and tries cannabis. What is the world coming to? No doubt, no journalist drinks anything but water, and all have difficulty even spelling marijuana. Oh please! ... Journalists are hypocrites, like all the rest of us.'[114]

Across the seven-year period from 1995 to 2002, Welby's 'Thought for the Month' in *Southam Parish Church News* displayed a strong doctrine of grace. He laid emphasis on the high ethical demands of Christianity and whole-hearted discipleship, but also the reality of human failure and the free offer of redemption and a fresh start through Jesus Christ. His concern was both for evangelism and active socio-political engagement. He aimed to persuade his readers of the truths of Christianity, both intellectually and experientially, while at the same time urging those who were already converted to transform their community and bear social responsibility as part of their Christian witness. He was clear that true conversion, and intimate relationship with Jesus Christ, must precede a Christian social ethic.

Widening Relationships

During his years in Southam, Welby began to establish a wider profile outside the parish, building especially upon his business background. As a result of his treasury experience, he became a non-executive director in June 1998 of the South Warwickshire General Hospitals NHS Trust, and chairman of its audit committee. The Trust was responsible for hospitals

114   Justin Welby, 'Thought for the Month', *SPCN* (February 2002).

in Warwick and Stratford-upon-Avon, with 2,000 staff, but Welby's time on the board coincided with a leadership crisis. In October 2000 the chief executive, Andrew Riley, was suspended on full pay after allegations that waiting-list numbers had been deliberately deflated so that the hospitals would meet government targets and receive bonus funding. He agreed to resign in January 2001, after negotiating a financial settlement with the Trust, though some said he had been 'made a scapegoat for political motives'.[115] Two weeks later the chairman, David Evans, followed Riley out of the door, having lost the confidence of the board. The bad news kept coming when doctors admitted in February that they had kept 92 organs from autopsies dating back to the 1970s, without permission. In this leadership vacuum, Welby suddenly found himself elected as the new chairman to deal with the turmoil and to re-establish public confidence in the hospitals, admitting in his first annual report that 'lessons had been learnt'.[116] With the Trust under intense scrutiny, he was determined that the best approach was 'transparency and openness'.[117] In his parish magazine he alluded to the troubles, touching on the issue of human fallibility, one of his regular themes:

> What do we expect of our doctors and health workers? They are after all human, and thus make mistakes. ... for all its faults the NHS still represents one of the clearest ways in which, as a society, we express care for one another. For that to go on we all need to show how much we value it, not just make more demands on it![118]

The Commission for Health Improvement published a scathing report after an inspection of the hospitals, giving the Trust the lowest rating for its performance in almost every

115 'Hospital Chief in Waiting Lists Inquiry', *Times*, 7 October 2000, p. 8; 'Health Boss Quits Over Cash Ruse', *Times*, 31 January 2001, p. 5; *Inappropriate Adjustments to NHS Waiting Lists* (London: National Audit Office, December 2001).
116 'Hospital Sorry For Blunders', *Leamington Courier*, 7 September 2001.
117 South Warwickshire General Hospitals NHS Trust Board Minutes, 1 March 2001.
118 Justin Welby, 'Thought for the Month', *SPCN* (March 2001).

area, and Welby admitted there was much work still to be done.[119] His chairmanship continued until early 2003, though it was a considerable time commitment (on average two days a week), and the Southam PCC expressed some concern about whether their rector should spend so much time away from the parish.[120] He earned £17,000 a year from his Trust work, equivalent to a second Church of England stipend. He saw none of the money because it all went into Coventry diocesan coffers, though some of it was set against the Southam parish share.

Meanwhile Welby was increasingly in demand for his expertise in financial ethics. In the oil industry in 1983 he had joined the fledgling Association of Corporate Treasurers (ACT) and in 1998 was appointed as its personal and ethical advisor, to help company treasurers facing ethical dilemmas. He became a regular contributor to ACT's magazine, *The Treasurer*, on topics such as 'Virtuous Treasurers', 'Knowing Right from Wrong' and 'Does Scrooge Prosper?'[121] In one article he wrote: 'Ethics is not just "what I feel" – or at least it should not be. ... The pressure to go with a majority, or not to make waves, is always enormous. ... There are few genuinely simple ethical questions. So much is about nuances, interpretation, and conscience.'[122]

At the same period Welby was invited to join the Finance Ethics Group of the Von Hügel Institute, a Roman Catholic research centre at St Edmund's College in Cambridge, concerned with the relationship between Christianity and social policy. It sought to harness the potential of Pope Leo XIII's encyclical *Rerum Novarum* ('About Revolutions', 1891) which emphasised social justice, human dignity and

---

119 *Report of a Clinical Governance Review at South Warwickshire General Hospitals NHS Trust* (London: Commission for Health Improvement, March 2002).
120 Southam PCC Minutes, 21 November 2001.
121 Justin Welby, 'Virtuous Treasurers', *The Treasurer* (January 2000), p. 66; Justin Welby, 'Knowing Right from Wrong', *The Treasurer* (February 2003), p. 47; Justin Welby, 'Does Scrooge Prosper?', *The Treasurer* (December 2006), p. 44.
122 Welby, 'Knowing Right from Wrong', p. 47.

the 'common good' – prominent themes in Welby's later discourse as Archbishop of Canterbury. The Finance Ethics Group brought together business executives, bankers and moral theologians to consider the issues of globalisation and the banks. Welby presented a paper on the ethics of financial derivatives, in which he had traded for many years at Enterprise Oil, and the inherent risks involved. He observed that the financial markets had grown remarkably in their complexity:

> Risk management is the buzz term in Treasury (always an empire-building profession), and its practice is an increasingly black art. At times one feels that the Treasurer's profession and the corporate finance sector in the City are engaged in a mutually rewarding process of finding ever more complicated ways to manage the risks that their methods are creating ever more prolifically. The only simple parts are the bill at the end and the rise in the Treasurer's pay.[123]

The language of risk-taking was later to become prominent in Welby's teaching about reconciliation and church growth, but it first began to take shape here in the context of stock markets and exchange rates. He argued that when faced by risk there was a proper balance to be struck between 'recklessness and terrified immobility'. An obsession with managing risk led to cowardice and paralysis of action, a lesson he would later apply to the Church of England.[124] Two years later, in 1999, Welby was in Santiago, Chile, lecturing at an international conference on financial globalisation convened by the United Nations Economic Commission for Latin America and the Caribbean (ECLAC) and the International Jacques Maritain Institute in Rome, which brought together policy-makers,

---

123 Justin Welby, 'The Ethics of Derivatives and Risk Management', *Ethical Perspectives* vol. 4 (July 1997), pp. 86–7. This paper was often republished in revised form: see Justin Welby, 'Is Modern Finance More Ethical?', *Finance & Bien Commun* (Autumn 1998), pp. 28–34; Justin Welby, 'Risk Management and the Ethics of New Financial Instruments', in Stephen F. Frowen and Francis P. McHugh (eds), *Financial Competition, Risk and Accountability: British and German Experiences* (Baskingstoke: Palgrave, 2001), pp. 119–35; in Dutch translation as Justin Welby, 'De ethiek van financiële derivaten en risicobeheer', *Ethische Perspectieven* vol. 19 (2009), pp. 4–19.

124 Welby, 'The Ethics of Derivatives and Risk Management', p. 91.

academics and financiers. He appealed for the rediscovery of commonly agreed virtues – prudence, transparency and social responsibility – as the foundations of an ethical structure for the global financial markets which were increasingly complex and dehumanised.[125]

Through the Von Hügel Institute, Welby established a new range of associations with Roman Catholic economists and theologians, especially in French-speaking Europe, which gave him a wider platform for his ideas and also helped to shape his personal spirituality. At the Finance Ethics Group he met Paul Dembinski, a Polish economist based in Geneva, founding-director of l'Observatoire de la Finance and the bilingual journal *Finance & Bien Commun*. Welby became closely associated with l'Observatoire, often lecturing at its conferences, sitting on its editorial board and on the jury of the Robin Cosgrove prize to promote ethical finance amongst young professionals. Through Dembinski he was invited to join l'Association Internationale pour l'Enseignement Social Chrétien (the International Association for Christian Social Teaching), of which Welby became vice-president in 1998. The group met once a year over a long weekend to examine the contemporary application of Roman Catholic social thought as expressed in papal encyclicals.

Through Dembinski, Welby was also introduced in 2000 to Nicolas Buttet, a Swiss Roman Catholic and former lawyer. Buttet had been living 'a dissolute life' until, in Welby's words, 'he heard Jesus calling him, saying "Come and follow me".' He worked briefly at the Vatican and then spent five years as a hermit in a stone hut on a rock-face near Saint-Maurice in Valais, 'eating whatever was brought to the door ... no heating, it was on the snow-line ... spending his time with the Lord'.[126] People began to come to Buttet to pray so in 1996 he founded

125   Justin Welby, 'Going with the Flow of the Market', in José Antonio Ocampo, Stefano Zamagni, Ricardo Ffrench-Davis and Carlo Pietrobelli (eds), *Financial Globalization and the Emerging Economies* (Santiago, Chile: ECLAC and the International Jacques Maritain Institute, 2000), pp. 303–9.
126   St Mellitus College, 2 December 2013.

the Eucharistein community in a local farmhouse, focused on redeeming people pushed to the fringes of society by drug and alcohol addictions or mental illness. Welby was bowled over by his first encounter, and described Buttet to his parishioners in Southam as 'So full of love for others that you could touch it. So utterly unconcerned with himself. So generous, and so committed to Jesus, he almost shone.'[127] Buttet was ordained as a Roman Catholic priest in 2003 and became Welby's spiritual director, one of the 'formative influences' on his life.[128] He was particularly impressed by Buttet's commitment to prayer, simplicity and care for the poor.

Through Buttet, Welby met another Roman Catholic who had a profound impact upon him, Cardinal Nguyen Van Thuan, president of the Pontifical Council for Justice and Peace. Thuan had been appointed archbishop coadjutor of Saigon (Ho Chi Minh City) in 1975 but was arrested by the Communist regime and imprisoned for twelve years, nine of them in solitary confinement, before being released in 1988 and sent into exile.[129] Welby described him as 'full of love for God and others, a lively sense of humour, and a face full of hope and strength'.[130] Thuan's example of faithfulness to Christ in the midst of extreme hardship became a familiar refrain in Welby's teaching, recurring often in his writings and sermons, including his installation in Liverpool and his enthronement in Durham.[131]

These new encounters were significant in shaping Welby's sacramentalism. He was particularly struck, for example, by

---

127 Justin Welby, 'Thought for the Month', *SPCN* (January 2001).
128 Lambeth Palace press conference, 9 November 2012, reply to a question.
129 André Nguyen Van Chau, *The Miracle of Hope: Political Prisoner, Prophet of Peace: Life of Francis Xavier Nguyen Van Thuan* (Boston: Pauline Books, 2003).
130 Justin Welby, 'Thought for the Month', *SPCN* (January 2001).
131 'Dean Justin's Sermon', *LCL* no. 52 (December 2007), p. 28; Justin Welby, 'Enthronement Sermon', 26 November 2011, www.durham.anglican.org. For other examples, see Justin Welby, 'The Gift of Reconciliation', *Guidelines* vol. 26 (September – December 2010), p. 82; Justin Welby, 'Marvel Amid the Mundane', *The Treasurer* (December 2011 – January 2012), p. 11; Justin Welby, 'Coping with Danger', *Guidelines* vol. 28 (January – April 2012), pp. 49–50; Justin Welby, 'Torture: Strictly Forbidden? The Spiritual Dimension', *The Friends Quarterly* vol. 40 (November 2012), p. 14.

the account of how Thuan worshipped in solitary confinement through saying daily mass with one grain of rice for bread and enough wine to fill the palm of one hand, which brought the political prisoner spiritual comfort and a tangible sense of the presence of God. Welby's strong bond with the Eucharistein community in Switzerland was likewise important. As the name suggests, at the heart of the community's spiritual life is perpetual adoration of the sacrament. On one occasion Welby arrived there at 11 o'clock at night, exhausted after a long flight, but went to the chapel and knelt in front of the sacrament for an hour and a half. He went to bed

> having met the Lord more genuinely than at any other time, pretty well, in my life and deeply at peace, despite everything that had happened to me, and renewed in vision and strength. Now I can't explain that. It doesn't fit into how I grew up as a Christian. But all I know is that God uses these things and he's gracious. And so I tend to be a bit of a spiritual magpie, and where something leads me closer to Jesus I say, 'Thank you, I'll have some of that.'[132]

Meanwhile, as Welby began to travel more widely in Africa he noticed the significance of the sacrament for those in peril. An abiding impression was visiting the swamps of the Niger Delta in 2004 where, 'in a town of utter poverty, serious violence and terrible killing, a colleague and I shared Communion with people who had nothing and could look forward to less, and found peace'.[133] Around the same period he began to receive holy communion daily as part of his personal spiritual discipline. This new range of friendships with Roman Catholics in France and Switzerland, and with Anglicans in Africa, provided a sacramental dimension to Welby's theological experience not typical for someone nurtured within English evangelicalism.

Welby's years in parish ministry were ones of growth not only for the local church, but also for his personal spirituality

---

132   Interview at New Wine Conference, 29 July 2013.
133   'Dean Justin's Sermon', pp. 28–9.

and ecumenical relationships. His gifts for bridge-building, obvious as a student at Cranmer Hall, were seen in Southam by the way in which he reconciled old and new styles of worship at St James and encouraged partnerships in evangelism with other denominations in the town. Although he showed evident abilities in leading and growing a congregation, his interests stretched far beyond the parish and the boundaries of Anglicanism. The international dimension to his work, which began to emerge in Southam, became particularly prominent. These aspects of Welby's character and experience were important in determining the future direction of his ministry. As the next step, he was talent-spotted by Coventry Cathedral in 2002 and recruited to help direct its international department in seeking reconciliation in areas of conflict.

Chapter 6

The Ministry of Reconciliation

On the night of 14 November 1940 the German Luftwaffe obliterated Coventry city centre during an intensive bombardment which marked an escalation in the Second World War and added a new verb to the dictionary: 'to coventrate'. Over 500 civilians were killed and the cathedral was destroyed alongside many homes and factories. Instead of calling for revenge, Provost Dick Howard spoke of reconciliation and forgiveness. Amongst the rubble lay medieval nails from the cathedral's fallen roof, three of which were bound together in the shape of a cross. The cathedral rose again, built afresh by Basil Spence during the 1950s, but the shell of the old remained, symbolising death and resurrection, devastation and renewal. The 'ministry of reconciliation' (2 Corinthians 5:18) became a particular vocation of the cathedral community.[1] From 1959 a *Litany of Reconciliation*, with the repeated refrain 'Father, forgive', was prayed in the ruins of the old cathedral every Friday at noon, the hour that Jesus was crucified. There were early initiatives towards Anglo–German reconciliation and the cathedral sent a team of young people to help rebuild Dresden, which had been carpet-bombed by the Allies. As other Christians began to capture the Coventry vision, the Community of the Cross of Nails (CCN) came to birth in the 1960s. It was overseen from 1974 by the director of the cathedral's International Centre for Reconciliation (ICR),

1   Richard T. Howard, *Ruined and Rebuilt: The Story of Coventry Cathedral, 1939–1962* (Coventry: Council of Coventry Cathedral, 1962); Basil Spence, *Phoenix at Coventry: The Building of a Cathedral* (London: Bles, 1962); Christopher A. Lamb (ed.), *Reconciling People: Coventry Cathedral's Story* (Norwich: Canterbury Press, 2011).

who was one of the residentiary canons. By the early twenty-first century there were approximately 160 CCN centres in 50 countries around the world working on local reconciliation projects as far flung as Cincinnati, Belfast, Cape Town and Khartoum.[2]

The focus of the cathedral's international ministry varied according to the canon in charge. The first director of the ICR, Kenyon Wright, had a particular interest in India. The third director, Paul Oestreicher, worked especially in Eastern Europe, behind the Iron Curtain. By the time he retired in 1998 international attention was no longer on Communism but on Islam, especially in the Middle East and in Africa. Therefore Bishop Colin Bennetts of Coventry appointed a specialist in religious dialogue between Christianity, Judaism and Islam as the new canon for reconciliation ministry. Andrew White, a 33-year-old London vicar, had been nurtured within the Holy Trinity Brompton network of churches, having served as Paul Perkin's curate in Battersea in the early 1990s. His first work with the ICR was in Israel, the West Bank and the Gaza Strip, where he demonstrated a genius for establishing relationships with hostile religious leaders from the diverse faith communities. The political situation in Israel disintegrated rapidly during 2000: the Oslo Accords lacked credibility; the Camp David Summit between Bill Clinton, Ehud Barak (Prime Minister of Israel) and Yasser Arafat (President of the Palestinian National Authority) proved a failure; and the al-Aqsa Intifada was declared, inflamed by Ariel Sharon's provocative visit to the Temple Mount in Jerusalem. Behind the scenes, White worked with Rabbi Michael Melchior (Israel's Deputy Foreign Minister) to bring together religious leaders in a peace initiative. In a context of escalating violence and the tightest security, a summit was held in January 2002 in Alexandria co-chaired by Archbishop George Carey and Sheikh Muhammad Sayed Tantawi, the Grand Imam of al-

2   Oliver Schuegraf, *The Cross of Nails: Joining in God's Mission of Reconciliation* (English translation, Norwich: Canterbury Press, 2012).

Azhar. After heated arguments and delicate diplomacy the 14 gathered leaders representing Judaism, Islam and Christianity signed the Alexandria Declaration which proclaimed that 'killing innocents in the name of God is a desecration of His Holy Name' and called for a religiously sanctioned ceasefire.[3]

Back home in Coventry diocese, Justin Welby was deeply impressed.[4] He wrote to congratulate White on his extraordinary achievement, promised the fervent prayers of Southam parish, and hoped that he might travel with White on one of his excursions, 'as bag carrier or anything'.[5] White promptly invited Welby to Israel and Palestine in March 2002, on a follow-up visit working towards the implementation of the Alexandria Process.[6] The adventure was, for Welby, 'a mind blowing, viewpoint changing, memory charging experience'. Some of the encounters were surreal. They met in Jerusalem with Torkom Manoogian, the Armenian Patriarch, who was seated on a red silk-covered throne wearing black robes and purple jewelled slippers while they ate Quality Street chocolates, drank Armenian brandy (strong) and Turkish coffee (very strong), and talked of politics and the independence of Armenia in the thirteenth century. Welby recalled: 'Sitting in extraordinary surroundings, wearing odd clothes, talking to people with remarkable titles, in even stranger clothes, about unusual events, I began to feel I had fallen into an episode of *Star Trek*.' There was drama, like being driven in a high-speed convoy through the dark countryside to Yasser Arafat's compound at Ramallah from which Israeli tanks had withdrawn only two days earlier. Welby's abiding impression,

3   Andrew White, *The Vicar of Baghdad: Fighting for Peace in the Middle East* (Oxford: Monarch, 2009), pp. 21–41; George Carey, *Know the Truth: A Memoir* (London: HarperCollins, 2004), pp. 391–7.

4   For Welby's testimony to White's courage and conviction, see Justin Welby, 'An Exceptional Vision', *LCL* no. 70 (July 2009), pp. 17–18; Justin Welby, 'Foreword', in Andrew White, *Father, Forgive: Reflections on Peacemaking* (Oxford: Monarch 2013), pp. 11–13.

5   Justin Welby to Andrew White, 25 January 2002, International Centre for Reconciliation [ICR] Archives, Coventry Cathedral.

6   Andrew White to Justin Welby, 31 January 2002, ICR Archives.

however, was of hearing the stories of desperate and fearful people, both Israeli and Palestinian, who longed for peace. He encountered Orthodox Christians from Bethlehem who despite poverty and persecution spoke confidently of their hope in Christ, and the rector of Southam was left pondering that 'It puts the issues of my life and work in perspective.'[7]

Shortly afterwards Welby was invited to join the team at Coventry Cathedral as White's co-director of international ministry. When offering him the job, Bishop Bennetts explained that he would spend two weeks a month travelling, mostly to areas of violent conflict, and would have to raise his own finances. Caroline said that 'such a crazy offer could only be from God', and so had to be accepted.[8] Welby and White forged a good working relationship, and a strong personal friendship, and Welby brought to the team particular experience in management and finance. He left Southam in October 2002 and was installed the following month as a residentiary canon, thus renewing friendship with John Irvine, Dean of Coventry from 2001.

Iraq, Nigeria, Burundi, Kenya

In the early days Welby and White made many of their trips together. Particularly memorable was their journey to Iraq in May 2003, shortly after Saddam Hussein's regime was toppled by the Allied invasion. They flew first to Amman in Jordan and then drove across the desert in convoy to Baghdad, instructing their driver to travel at at least 110 miles per hour on the most dangerous stretch of road between Ramadi and Falluja. In the capital they met in Saddam's old Republican Palace with the Coalition Provisional Authority who wanted

7   Justin Welby, 'Thought for the Month', *SPCN* (May 2002).
8   Williams, 'Of Secular and Sacred', p. 44.

Iraq's religious leaders to help in the task of rebuilding. St George's Anglican Church in Baghdad had somehow survived the bombardment, though it had been sacked by looters, so the two canons decided to 'reopen' it. With a congregation of about 50, mostly diplomats and military, Welby led the service and White preached from Haggai 2:9 ('"The glory of this present house will be greater than the glory of the former house", says the Lord Almighty. "And in this place I will grant peace", declares the Lord Almighty'), a verse carved in stone at Coventry's bombed cathedral. There was warning of a major bomb threat to the church, so during the service it was surrounded by tanks and armoured personnel carriers, while Apache helicopters hovered overhead.[9] Despite the dangers, Welby described the trip as 'a wonderful celebration of liberation and the renewal of hope'.[10] There was also a return to Israel, sometimes stressful but punctuated, in retrospect, by humour. He found himself 'looking up the barrel of a gun at a roadblock' near Bethlehem when his mobile phone rang. After an embarrassed pause he answered it, only to hear, 'Warwick Glass here, Mr Welby. Can we fit your new window this afternoon?'[11]

Welby and White agreed to divide the reconciliation work between them. White took responsibility for the Middle East, especially Israel/Palestine and Iraq.[12] Welby focused on Africa, especially Nigeria, where he had first travelled with Elf Aquitaine in the late 1970s. Coventry diocese had a particularly close relationship with Kaduna diocese, in central Nigeria, the location of intense tribal and religious violence between Muslim and Christian communities. Tensions were heightened by the implementation of Sharia law in 2001 and by

9   Andrew White, *Iraq: Searching for Hope* (London: Continuum, 2005), pp. 25–37.
10   Justin Welby, 'International Department of the Diocese and Cathedral', *The Corporation of Coventry Cathedral: Annual Reports for 2003*, p. 38.
11   Justin Welby, 'Guns, God and Staying True to Yourself', *The Treasurer* (January – February 2006), p. 46; 'Meet the Dean Designate', p. 5.
12   For an assessment, see R. John Elford, 'Andrew White in Iraq', in R. John Elford (ed.), *Just Reconciliation: The Practice and Morality of Making Peace* (Bern: Peter Lang, 2011), pp. 85–106.

rhetoric surrounding the Miss World beauty pageant in Abuja the following year. In three days of rioting in November 2002 several thousand people were killed and 25,000 left homeless. Three months earlier Andrew White had brought together 22 senior Christian and Muslim clerics to sign the Kaduna Peace Declaration, modelled on the Alexandria Declaration. Welby inherited this work, seeking to facilitate the implementation of the Kaduna Declaration. One of his first involvements was a conference for Anglican clergy in January 2003 on the theme of reconciliation, based on the book of Jonah: 'It was bitter and difficult, with many of the clergy very hurt by the events which they had seen. Churches had been burnt, parishioners killed and injured, they were seeking revenge not reconciliation.'[13] Welby quickly established a close friendship with Josiah Idowu-Fearon (Bishop of Kaduna from 1997 and the first Archbishop of Kaduna province from 2003), whom he praised as 'a man of outstanding character, integrity and vision'.[14] Idowu-Fearon modelled for his clergy a passion to reconcile and willingness to dialogue with Muslim leaders. As part of this peace-making ministry, in 2004 Kaduna diocese launched Jacaranda Farm, 80 hectares with a health centre attached, providing agricultural training for unemployed Christian and Muslim young men, who worked side by side. Its crops included mangos, cashew nuts, oranges, grapes, passionfruit, maize and sugarcane; and Abiodun Ogunyemi (Archdeacon of Kaduna, and later Bishop of Damaturu) spent six months in Britain working with the ICR at Coventry to publicise the project.

The success in Kaduna led to invitations elsewhere. After riots in Plateau State, centred on Jos, the state governor in 2003 asked Welby and his Coventry team to facilitate community reconciliation. They commissioned research into the root causes of the violence through the Centre for Conflict

---

13   Justin Welby, 'Reconciliation in Nigeria', in R. John Elford (ed.), *Just Reconciliation: The Practice and Morality of Making Peace* (Bern: Peter Lang, 2011), p. 65.
14   Justin Welby to Christopher Graves, 1 October 2003, ICR Archives.

Management and Peace Studies at the University of Jos. They organised peace-building and skill-training workshops for over a thousand disaffected Christian and Muslim youth. In collaboration with the State Security Service they financed an early warning system in the form of satellite telephones for key community leaders across the religious and ethnic divide, to enable quick communication in the event of crisis. Because newspapers were often complicit in escalating violence, they also gathered journalists from ten states across central Nigeria to teach how the media can alleviate rather than aggravate tensions. A fresh outbreak of civil strife in Jos in 2005 left 4,000 people dead and over 100,000 homeless. But this holistic ministry of peace-making continued, by restarting schools and offering training in agriculture, as Welby noted: 'The good news of reconciliation is tangible. ... It was Christian led, locally directed, empowered women, and subverted the power structure of gun running.'[15]

In the south of the country, in the Niger Delta, Welby was invited by the Nigerian government to act as an international mediator for their Peace and Security Strategy, bringing together indigenous communities, oil companies and local officials. Crude oil was first discovered in the delta in 1956, near Port Harcourt, and had been fought over for a generation. Shell had the largest stake, alongside other major companies like Exxon Mobil, Texaco and Welby's former employers, Elf Aquitaine. Decades of mismanagement had led to environmental degradation, with polluted waters, ruined agriculture, depleted fishing and acid rain. Though Welby had witnessed much abject poverty during his African travels, in the swamps of Ogoni he saw 'poverty unlike anything I had seen before'.[16] Local militias controlled large areas, financing their operations through bunkering (stealing illegally produced oil) worth billions of dollars a year. Violence and kidnapping

---

15   Justin Welby, 'Good News for the Poor', a talk for the Anglican Alliance for Development, 30 April 2012, www.durham.anglican.org.

16   'Meet the Dean Designate', p. 5.

were endemic. Corruption took place, in Welby's words, on 'a breath-taking scale' in which politicians and oil companies were deeply implicated, 'caught in a devil's partnership'.[17] The Movement for the Survival of the Ogoni People (MOSOP) campaigned against the multitude of injustices, especially against Shell, and several leading activists were summarily executed in the mid-1990s, including the playwright and poet, Ken Saro-Wiwa. The initial appeal for help from the ICR at Coventry came not from MOSOP, or from the local Nigerian churches, but from employees of Shell. From 2004 Welby's team spent considerable time researching the issues in depth and establishing relationships on all sides, with more than a hundred meetings in a year, before a formal Ogoni Reconciliation Process was announced by President Obasanjo in May 2005 facilitated by a Roman Catholic priest from Kaduna.[18] Although progress in Nigeria was very slow, Welby reported back to Coventry Cathedral that there were 'huge opportunities for the ministry of reconciliation to make great differences to the quality of life of a wonderful country'.[19]

Welby's abilities as a French-speaker provided further openings in Francophone central Africa, a region torn apart by genocide and a decade of on-going ethnic bloodshed between Hutu and Tutsi. In Burundi, which Welby visited for the first time in November 2003, an estimated 300,000 civilians had been killed in the civil war over the previous ten years. He established links with Pie Ntukamazina, Bishop of Bujumbura, the Burundian capital whose cathedral of Sainte Trinité was involved in reconciliation ministry. It welcomed a mixed Hutu and Tutsi congregation, and sponsored the Centre de Paix (Peace House). Welby made contacts with the Université Lumière in Bujumbura, a private Christian

17   Justin Welby, 'International Companies in Places of Instability: The Issue of Mutual Capture', in Barbara Fryzel and Paul H. Dembinski (eds), *The Role of Large Enterprises in Democracy and Society* (Basingstoke: Palgrave, 2010), pp. 90, 92.
18   'Coventry Aids Peace Process in Oil-Fields', *Church Times*, 10 June 2005, p. 8; Justin Welby, 'Peace in Six Hard Steps', *Church Times*, 26 August 2005, p. 8.
19   Welby, 'International Department', p. 38.

university which was both ecumenical and inter-ethnic. To formalise their relationship with the ICR in Coventry, both the cathedral and the university joined the CCN network. He also met for the first time Bernard Ntahoturi, Bishop of Matana and Anglican provincial secretary, who in 2005 was elected Archbishop of Burundi, one of the primates of the Anglican Communion.[20] These local partnerships brought introductions to all levels of Burundian society. For example, in July 2004 Welby led a two-day workshop in the capital for high-ranking politicians and government officials, opened by the Vice-President, in preparation for national elections. Speaking entirely in French, Welby mapped out a process from conflict to reconciliation, including four case studies of good practice: Anglo–German reconciliation after the Second World War, the Truth and Reconciliation Commission in post-apartheid South Africa, the Good Friday Agreement in Northern Ireland, and the Alexandria Process in the Middle East. The dangers of working in that environment were illustrated just a week afterwards when Bishop Ntukamazina was abducted along with other church leaders by rebel gunmen while returning from a confirmation service. He escaped with his life after a long gun battle when his captors were attacked by another rebel group.[21] A few days later over 150 civilians of all ages were massacred by rebels at Gatumba, a refugee camp on the border between Burundi and the Democratic Republic of the Congo.

In January and May 2005, Welby was invited to Kenya by Peter Anaminyi from the international Christian radio station, Feba Radio Kenya, to help facilitate a meeting of senior Christian and Muslim leaders in the north of Mombasa. The initiative was funded by the British High Commission in an attempt at pre-emptive reconciliation to prevent inter-religious violence. Welby took with him two key leaders he

20   Interview with Bernard Ntahoturi, 25 October 2013.
21   See letter from Bishop Ntukamazina about his ordeal, Anglican Communion News Service, 16 August 2004, www.anglicancommunion.org/acns.

had encountered in Kaduna, Pastor James Wuye and Imam Mohammed Ashafa, co-directors of the Interfaith Mediation Centre in Nigeria.[22] In Kenya he met Eliud Wabukala, Bishop of Bungoma and chairman of the National Council of Churches of Kenya (NCCK), and a few months later Wabukala travelled to Coventry to discuss further peace initiatives and stayed with the Welbys in their home.[23] It was to prove another significant connection because Wabukala was elected Archbishop of Kenya in 2009, one of the Anglican Communion's most prominent conservative leaders and a vocal critic of Canterbury. These years travelling in Africa as a cathedral canon, meeting future Anglican primates, were to prove invaluable for Welby's burgeoning global relationships.

In *The Treasurer* Welby reflected on three ways in which his background in treasury management had helped to prepare him for this ministry in conflict resolution. First, conflict resolution required the ability 'to synthesise a lot of information quickly and under pressure', which was

> very similar to the process of pulling together information before deciding the timing of an issue of debt, or even a significant forex [foreign exchange] transaction: you know what you know, you know there is a lot that has escaped you, but you have to take a view and make a decision.

Second, conflict resolution like finance required 'flexibility in attitude, in analytical models, in planning and in execution'. At Enterprise Oil, Welby had learned to deal with the unexpected, such as a sudden collapse in barrel price or fluctuations in exchange rates, and the need for rapid changes of plan. In the same way, in the Niger Delta flexibility was vital and constant analysis of the key questions, 'What are the factors causing conflict? What are the motives of the main actors? What are the likely outcomes? What are the spoilers?' Third, in both lines

---

22   See further, *The Imam and the Pastor* (FLT films, 2006); *An African Answer* (FLT films, 2010).

23   Interview with Eliud Wabukala, 26 October 2013.

of work 'determination is essential'. Treasury management at Enterprise Oil required resilience to broker deals, sometimes over many months amidst numerous obstacles, and to keep pushing forward towards key goals. A similar steely character was needed in reconciliation ministry: 'Determination is the only way to end conflicts, or even to start negotiations. Once the basic agreement is there, you can be sure that people will try and spoil it.'[24]

Much of Welby's work in Nigeria, Burundi and elsewhere placed him in positions of grave personal danger. More than once he was caught in riots, and could testify from personal experience that 'crowds in fury are terrifying'.[25] On a dozen occasions he found himself in situations where the militia was in control and anything might happen. Twice from Nigeria he telephoned Caroline at home in Coventry and asked her to pray, fearing that he may have miscalculated the risks and might be dead within minutes. At the height of the violence in Plateau State in 2004 Welby drove in convoy with armed escort to Wase, a Muslim-controlled town about two hours from Jos. In a tense atmosphere, as he was meeting with the local emir, his Muslim driver outside overheard three young men with AK47s discussing whether to kill their English visitor. They left by a different route. With a colleague from Coventry, Jonathan Evans, Welby travelled against advice to Nembe deep in the swamps of the Niger Delta, two hours journey by speedboat from Port Harcourt. There a young militia leader high on alcohol and drugs told his accomplices to take Welby and Evans outside and shoot them, and their lives were redeemed only when a local elder spent half an hour pleading on their behalf. The two Englishmen were held by the militia overnight, pondering their fate, but were released the next day. On another occasion Welby was taken out to dinner in a hotel at Port Harcourt by a Nigerian oil contractor involved in bunkering and given subtle death threats at the

24   Welby, 'Guns, God and Staying True to Yourself', p. 46.
25   Welby, 'Coping with Danger', p. 46.

table.[26] He learnt that he had a price of $30 on his head and later joked that, in comparison to the $250,000 contract to kill Andrew White in Iraq, 'I couldn't decide whether to be insulted or afraid.'[27] But he took the threat seriously and quickly left the area.[28] Some of Welby's activities negotiating with Islamist insurgents were carried out under strict secrecy and therefore were open to misinterpretation and raised concerns for Nigerian national security. While visiting a mosque in Borno State in north-east Nigeria in 2005, at the invitation of the state governor, he was arrested by the State Security Service, Nigeria's intelligence agency. After being held for several hours, and interrogated, he was released and allowed to drive back to the state capital Maiduguri, only to be detained again the following morning over breakfast and put on an aeroplane south, much to his annoyance. Andrew White seemed to be 'impervious' to these dangers, but Welby found the ministry increasingly difficult for both him and his family with frequent absences from home.[29] After three years, he had spent a total of 15 months overseas, built up 'a contact list of some very surprising and violent people, enjoyed a bit of success and experienced a lot of frustration'. He had established relationships 'with killers and with the families of their victims, with arms smugglers, corrupt officials and more'.[30]

26   Justin Welby, 'Reconciliation and Forgiveness', part 1, New Wine seminar 2004 (with Jonathan Evans), audio recording; Justin Welby, 'Blessed are the Peacemakers', part 1, New Wine seminar 2006, audio recording.
27   Welby, 'Guns, God and Staying True to Yourself', p. 46.
28   Welby, 'Coping with Danger', p. 47.
29   'Meet the Dean Designate', p. 4.
30   Welby, 'Guns, God and Staying True to Yourself', p. 46.

The Six Rs

Coventry's International Centre for Reconciliation developed a systematic method for their work in conflict situations, summarised by six Rs – Researching, Relating, Relieving, Risking, Reconciling and Resourcing. Although first addressed to war zones in Africa and the Middle East, the basic approach could equally be applied to ecclesiastical divisions. Indeed Welby's attitude to reconciliation within the Church of England and the wider Anglican Communion was heavily influenced by this Coventry framework which provided him with a ready-made set of analytical tools. His exposition of the six key principles is therefore significant beyond its primary context in Nigeria.

First came Researching, the need to understand the deepest roots of a conflict by listening very carefully to all sides without jumping to conclusions:

> It is essential to begin by putting aside judgement. Apparent causes and rights and wrongs may very often, with further examination, prove to be too simple. It is essential to include both sides in the research, even if the initial impression is that one side is more to blame. In order to be able to hear what people are saying truly, the researcher must empathize with the suffering of the people to whom he is talking, and try to see what they were seeing through their eyes. Research must be repeated again and again: the principle of iteration is essential. Above all, anyone involved in reconciliation who is an outsider, must assume persistent ignorance and inability fully to comprehend what they are seeing and hearing.

This patient research bears strong resonance to the 'listening process' and *'indaba'* advocated amongst Anglicans by the Lambeth Conferences of 1998 and 2008. Welby drew parallels with the story of the prodigal son (Luke 15) where the father was 'looking, searching, listening, waiting. There was no rush to judgement, but rather a willingness to receive, to be vulnerable.' The researcher must also identify 'spoilers', those people or organisations with 'a vested interest in the continuation of the conflict, rather than in its resolution' (such as arms traders or criminal gangs), and establish a plan to deal with them.[31]

The second R was Relating:

> All effective reconciliation depends on facing the truth. Both sides have to face the truth about themselves, to look in the mirror and see who they are and what they have done. They have to re-imagine a new face, not arising from victory, but from a transformation of conflict. ... Relating should be indiscriminate (almost), that is to say one does not relate to people because they are good but because they are there. In the same way God reaches out to human beings not for their merit but out of His love.

The reconciler must be willing to be personally vulnerable in forging genuine relationships:

> They have to relate to a person, not an office. One cannot see a 'militia leader'. One has to see a named individual with feelings, emotions in whom the blood flows and who has worries and loves like everyone else. Relationships must be affective. They need to show signs of personal engagement, to affirm, to encourage and to be warm in their expression. Such relationships will necessarily be emotional. Conflicts are emotional places to be in. ... The foundation of relating is that the very existence of a relationship is more important than the process of reconciliation.

Welby saw this ministry of reaching out across barriers, even to those who had done major wrong, as an extension of the gospel. In the parable, the elder brother wanted due process before he would engage, refusing to come in until his father had promised to exert family discipline by admonishing or punishing the prodigal. But the father drew his younger son back into the family through relationship, seeking his fullness of life. Welby concluded that relationships must come before justice and the righting of wrongs, not vice versa: 'Justice cannot be established in depth and with confidence in the

---

31   Welby, 'Reconciliation in Nigeria', pp. 72–3.

absence of profound relationships, in which trust has begun to emerge.'[32]

The third part of the process was Relieving, the alleviation of the socio-economic roots of conflict. This commitment to a community's material wellbeing was a validation of genuine relationships and concern for the whole person. The fourth was Risking. Welby had first appropriated the language of risk in his writings on finance in the 1990s, but it evolved into an especially significant part of his discourse when applied to other contexts. For example, in 2000 he told his Southam parishioners, 'We cannot eliminate risk. It is a part of life, and the risk of life always ends at some point in death. Disease or accident will one day catch all of us.' The wrong response to risk was to take fright and refuse to dare to do anything. The right response was to trust in the sovereignty of God, 'a safety net stronger than any risk', because 'even when the risk goes wrong, even when life throws the worst at us, God is still there'.[33] Likewise, in reconciliation ministry there were serious risks, which Welby elucidated. In areas of armed conflict there was the obvious personal danger of being injured, kidnapped, or even murdered. But beyond such 'heroics' was the risk of misunderstanding because the reconciler must endure 'the "scandal" of talking to evil people'. When asked 'Why do you meet bad people?', Welby replied, 'It's the bad people who are causing the trouble.' There was also the risk of failure which might accelerate the conflict and deepen hatreds. Nevertheless, he insisted that 'without risk there will be no reconciliation'. Turning again to the parable of the prodigal son, he commented that 'the older brother takes no risks. He will not even risk meeting his younger brother but stays outside, further demonstrating his independence and self-will. By contrast, the father risks everything.'[34]

32   Welby, 'Reconciliation in Nigeria', pp. 74–5.
33   Justin Welby, 'Thought for the Month', SPCN (July 2000).
34   Welby, 'Reconciliation in Nigeria', p. 79.

The fifth R was Reconciling, the point at which the issues of justice, restitution and forgiveness first emerge. Welby emphasised that rapid reconciliation was illusory. It was a long-term process, never an event. Summits between leaders, and the signing of peace accords, were helpful in creating momentum but never sufficient. He warned against *declarationitis*, 'the disease of making declarations and concluding that by doing so we have changed the world. It is as though, by some strange semiotic mechanism, talking enough about reconciliation can lead to its happening.'[35] The sixth and final component was Resourcing, enabling communities to address their local conflicts without assistance from outside agencies. These six parts of the reconciliation process were not linear but a 'complex matrix'.[36]

Welby drew an important distinction between reconciliation and arbitration or mediation. Its purpose was not to resolve conflict or end disagreement, but to enable warring parties 'to continue to disagree without violence or mutual destruction'.[37] He observed that reconciliation was 'at the very heart of the gospel', demonstrated supremely in the cross of Christ which brought sinners into relationship with God. Christ's shed blood was 'the fountain of reconciliation with God, from which all other reconciliation flows'.[38] Therefore the church was to be 'the body of reconciled reconcilers':

> Christians should not just be recipients of reconciliation they should also be the source of rivers of reconciliation flowing to the places of conflict and trauma around them in their own families, in their workplaces and communities and across the entire experience of human kind.[39]

Elsewhere, Welby said: 'the idea that God's reconciliation with us can be contained simply within the Church is ridiculous –

35   Welby, 'The Gift of Reconciliation', p. 85.
36   Welby, 'Reconciliation in Nigeria', p. 71.
37   Welby, 'Reconciliation in Nigeria', p. 66.
38   Welby, 'The Gift of Reconciliation', pp. 80, 83; Justin Welby, 'The Book of Lamentations: Five Addresses for Holy Week', Coventry Cathedral 2006, p. 11.
39   Welby, 'Reconciliation in Nigeria', p. 67.

God's far too generous for that and his grace should overflow into the world around us.'[40]

Reconciliation Begins at Home

Measured by financial turnover alone, the work of Coventry's International Centre for Reconciliation was booming. In 2001 its income was £205,000 (amounting to 17 per cent of the cathedral's total income). By 2003 there were 16 full-time members of staff and income had more than doubled to £587,000. In 2004 it more than doubled again to £1,227,000.[41] That year saw major new initiatives by Welby in Burundi and the Niger Delta, and by White in Baghdad with the launch of the Iraqi Institute for Peace to promote dialogue between Sunni and Shia religious leaders. Much of the finance came in the form of grants from Shell Nigeria, to support the work in Ogoniland, and from international government agencies like the Foreign and Commonwealth Office and the United States Institute for Peace. But this rate of growth was unsustainable and potentially placed the finances of the whole cathedral at risk. Welby admitted that the reconciliation ministry was 'dependent upon very large donations from a very few sources'.[42] The following year the work collapsed.

In June 2005, after seven years based in Coventry, White moved permanently to Iraq as vicar of St George's, Baghdad. His ministry was now funded independently through the Foundation for Relief and Reconciliation in the Middle East (chaired by Lord Carey). The cathedral's international ministry was downsized and there was a change of focus, away from flak-jackets and dodging bullets in war zones to reconciliation

---

40   'Meet the Dean Designate', p. 5.
41   Corporation of Coventry Cathedral, annual reports for 2002–04.
42   Welby, 'International Department', p. 39.

at home. Since the funding had run out, all the employees at the ICR were made redundant, mainly young interns. There were warning signs of this imminent collapse which had gone unheeded, and the dismissal of staff was a major knock-back for which Welby felt personally responsible, an emotionally draining episode. He admitted: 'I failed quite badly as a result of a series of mistakes ... I learned not to let situations drift.'[43] He called it an 'experience of grief',[44] and reflected:

> the pressures of achievement, or working towards targets, or trying to get things done, are the ones that knock us off course. I had a significant failure this autumn, and struggled profoundly, emotionally, in terms of stress and trying to know what to do. At times like that, and just as much in the pressure of success, we can find we are no longer the people we want to be or even feel comfortable being. My aim for 2006 is to keep my core values in the centre of what I do, and maintain the boundaries that tell me where I am going wrong.[45]

Previously in his Southam parish magazine he had written about the role of such crises in Christian discipleship:

> Crises are opportunities. They are times for thinking about the foundations of our lives. What do I depend on? What is the rock in my life that I cling to, or the light that I am guided by? Crises strip from us everything that is false, or weak, or not essential. ... the more I see of crises, the more I know that whether they come from great world events or small personal upheavals, the only rock and light that is always there for us is Jesus.[46]

As a result of the crisis at the ICR, Welby offered to resign and return to parish ministry. Yet Bishop Bennetts and Dean Irvine were keen to keep him at the cathedral, and gave him a residentiary canonry funded by the Church Commissioners, which by coincidence had come free that summer with the

43   'Justin Welby', *Alpha Journal* (October 2013), www.alpha.org/journal.
44   Welby and Welby, 'Grief'.
45   Welby, 'Guns, God and Staying True to Yourself', p. 46.
46   Justin Welby, 'Farewell', *SPCN* (October 2002).

departure of Stuart Beake to be Archdeacon of Surrey. So
Welby was installed in November 2005 as the cathedral's sub-
dean, Irvine's deputy. His primary focus was now the day-to-
day running of the cathedral and local reconciliation projects
in Coventry city and diocese, and he was only allowed to visit
Africa on a much less frequent basis. One of the criticisms of
the ICR had been that making peace in the Middle East or
Africa was all very well, but not if divisions closer to home were
ignored. It was known by some disaffected local congregations
as 'the cathedral which reconciled the world and alienated the
diocese'. Part of Welby's new role was to work in areas of
deprivation in Coventry to bring different ethnic and religious
groups together, in collaboration with organisations such as
the Coventry Community Forum. His team was involved in
local schools and in running conferences for young people on
issues like peace-building and interfaith dialogue. He was also
deployed by Bishop Bennetts to help local Anglican parishes
where relationships had broken down. Further afield, he was
recruited to the board of the Dresden Trust, founded in 1993
to build cultural and educational links between Britain and
Dresden in a spirit of peace and co-operation.[47]

Disagreement without Rancour

Welby's years at Coventry Cathedral within a theologically
mixed but harmonious staff team were significant in shaping
his understanding of the ideals of Anglican comprehensiveness
and the nature of 'good disagreement'. The cathedral itself
aimed to be a model of reconciliation. Its tradition had long
been liberal catholic, but since Irvine's arrival as dean in
2001 evangelicalism was better represented both amongst

47   Information from Alan Russell, 8 January 2014.

the congregation and within the chapter. It catered for a wide cross-section of people, offering services ranging from high mass to charismatic praise. There were 'wildly different views' within the cathedral community, Welby acknowledged, on key questions such as the authority of Scripture, Christian morality and the purpose of the church.[48] Even the senior staff were 'deeply divided' on sexual ethics and the Jeffrey John Affair of 2003 created ripples at the cathedral, where a significant number of the congregation were gay.[49] Jeffrey John (chancellor and canon theologian at Southwark Cathedral), a vocal advocate for the blessing of same-sex unions, was nominated in May 2003 as the new Bishop of Reading, to the consternation of evangelicals in Oxford diocese and throughout the Church of England. John had a long-standing male partner (also an Anglican clergyman), but gave assurances that they had lived celibately for more than a decade and that he would uphold the church's official teaching in the House of Bishops' report, *Issues in Human Sexuality* (1991). The appointment was greeted with furore. Protest letters rained down, bishops broke ranks and the secular press had a field day. After seven weeks of mounting pressure from across the Anglican Communion, and amidst mutual recriminations, John was forced by his friend Archbishop Rowan Williams to withdraw his acceptance of the position.[50] In Welby's words, homosexuality acted as 'a lightning conductor' in the power struggle between evangelicals and liberals for dominance in the Church of England. Within the Coventry Cathedral chapter there was a 'full and frank exchange of views' on the subject and he asked, 'How can we go around the world trying to talk about reconciliation ... when we don't live it out in our own

---

48   Welby, 'Reconciliation and Forgiveness' (2003), part 2.
49   Welby, 'Reconciliation and Forgiveness' (2004), part 1.
50   Stephen Bates, *A Church at War: Anglicans and Homosexuality* (London: Hodder and Stoughton, 2005), pp. 196–228; John S. Peart-Binns, *A Heart in My Head: A Biography of Richard Harries* (London: Continuum, 2007), pp. 205–21; Rupert Shortt, *Rowan's Rule: The Biography of the Archbishop* (London: Hodder and Stoughton, 2008), pp. 264–77; Andrew Goddard, *Rowan Williams: His Legacy* (Oxford: Lion, 2013), pp. 93–107.

community?' Some at the cathedral did not want to invite evangelicals to preach, 'because they're homophobic European versions of the Taliban'; others refused liberals, 'because they don't preach the gospel'. Welby was of the opinion that 'we're going to have to take some risks if the cathedral community is going to find a safe place to work out its issues in a reconciled way, not with conflict'.[51]

Welby made his own position clear, that 'sexual practice is for marriage, and marriage is between men and women, and that's the biblical position'. Such a view was pastorally difficult, 'but it's what the Bible says'. Therefore the question of right and wrong in the Jeffrey John Affair 'matters enormously ... truth is essential'. Nonetheless, he was perturbed at the manner in which John's nomination as a bishop was debated by the church: 'the public arguing through the columns of the Times, the Telegraph and over the BBC has not helped evangelism. ... I'm not saying that the issue isn't important, it's just not the right way of doing it.' He reiterated that whatever people might think about the principles at stake, 'it cannot be right that the secular press is a substitute for dialogue between Christians, a vitriolic go-between that makes our communication with other people who follow Christ more difficult not more easy'.[52]

In this context, Dean Irvine created space for 'an open conversation' about homosexuality during a Sunday evening service in January 2004. Welby debated the issue with his friend, Adrian Daffern (the canon precentor), seeking to model to the congregation a generous and prayerful approach to theological disagreement.[53] They did not try to settle the substantive question over what the Bible teaches about homosexuality, but rather to demonstrate that friends could disagree without rancour. Welby began by observing that in

51   Welby, 'Reconciliation and Forgiveness' (2003), part 2.
52   Welby, 'Reconciliation and Forgiveness' (2003), part 2.
53   Justin Welby and Adrian Daffern, dialogue at Coventry Cathedral, January 2004 (audio recording).

Southam parish he had only preached once about sex in seven years, 'so it's not an obsession. ... Can the church actually talk about anything else? ... There are plenty of other sins that matter. ... There are a lot of serious issues which, in the words of the New Testament, quench the Holy Spirit of God, which we tend to overlook.' Speaking from 'an evangelical tradition', the key issue for Welby was the authority of Scripture. He acknowledged that sometimes the church had been captive to non-Christian views, foolishly trying to defend slavery or apartheid from the Bible, for example. Nevertheless, he observed that in the great periods of renewal in Christian history, the call was always 'back to the Bible':

> as they've gathered round the Bible and prayed under the guidance of the Spirit, they have understood afresh the word of God for their time. The word doesn't change but God applies it afresh in our hearts in each generation. ... One of the most precious experiences of my Christian life is sharing the Bible with others and being excited afresh by the word of God.

He asserted: 'the Bible is actually clear that homosexual practice is not permitted, is against the will of God'.

Daffern gave the example of a gay couple, friends whom he had introduced to each other, one of them an Anglican clergyman in a parish in south London which was 'on any measure blessed by God, a most remarkable ministry, with a thriving church, with amazing things going with young people and the community, and with a passionate, passionate commitment to evangelism, to the gospel of Jesus, and yet they are gay'. Welby was not convinced by this argument from fruitfulness, and replied that he was increasingly conscious that

> if the success of my ministry depended on my own good behaviour, I would be a total and complete failure from beginning to end, and nothing would have ever happened at any time in my ministry. The fact is that God's grace works despite human failure and that therefore, it seems to me, to look at a ministry and say 'that's very successful', tells

us wonderful things about God's grace but not necessarily wonderful things about the ministers – it may very often, but it doesn't necessarily. It doesn't follow that because the ministry's a success, the ministers are good.

This was the inverse of his subsequent controversial aphorism as Archbishop of Canterbury that 'where you have a good vicar you will find growing churches'. A good vicar might mean a growing church, but according to Welby a growing church did not necessarily mean a good vicar. He continued:

> Pastorally I would love to say, 'It's fine'. ... I know gay Christian couples who I respect hugely for their spirituality, and in many ways consider infinitely better people than I am – but what I've also discovered in my life since I was a Christian, despite some real failures of the most desperate kind, is that God knows best. ... God speaks through Scripture, and if we follow what Scripture says that is the best love that there is. And although we constantly fail to do that, if we at any point say, 'Well, in this particular area, actually because of more recent understandings or whatever, we're going to do something different', that pastorally, however we feel, however hard it is – and I can't begin to describe how difficult it is to say this – however hard it is, we will be letting down the people that we are dealing with pastorally, because God knows best and the Scripture in the end is clear.

'What about people's feelings?', Welby asked. 'In my parish anything that required confrontation, that required saying to someone that things weren't right, I found indescribably utterly totally painful, because of my own consciousness of my own weakness and my own consciousness of how easy it is to be hypocritical.' Nonetheless he insisted, 'Truth is essential. We have to arrive at truth.' Faced with this pastoral dilemma, he urged:

> it is essential that as Christians we enter into the feelings of those we're dealing with. We are not at liberty to stand at a distance and say, 'This is right, you lot have got to bear the consequences'. ... I think that as a principle of behaviour,

we're called to enter into each other's pain, and the pain on both sides is enormous.

He spoke not only of the pain of gay people within the Coventry Cathedral community, but also the pain experienced by conservative Anglicans in Africa. For example he had attended an ordination service in Nigeria in the summer of 2003 at which the bishop described developments amongst Anglicans in North America and the United Kingdom. Welby remembered: 'I've never heard 2,000 people groan in pain before. There was a gasp.' Speaking to his own cathedral congregation he concluded: 'I see and I feel the pain of fellow members of this community. But I come back to the fact that I believe at the bottom of my heart that what the Bible says is true ... genital sex between people of the same gender is not permitted by Scripture.'

The dialogue was deliberately inconclusive, but ended with a call from both men for Christians to stick together despite their disagreements. Daffern explained:

> it's a wonderful thing in this cathedral that we have a team of clergy who are passionate about their love for Jesus, and their longing to see this place be alive for God, and yet within the team we have our differences on some issues. And I think that makes us stronger not weaker, because we stay together, we pray together, we study Scripture together, we love each other. ... It's amazing what God is doing in us.

He called for 'transparency and integrity' within the church. 'Even if we disagree, we cannot allow this to break us from our unity in Christ. And that means we have to demonstrate to the world that we're not just obsessed with sex.' Daffern reiterated:

> If we can model to the church, if we can say, 'We're Coventry Cathedral, and we disagree on this one issue, but we're not going to let it break us, we're going to keep searching for the truth, and sometimes that's going to be painful and sometimes that may mean we get cross with each other ... but never mind

that, we believe in Jesus and we're going to affirm the love of Christ, and we're going to trust the work of the Spirit, and we're going to stay together', my goodness me, can you imagine the impact that would have on the wider church with so much brokenness and people walking out ... If we can say, 'We disagree but we're going to try to hold together and try to work this out', I think that would be an amazing message to send out and I would love that to happen.

Likewise Welby observed that the Corinthian church in the first century was dysfunctional, divided over major issues like sexuality and the resurrection, yet the Apostle Paul wrote to them with some of the New Testament's most sublime exhortations on love and unity, and despite their failures always thanked God for them (1 Corinthians 1:4). 'As fellow Christians, the fact that we belong to each other ... is not our choice,' Welby declared. 'We are related to every Christian that exists anywhere. Fellowship is God-given.'

The Welby–Daffern dialogue was intended as a model which might be replicated elsewhere in the Church of England. In front of an evangelical audience at New Wine that summer, Welby reflected upon their engagement: 'in God's grace we managed to disagree profoundly, but without bitterness, without rancour. I cannot deny he's a Christian, he loves the Lord Jesus Christ. I disagree profoundly with some of his interpretation of Scripture and am quite happy to say so in public', but their conversation had taken 'the sting out of the debate' and 'had an immense effect in bringing people towards Jesus Christ.' Although the question was not settled and conflict within the cathedral about homosexuality did not end, 'the division has had some of its bitterness drawn from it, because it's been recognised, acknowledged and discussed openly'. He lamented that the Church of England's 'destructive' arguments were 'a diversion of effort', a distraction from the task of 'seeking to win the 92 per cent of this population who never go near a church and find the whole debate completely incomprehensible'. Nothing, he warned, was 'a great sapper of spiritual passion' than public division.[54]

Unity, Diversity and Truth

In seminars on reconciliation and forgiveness at New Wine in 2003, 2004 and 2006, Welby unpacked his approach to church unity in more detail. When asked where he drew the line, he replied: 'I'm an orthodox Bible-believing evangelical ... Scripture is my final authority for all matters of life and of doctrine.' Yet it was vital, he insisted, to avoid 'proof-texting' (dragging Bible texts out of their context) and to study, pray and learn together. 'So I draw lines, but I draw them reluctantly and after a lot of listening.' If the people on the other side of the controversy were also Christians, then according to the New Testament 'I'm obliged to love them. I do not have any alternative. I may correct them with gentleness. ... I may debate and discuss with them. But I cannot hate them. It is not an option that God in Scripture has left me.' He noted again that the Apostle Paul may have dealt with the Corinthians 'jolly severely' because of their doctrinal errors, but he still treated them as 'fellow members of the family of God' and did not cut himself off from them. 'Splitting is addictive', Welby warned, as witnessed by the history of Protestantism since the Reformation.[55]

Hand in hand with this passion for unity, Welby insisted that truth must not be sacrificed for the sake of keeping Anglicans together: 'Jesus revealed the truth. Truth is at the heart of what it is to be a Christian. It is not a negotiable.' He continued:

---

54   Welby, 'Reconciliation and Forgiveness' (2004), part 2.
55   Welby, 'Reconciliation and Forgiveness' (2003), part 2.

Are truth and unity opposites, are they competing, do they fight each other? ... You often hear that said, but read the Bible! Jesus reveals the truth and Jesus prays that we may be one. Was Jesus wrong? It must be possible for us to live in truth and unity. That is the will and purpose of Christ. There is no competition between truth and unity. They are both given by God, and they are to be held together like mercy and justice. ... We are called to preach truth and live in unity.[56]

Reconciliation, he suggested, was 'a foretaste of the kingdom' and 'makes the gospel visible'. As a command of Christ, it was 'not an optional extra' but 'a fundamental part of the package of being saved'. Division between Christians was 'desperately damaging' and a 'scandal to the gospel', whereas a reconciled church 'attracts the unbeliever'. When Christians were seen to work together in fellowship, 'the world sits up and takes notice'.[57]

Welby's international travels gave him a wider appreciation of a theology of unity in diversity, whether ministering at the Lord's Table to a multi-lingual congregation in Baghdad or experiencing the unique Epiphany celebrations of Orthodox Christians in Bethlehem. He challenged his New Wine audience to think through their ecclesiology more carefully, suggesting that although evangelicals knew in theory that the church was the people not the building, too often they meant 'it's our kind of people, it's the people we agree with'. On the contrary, he declared, 'Difference is part of being Christian.' Therefore the key was to find 'a safe way of disagreeing'.[58] He encouraged his hearers to identify peace-makers in their congregations who were good at building relationships across the divide, 'who aren't tribal'.[59] Welby drew an important distinction between reconciliation and the end of argument: 'Reconciliation is conflict transformed, not concluded. It's

56   Welby, 'Blessed are the Peacemakers', part 1.
57   Welby, 'Reconciliation and Forgiveness' (2003), parts 1 and 2; Welby, 'Reconciliation and Forgiveness' (2004), part 2; Welby, 'Blessed are the Peacemakers', part 1.
58   Welby, 'Reconciliation and Forgiveness' (2003), part 2.
59   Welby, 'Reconciliation and Forgiveness' (2004), part 2.

conflict with words, not with AK47s.'[60] Again he repeated, 'Conflict itself is not bad, it's only bad when it gets out of control.'[61]

As of supreme importance, Welby insisted that Christians must learn to disagree 'in a way that honours the gospel', not arguing with 'the world's weapons' (2 Corinthians 10:3). Disputes must be dealt with internally, not in the secular press. 'If people hear Christians disagreeing vitriolicly and savagely, in public at each other, with cruelty and not with grace, not merely with firmness but with real viciousness, they are not going to be converted. It is not going to show them the gospel.'[62] Digging trenches and firing mortars at each other 'will neither convince the world, nor will it solve the problem'. Instead it was necessary to find 'a place where people can disagree incredibly vehemently but safely', out of the public gaze, where they can speak freely and be listened to carefully, 'without being condemned as in some sense less than human'.[63] Even when Christians disagreed 'rightly and passionately', their attitude must be one of servanthood. Jesus, the master, washed the feet even of Judas, Welby observed.[64] One of his key Bible texts was 2 Timothy 2:24–25, 'the Lord's servant must not be quarrelsome but kindly to *everyone* ... correcting opponents with *gentleness*. God may perhaps grant that they will repent and come to know the truth.' These verses encapsulated the importance of Christian truth, a godly attitude to opponents within the church, and the role of the Holy Spirit in bringing repentance and renewal.[65]

The continual escalation of conflict within the Anglican Communion bore striking resemblance to what Welby had witnessed in war zones, 'only without guns'.[66] Parallels to

60　　Welby, 'Reconciliation and Forgiveness' (2004), part 1.
61　　Welby, 'Blessed are the Peacemakers', part 1.
62　　Welby, 'Blessed are the Peacemakers', part 1.
63　　Welby, 'Reconciliation and Forgiveness' (2003), part 2.
64　　Welby, 'Reconciliation and Forgiveness' (2004), part 1.
65　　Welby, 'Reconciliation and Forgiveness' (2003), part 2.
66　　Welby, 'Blessed are the Peacemakers', part 1.

the Jeffrey John crisis were played out in North America. In May 2003 a gay couple in Vancouver had their relationship blessed using a liturgy authorised by Michael Ingham (Bishop of New Westminster), as mandated by his diocesan synod. Meanwhile in November 2003 Gene Robinson, a clergyman in a same-sex partnership, was consecrated by The Episcopal Church as Bishop of New Hampshire.[67] The consecration went ahead despite warnings from the Anglican primates meeting at Lambeth Palace that it would 'tear the fabric of our Communion at its deepest level' and 'jeopardise our sacramental fellowship with each other'.[68] With schism threatened throughout the Anglican world, Archbishop Williams appointed a Lambeth Commission on Communion, chaired by Robin Eames (Archbishop of Armagh), which published *The Windsor Report* in October 2004. It called for a moratorium on same-sex blessings and on the consecration of bishops in same-sex unions, and set in process the drafting of an Anglican Communion Covenant. Several commentators began to question the future of the Archbishop of Canterbury's representative role as Anglicanism's *primus inter pares* (first amongst equals). Although Welby was a self-confessed 'fan of Rowan Williams', he believed it was a fair question for Nigeria (by far the largest Anglican province) to ask why in a post-colonial world the Communion 'should be run by a white man in Lambeth'.[69]

Challenged by a comment from a gay American priest that Anglicans needed as much help in reconciliation as did the militias of the Niger Delta, Welby began to invest his energies in bringing members of the global church together. In light of *The Windsor Report* he convened two private gatherings of Anglican theologians, bishops and archbishops at the Community of the Cross of Nails in Coventry in November

---

67   Bates, *Church at War*, pp. 229–75; Elizabeth Adams, *Going to Heaven: The Life and Election of Bishop Gene Robinson* (New York: Soft Skull Press, 2006); Gene Robinson, *In the Eye of the Storm* (Norwich: Canterbury Press, 2008).
68   Statement by Anglican primates, Lambeth Palace, 16 October 2003.
69   Welby, 'Blessed are the Peacemakers', part 1.

2005 and July 2006 to listen to each other's concerns. Welby was the chief organiser, though the formal invitations came from Bishop Bennetts and Dean Irvine. The meetings were facilitated by a Swedish theologian, Runar Eldebo (Professor of Homiletics at Stockholm School of Theology), and aimed to build trust, respect and better understanding amongst those who attended. One practical result, inspired by the Coventry consultation, was 'The Bible in the Life of the Church', a project initiated by David Moxon (Archbishop of New Zealand).[70] During three years of intensive field research, it analysed the wide variety of hermeneutical approaches to the Bible evident within the multiple contexts of the global Anglican family. Its report, entitled *Deep Engagement, Fresh Discovery*, was welcomed at the Anglican Consultative Council (ACC 15) in Auckland in November 2012.[71]

Following St Benedict

Although Welby had good relationships with new Roman Catholic communities like the Eucharistein monastery in Switzerland, his strongest personal attachment was closer to home with the Anglican Benedictines. He first encountered the order as an ordinand in the early 1990s when he spent four days on retreat at Elmore Abbey near Newbury, in Berkshire, at the recommendation of his stepfather. Having been erased from the Church of England at the Reformation, the Benedictine movement was re-integrated within Anglicanism during the monastic revival of the nineteenth and early twentieth centuries. In its heyday in the 1940s and 1950s, the most prominent community at Nashdom Abbey

---

70   Letter from David Moxon, 8 January 2013.
71   Clare Amos (ed.), *The Bible in the Life of the Church* (Norwich: Canterbury Press, 2013).

near Maidenhead was a powerhouse of Anglo-Catholicism, boasting such luminaries as the liturgical scholar Gregory Dix. By the time Welby discovered the community, however, numbers had dwindled, Nashdom had shut and the surviving monks moved to Elmore. Yet it remained a small bastion of Anglo-Papalism, celebrating the Roman eucharistic rite (before switching to *Common Worship* in 2002) and using the prayers of the Roman breviary.[72]

During his first retreat Welby found the liturgical rigour of the community difficult to cope with, 'the regularity, the vast chunks of psalms, the lack of spontaneous worship'. But he soon came to find the discipline a help not a hindrance:

> There are also moments of awe, as through sheer repetition the word of God penetrates my thick skull, and I see afresh. Above all, for me, there is the encouragement of ordinary people seeking to live out a life of integrity in community, with Christ at the centre, guided by a Rule of incandescent common sense.[73]

Welby was a regular visitor to Elmore and in 2004 became a Benedictine oblate (similar to the 'third order' amongst the Franciscans and Dominicans), committing himself to follow Benedict's Rule in his daily life.[74] To his Southam parishioners, he explained that the Rule was 'full of good stuff' and remarkably contemporary as an antidote to stress. He pointed especially to Benedict's emphasis upon a balanced lifestyle (a mixture of work, prayer and rest), stable relationships, and freedom from chasing after possessions.[75] He later became a trustee of the community and oversaw the move of the four remaining monks from Elmore to Salisbury in September 2010.

---

72   Petà Dunstan, *The Labour of Obedience: The Benedictines of Pershore, Nashdom and Elmore: A History* (Norwich: Canterbury Press, 2009).
73   Justin Welby, 'Benedict and Bible', Coventry Cathedral, Lent 2004.
74   Augustine Morris, *Oblates: Life with St Benedict* (Newbury: Elmore Abbey, 1992); Gervase Holdaway (ed.), *The Oblate Life* (Norwich: Canterbury Press, 2008).
75   Justin Welby, 'Thought for the Month', *SPCN* (September 2001).

Coventry's original cathedral, for the medieval diocese of Coventry and Lichfield, was a Benedictine foundation in the eleventh century. This spiritual heritage remained important at the cathedral and the Community of the Cross of Nails followed a special 'Coventry Discipline', written by Provost Williams in the 1960s and based on Benedict's Rule. During Welby's years as a cathedral canon and sub-dean he therefore had opportunity to teach more extensively about Benedictine principles. He wrote a cathedral study course for Lent 2004 on 'Benedict and Bible' and undertook a wholesale revision of the CCN's discipline in 2007, reinvigorated and recast in softer focus as 'A Coventry Way'. Welby saw Benedict's Rule as a practical commentary on Scripture, based on life experience, laying down principles not just for running a monastery but any Christian organisation. He welcomed especially its focus on Christ and its call to listen carefully to God through the Bible: 'I find that the excitement of a fulfilling job can cause so much noise and thinking in my mind that listening is drowned out.' Particularly counter-cultural was Benedict's emphasis upon obedience, as Welby noted: 'I am very challenged by it. As a canon I have sworn obedience to the Queen, the Bishop and the Dean (the last two with explicit qualifications!). ... I don't do obedience very well. Nor do many people.' Yet he admitted that obedience to those in authority was essential for the flourishing of a Christian community and a reflection of their obedience to God.[76]

Moral philosopher Alasdair MacIntyre suggested in *After Virtue* (1981) that Europe and North America at the end of the second millennium had entered 'the new dark ages', parallel to those which followed the demise of the Roman Empire, except that 'the barbarians' were not beyond the frontiers but already in government. Therefore what was needed to sustain intellectual and moral civilization was a new

---

76   Welby, 'Benedict and Bible'.

St Benedict.[77] This idea appealed to Welby who saw it as an encouragement for the Western church facing cultural eclipse. He praised Benedict as 'an inspiring source of hope and vision for a church facing challenge, change and decline', because the monk 'saw much worse than we can imagine, but held to a vision of a God whose purposes are good'. In particular, with clear contemporary application, Welby observed that Benedictine communities played 'a crucial part in re-evangelising Europe' from the sixth century onwards.[78] This chimed with Welby's own ambitions to reverse the decline in his generation. As Archbishop of Canterbury, he would again point to the evangelistic endeavour of British Christians in the 'dark ages' as a model for the twenty-first-century church.

Holy Trinity, Coventry

During his final months in Coventry in 2007, Welby was asked by Bishop Bennetts to review the relationship between the cathedral and its near neighbour, Holy Trinity, Coventry (HTC). The buildings are just yards from each other, practically on the same site in the city centre, though for most of the twentieth century their two Christian communities were entirely independent, sometimes rivals. In the 1950s some at Holy Trinity had hoped that it would become the new cathedral and resented the vast sums of money spent on erecting Basil Spence's cavernous replacement next door. The arrival of John Irvine as dean in 2001 signalled the start of a much closer relationship, because unlike his predecessors he was more in sympathy with HTC's evangelical and charismatic ethos. Irvine

---

77   Alasdair MacIntyre, *After Virtue: A Study in Moral Theory* (London: Duckworth, 1981), p. 245.
78   Justin Welby, 'Why Bother with St Benedict?', *Cathedral News: The Newsletter of the Friends of Coventry Cathedral* (August 2005), pp. 4–5.

and Keith Sinclair (vicar of HTC) worked closely together and Irvine's wife, Andrea, was ordained in 2002 as Sinclair's curate. Three HTC incumbents in a row were promoted to the episcopate – Graham Dow to Willesden in 1992, David Urquhart to Birkenhead in 2000, and when Sinclair moved in 2007 to become the next Bishop of Birkenhead there was an opportunity to pause and take stock.

The overlap between the ministries of the cathedral and HTC was increasingly obvious. Both had a strong choral tradition and informal evening services, both worked with families and students, both ran Alpha Courses. They were fishing in the same pool. Welby was asked to lead a consultation process before the next vicar was appointed, and was formally licensed as HTC's priest-in-charge on 1 April 2007. He saw it as an opportunity to reassess 'how God's calling to us all can best be carried out, while respecting the traditions and individual identities of both worshipping communities'. His hope was for 'flourishing Christian communities in the City centre, living out their discipleship in radical new ways'.[79] Amongst the HTC congregation there was some 'grumbling and paranoia', even 'conspiracy theories' at the sub-dean from the cathedral being imposed upon them, but Welby repeated that he had 'no agenda' and it was not a 'takeover'. At the church's annual meeting he exhorted them to engage fully with the process:

> The nature of God is to turn the world upside down. He bursts into our lives when it is going well and bad [sic]. The next twelve months are a turning point for HTC. It is a new step and a time for a fresh vision. We do not know the mind of God yet, but it will be more wonderful than we can imagine. ... If we are listening to God, then you will be prepared for radical change. Not abandoning the past, but building on it.[80]

79   Letter from Justin Welby, *Holy Trinity Coventry Update* (March 2007).
80   'Summary of Chairman's Report to the Annual Meeting of Parishioners', *Holy Trinity Coventry Update* (May 2007).

During the consultation (attended by about 110 people from the parish church, but only about 25 from the cathedral), they were asked to imagine 'a Golden age for mission' in Coventry city centre. The conclusions were modest. There were obvious areas for potential collaboration, in children's and youth work, tourism, healing ministry, social action and evangelism, but 'Any idea of merger is out of the question without a radical change and surrender of rights and power by one side or the other; the history and cultures are too different.' One proposal was for the next vicar of HTC to be also a residentiary canon at the cathedral, perhaps even the next sub-dean, but this came to nothing. Welby wanted to push further, as seen by repetition of two of his favourite words, 'radical' and 'risk'. He floated the prospect of a 'really radical' transformation, with HTC taking charge of regular Sunday and mid-week worship and the cathedral taking charge of major celebrations, conferences and courses. This would bring 'much more flexibility, but it would be a very risky route. It would involve doing church very differently, risking the comfort of the daily routine for the challenge of reaching out to city, diocese and world in new ways.'[81] The relationship between Coventry Cathedral and HTC was an unfinished project. It was one example of reconciliation ministry at a local level, but there was little enthusiasm amongst the congregations for practical reorganisation, let alone radical revolution. The fruits of the consultation were limited and Welby's gifts were soon in demand elsewhere.

In February 2007 a brown envelope arrived on the doormat, bearing the title 'On Her Majesty's Service'. Caroline Welby instinctively thought it was a tax demand, but inside was an invitation from Downing Street offering Justin the deanery of Liverpool Cathedral. There had been no interviews, and he had no idea he was being considered for the post, or

---

81   Justin Welby and David Williams, 'Holy Trinity / Cathedral Consultation Conclusions and Recommendations', *Holy Trinity Coventry Update* (October 2007).

even that the deanery was vacant.[82] Bishop Bennetts was particularly active in ensuring that able clergy in his diocese, suitable for promotion to senior posts, were commended to the appointments secretaries of the Archbishop of Canterbury and the Prime Minister. In 2007 three Coventry clergymen were elevated to suffragan bishoprics in quick succession – Birkenhead (Keith Sinclair), Wolverhampton (Clive Gregory) and Jarrow (Mark Bryant). Welby's name was on the same list. Nevertheless, he did not immediately jump at Liverpool because he and Caroline were not sure they wanted to spend the rest of their ministry in a cathedral setting. Another possibility was the vacant bishopric of Cyprus and the Gulf, part of the vast Anglican province of Jerusalem and the Middle East which stretches from Algeria to Somalia and Iran. The diocese encompasses Anglican congregations both in Cyprus (with headquarters at Nicosia) and in the Muslim-dominated states of Iraq, Kuwait, Saudi Arabia, Bahrain, Qatar, the United Arab Emirates, Yemen and Oman. Its bishop, Clive Handford, retired in April 2007 and Welby was considered a fitting successor given his international experience, though he played down his chances in typical fashion. Standing only five feet and nine inches tall, he used to quip, 'I'll never be a bishop, I'm too short!' He allowed his name to be put forward, and was shortlisted for the post, but withdrew before the interviews because the Welbys felt that the inevitable long months of travel around a diocese covering over 1.3 million square miles would put too much strain on their family life. After some months of prayer and seeking advice, they decided to continue ministering in an English cathedral and accepted the offer of Liverpool which was announced publicly by Downing Street in June 2007.

---

82   'Meet the Dean Designate', pp. 5–6; *Travellers' Tales*, 31 March 2013.

Chapter 7

Liverpool Cathedral

The Anglican cathedral in Liverpool, looking over the city from the top of St James' Mount, is the largest church in Britain and the fifth largest in the world. The vast neo-Gothic edifice was begun in 1904 in the days of Bishop Chavasse but not completed until 1978, long after the death of its architect, Sir Giles Gilbert Scott. Its magnificent Willis organ is the largest pipe organ in Britain, bigger even than the one in the Royal Albert Hall. Its massive bells, high in the tower, are the heaviest peal in the world.[1] Yet this remarkable Christian building is situated in the midst of some of the most socially deprived communities in Britain. The demise of Merseyside's traditional industries in the 1970s and 1980s, and the closure of its docks and factories, led to spiralling rates of unemployment, social unrest and economic collapse, the effects of which were still being felt 30 years later. By the turn of the new millennium, there were green shoots of recovery in some areas of the city. After decades of depression, Liverpool tried to reinvent itself, no longer as an industrial powerhouse but as a tourist centre and a World Heritage Site, ripe for urban regeneration. In 2007 the city celebrated the 800th anniversary of the founding of the borough, and in 2008 it was named European Capital of Culture, which pumped millions of pounds into the local economy though little of it reached areas like Toxteth. Poverty and wealth coexisted side by side. *Cities Unlimited* (2007), a remarkable report by the think-tank Policy Exchange, claimed there was no realistic hope of regenerating cities like

1   Peter Kennerley, *The Building of Liverpool Cathedral* (new edition, Lancaster: Carnegie, 2008).

Liverpool, so the population should be encouraged to move to the economic hub of London and the south-east, especially to Oxford and Cambridge.[2]

Justin Welby was Liverpool Cathedral's sixth dean. He inherited an iconic tourist venue that attracted nearly half a million visitors a year and employed a staff of 80, supported by 250 volunteers. Immediately before his arrival, the cathedral community had experienced some difficulties. The financial outlook was bleak. There had been dysfunctional relationships, including within the cathedral chapter, and a formal Visitation by James Jones (Bishop of Liverpool) during 2006–07 to investigate the problems. Welby's expertise in finance and reconciliation were therefore obvious assets, and his first tasks were to steady the ship and rebuild confidence.

Safety and Risk-Taking

At his installation, on 8 December 2007, Welby announced his vision for the cathedral community with three central priorities.[3] It was to be a place of freedom in worship, risk-taking and generosity. As in Southam parish church, so in Liverpool Cathedral, Welby made clear his intention to encourage worship 'in many different styles', 'styles modern and traditional, silent and full of sound. In worship will be found the presence of God and with Him and Him alone there is hope for our fears, healing for our wounds, sense in our lostness, forgiveness in our failings.' Gently hinting that choral music would not maintain its monopoly, he observed that 'The style is far less important than the substance: of a

---

2   Tim Leunig, James Swaffield and Oliver Marc Hartwich, *Cities Unlimited: Making Urban Regeneration Work* (London: Policy Exchange, 2007).
3   'Dean Justin's Sermon', pp. 26–30.

heart turned towards God.' Second, the cathedral would be 'a place of risk':

> Jesus sent his disciples out to heal and transform – to take risks; to bring people into the presence of the living God. Christians are to be people who go out and make a difference because of the power of God and the love of Christ. Whatever else Christianity may be, it is fire and passion not comfort and ease. Risk means taking chances with things that may and will fail, whether styles of worship, or new forms of church life, or in reconciliation amongst people who are in conflict, or in offering generous hospitality and love.

Risk, according to the new dean, meant 'saying what is true when it is unpopular', going out with the good news of Jesus Christ, 'not being afraid of the incredible consequences of that message for every aspect of life, public and private. If we trust Christ we can do no less than take risks.' Third, he wanted the cathedral to be a place of generosity, which was far wider than merely hospitality and welcome:

> God's generosity to us was to give the life of His son Jesus so that we might know God. Christians should be as lavish as God with their love to each other and in the world around. ... Generosity listens, and affirms with passion the God-given value of the human being in each encounter, whether we agree with the person we encounter or not. Generosity forgives others, knowing our own weakness and the forgiveness we receive from God. Generosity reaches out, and obeying Jesus, goes with the Gospel of salvation and hope. ... Churches must be Christ centred, consciously and explicitly, full of passionate love for Jesus, or they are nothing.

Six months into the post Welby reiterated that Liverpool Cathedral was to be a 'thriving, accepting, holy and outgoing community'. He warned against the temptation for Christians to become 'inward looking and self obsessed'. Their calling was to be missionaries into the wider community: 'Ironically, one of the ways in which the Cathedral building is used is by leaving it. It is not a prison but a base.' He also began to develop further the language of risk, now a dominant theme in his discourse. Welby proposed a new slogan, 'This Cathedral should be a safe place to do risky things', which he interpreted: 'Safe because a fervent and flourishing spirituality becomes a safety net for when we fall, and a resource for when we need renewal. Safe because you can succeed and fail and be loved. Safe because you can say controversial things and be accepted.' But also risky, because Christian discipleship, the way of the cross, 'means facing tough issues, asking hard questions, reaching out in mission to dark places. In four words, *doing what Jesus does*.'[4]

Welby's characteristic approach of decisive leadership, interwoven with collegiality and consensus (as seen, for example, in Southam) was evident in the way he negotiated the cathedral's change of direction. It was a management style he had learnt at Enterprise Oil, and in *The Treasurer* he described his role as Dean of Liverpool as 'chief executive of a business'.[5] The Welbys invested many evenings in hosting cathedral volunteers and their partners to dinner at the deanery, in groups of a dozen, to build friendships around the table – an approach they had found fruitful in the parish 12 years before. In October 2008 he also launched a formal consultation process to which all were invited to contribute. The difficulties they faced were evident – a vast building which was seldom even 15 per cent full, except for special services; a high average age, with very few families and young people outside the choir; a poorly paid staff and coffers which were running dry. Yet it was also 'a golden age of opportunity', with a landmark building in one of the world's great cities, and a gospel message of transformative power. 'In short, the times demand a fresh vision.'[6]

4   Justin Welby, 'Honouring the Builders', *LCL* no. 59 (July 2008), pp. 2–3.
5   Williams, 'Of Secular and Sacred', p. 43.
6   Liverpool Cathedral Consultation 2008; 'Consultation in Context', *LCL* no. 66 (March 2009), p. 8.

The cathedral community emerged from the consultation with a corporate vision which all had helped to shape – but the headline motto, often quoted, was almost identical to the one Welby had himself proposed months earlier: 'a safe place to do risky things in Christ's service'. Capturing the image of the cathedral's soaring columns, the priorities were expressed as four 'pillars of growth'. First, mission and evangelism, drawing people 'to living faith' and proclaiming 'a radical gospel of regenerative transformation for society and individuals'. Second, 'vibrant and inclusive' worship in many styles, enabling everyone to encounter Christ. Third, education and reflection, to 'grapple intelligently with the hardest questions of contemporary life' and contribute to public debate. Fourth, an 'eclectic spirituality' which nurtured Christian growth. These were the priorities by which Welby wanted Liverpool Cathedral to be measured, 'to drive us forward in God's mission'.[7]

The three events which most captured the public imagination, and hit the headlines in the secular press, during Welby's years in Liverpool were all justified on the basis that the cathedral wanted to be 'a safe place to do risky things in Christ's service'. In May 2009 the tune to John Lennon's anthem, 'Imagine', was rung from the cathedral bells as part of the Futuresonic arts and music festival.[8] Yoko Ono said the idea was 'so beautiful, it made me choke up'.[9] The song was generally considered atheistic, with its call to 'imagine there's no heaven, it's easy if you try', and Welby was inundated with critical emails from around the globe. He explained why they had taken the risk: 'I'd say the song is the right destination – justice and peace – but the wrong route. ... We didn't agree with the lyrics, but the more we looked at it, the more we

7   For this vision statement, see *Liverpool Cathedral Annual Review* (2009), p. 3; and Liverpool Cathedral Development Plan 2010–13, appendix 1.
8   'Message of Peace to Ring Loud and Clear', *Liverpool Daily Echo*, 14 May 2009, p. 16.
9   'Beautiful Plan Moved Me to Tears Says Yoko', *Liverpool Daily Echo*, 6 March 2009, p. 6.

thought the song has an awful lot that connects with issues that people genuinely feel.'[10] Equally risky was the cathedral's decision in February 2011 to host a political rally for the first time in its history, organised by the Merseyside Trades Union Council in protest at government cuts. Veteran socialist Tony Benn addressed a crowd of 2,000 people, with their placards and banners, with a rallying cry against the Coalition. Again Welby was forced to defend the chapter's judgement, explaining that it was 'nothing to do with party politics':

> Christians are told a lot by God about justice, it's a key theme of the Bible. We all know if people are being shoved aside economically, then those are the bonds of injustice and they need breaking. The whole of Merseyside is suffering bigger cuts than the rest of the UK and at a speed that makes it impossible to adjust and care for those affected, which is most of us in the region. The way things are being done here is wrong.[11]

Eyebrows were raised again, two months later, when the cathedral hosted a dance party organised by the record label Dig Deeper and Liverpool club Freeze, for 400 fans of the internationally renowned DJs Hernan Cattaneo and Danny Howells. It was viewed by the chapter as an opportunity for outreach, and a 'Spirit Zone' was provided instead of the usual 'Chill-Out Area'. It coincided also with a day of music workshops at the cathedral for teenagers in Toxteth.[12] The cathedral's new priorities, corporately agreed, liberated the dean and chapter to push the boundaries in innovative ways such as these. It won the cathedral a higher profile in the city and helped to reach sectors of the population who normally had little connection with church. The momentum

10   Pat Ashworth, '"Risky" Lennon Tune Ties Knots in Tower', *Church Times*, 22 May 2009, p. 5.
11   '2,000 Pack Cathedral to Hear Benn Condemn Spending Cuts', *Liverpool Daily Post*, 7 February 2011, p. 6.
12   Richard White, 'Letter of the Month: In Christ's Service?', *LCL* no. 81 (March 2011), pp. 4–5; 'It's God's House' and 'We'll Be Dancing in the Aisles!', *Liverpool Daily Echo*, 25 March 2011, pp. 3, 13.

thus explicitly began to shift, from caution to risk, and from maintenance to mission.

Fresh Expressions

Finance was a major headache throughout Welby's tenure. The operating deficit in 2009 was £308,000, which was typical of other years.[13] As the cathedral's development plan stated, 'Put starkly, on the basis of our recent performance we have another 6–8 years of reserves; after that, there is nothing left.'[14] Although there were doubts about the cathedral's future viability, the chapter embraced the idea that evangelism was the key: 'Our overarching priority is to grow. ... Cutting our work, mission and ministry may make short term savings, growth offers us security and confidence over a longer term.'[15] Unlike parish churches, which were generally in decline across the country, cathedrals were growing. National trends showed a 30 per cent rise in cathedral attendance during the first decade of the twenty-first century.[16] But Welby's team was determined to pray and work for a far greater increase, partly in response to the Bishop of Liverpool's Growth Agenda set for the diocese. In March 2010 the chapter announced their ambitious target to double the number of worshippers within just five years, from about 400 on an average Sunday to 800. This would not be by recruiting from other churches but by evangelisation of the cathedral fringe and non-Christians in

13 *Liverpool Cathedral Annual Review* (2009), p. 4.
14 Liverpool Cathedral Development Plan 2010–13.
15 *Liverpool Cathedral Annual Review* (2011), p. 17.
16 *Church Statistics 2010/11* (London: Archbishops' Council, 2012), p. 33. For Liverpool figures, see Lew Eccleshall, 'How Do We Fare Compared to the National Average?', *LCL* no. 70 (July 2009), pp. 13–15.

the local community.[17] Alpha Courses became a frequent part of the cathedral programme.

Welby believed that one essential to growth was the provision of contemporary worship alongside more traditional forms. Central to this strategy was the recruitment of Richard White as canon for mission and evangelism in September 2009. His job title explicitly named 'evangelism' not just generic 'mission' to indicate that proclaiming the message of Jesus Christ was vital not merely social reform. White was previously a pioneer minister with the 'fresh expressions' Dream Network, familiar with experimental worship and outreach to a younger generation.[18] Although Welby promised that Liverpool Cathedral would remain a place of musical and liturgical distinction, with a strong choral tradition, he hoped for a 'mixed economy' (Rowan Williams' phrase for 'fresh expressions' and 'inherited' church patterns existing side by side).[19] In a series of sermons on the role of a cathedral in post-modern Britain, Welby explained:

> Some love incense and mystery, rich robes and symbol. Others thrive on participation, all contributing. They are usually different churches, each church is like a bus with a sign on the front, 'bells and smells', 'happy clappy'. ... But the Cathedral is the mother church, the unifier, we cannot have a single style, a single destination sign. ... So we have clergy from all traditions, and they bring skills in different sorts of worship, from chasubles and incense to bands and informality, but always seeking excellence.

He wanted everyone in Liverpool diocese to be able to say, 'that is my Cathedral'.[20] The dean laid special emphasis upon being 'non-tribal', an explicit rejection of ecclesiastical partisanship and a telling choice of words given his first-hand experience of destructive tribal conflict in an African context.

---

17   Richard White, 'Prepare to Double', *LCL* no. 76 (May 2010), pp. 16–17.
18   'Supporting Mission and Evangelism', *LCL* no. 69 (June 2009), pp. 16–17.
19   *Liverpool Cathedral Annual Review* (2009), p. 13.
20   Justin Welby, 'Four February Sermons: The Post-Modern Cathedral', part 1, 6 February 2011, www.liverpoolcathedral.org.uk.

His desire for an eclectic Anglican comprehensiveness bore strong resonance with the relaxed ecumenical ethos of HTB and the Alpha Course.

There was a deliberate attempt to accommodate a variety of styles. In October 2009, for example, 1,000 pilgrims of all ages gathered in the cathedral around the icon of Our Lady of Walsingham and engaged in such activities as prayer in the presence of the blessed sacrament and an exuberant 'youth mass', which was not to everyone's taste.[21] By March 2010 Welby, in collaboration with his canon precentor, Myles Davies, began to shake up the pattern of the main Sunday eucharist, moving furniture and experimenting with changes of voice and location. He observed:

> The Cathedral building has a distinctly rough personality. When there is a service, if the liturgy does not make use of the space, subdue it and dominate it, the building snorts contemptuously and sweeps the liturgy aside. It is a fabulous servant of the worship of God, but takes hard thinking and much imagination before it will agree to serve.

The dean acknowledged that change was 'often uncomfortable, unsettling', but then 'So is Christian faith'. He wanted an 'inspiring liturgy that is at once ancient and modern'.[22] A year later, from March 2011, people were offered a clear choice at the main Sunday eucharist. They could attend the traditional choral service as usual, or they could go downstairs to 'Zone 2' (overseen by White), where the worship was informal and interactive, arranged in 'café style'. The two congregations joined for the eucharistic prayer and to receive communion together.[23]

Learning again from his days at HTB, Welby hoped that the cathedral itself would one day begin to plant new

---

21 *Liverpool Cathedral Annual Review* (2009), p. 13.
22 Justin Welby, 'Using Our Great Space Imaginatively in Liturgy', *LCL* no. 74 (March 2010), pp. 11–12. See also, Justin Welby, 'Trying Something New', *LCL* no. 57 (May 2008), p. 8.
23 Richard White, 'A New Worship Zone', *LCL* no. 80 (January 2011), pp. 8–9.

churches. He also began to investigate the possibility of a new theological college.[24] The cathedral's School of Theology was launched in September 2010, in partnership with St Mellitus College in London (closely connected to the HTB network of churches), to educate Christians on Merseyside in the Bible and theology.[25] Soon after Welby had left Liverpool the Church of England's Ministry Council agreed to St Mellitus training ordinands at the cathedral, in partnership with the five Anglican dioceses in the north-west, from September 2013.

Another of Welby's dreams was to establish an ecumenical religious community, perhaps in a house on Hope Street, halfway between the Anglican and Roman Catholic cathedrals. He celebrated that in France and Switzerland new religious communities were springing up, with many joining, 'replacing the decaying and emptying monasteries with a vigour as great as at the time of Benedict or Francis'.[26] He hoped that in Liverpool such a work might be pioneered by Chemin Neuf (New Way), an ecumenical religious order drawing members from many different denominations, though dominated by French-speaking Roman Catholics. It was founded in Lyon in 1973 by Laurent Fabre, a young Jesuit who had experienced charismatic renewal. By the early twenty-first century Chemin Neuf had over 1,200 members in 26 countries and nearly 10,000 associate members. Its theological emphases were simplicity of life, Ignatian spirituality, 'baptism in the Holy Spirit', mission and Christian unity. It enthusiastically welcomed the Alpha Course as an evangelistic tool and was the first to run Alpha amongst Roman Catholics in France.[27] Welby first encountered the community in 2006 when speaking at a Chemin Neuf conference on reconciliation at

24   Liverpool Cathedral Development Plan 2010–13.
25   'School of Theology', *LCL* no. 78 (September 2010), p. 16.
26   Justin Welby, sermon at Liverpool Cathedral, 1 August 2010, www.liverpoolcathedral. org.uk.
27   Timothy Watson, '"Life Precedes Law": The Story So Far of the Chemin Neuf Community', *One in Christ* vol. 43 (Summer 2009), pp. 27–51.

the Centre Siloé at Montagnieu near Lyon. His dreams for a community house in Liverpool were not realised, though his last appointment was of Tim Watson, an Anglican member of Chemin Neuf, as curate of Liverpool Cathedral from August 2011. Welby preached at Watson's ordination at Sablonceaux Abbey in France during a Chemin Neuf community week.[28]

Archbishop's Envoy

Although he had his hands full running a cathedral, Welby continued to be in demand internationally for his expertise in conflict resolution. He was invited to Nairobi and Eldoret, in the Kenyan Rift Valley, in early 2008 in the aftermath of the post-election violence. There he met with Anglican church leaders, including Archbishop Benjamin Nzimbi, and helped to put together a strategic plan for a reconciliation process.[29] Meanwhile Welby had a growing reputation as an authority on Nigeria. In 2006 and 2009 he spoke at seminars organised by the US State Department, and in 2008 and 2011 was flown out to Washington to brief the incoming American ambassadors to Abuja.

Welby also found himself drawn more deeply into Anglican Communion affairs as one of the Archbishop of Canterbury's trusted advisors. Rowan Williams was increasingly frustrated at the heightened rhetoric within the global Communion, especially in the controversy over sexuality, and appealed to the Anglican primates in his 2007 advent letter for a new form of dialogue:

> A great deal of the language that is around in the Communion at present seems to presuppose that any change from our current deadlock is impossible, that division is unavoidable

28   'Welcome to Tim', *LCL* no. 84 (September – October 2011), p. 7.
29   Justin Welby, 'Kenya: Steps to Reconciliation', *LCL* no. 55 (March 2008), pp. 3–6.

and that any such division represents so radical a difference in fundamental faith that no recognition and future co-operation can be imagined. I cannot accept these assumptions, and I do not believe that as Christians we should see them as beyond challenge ...[30]

Williams called for 'facilitated conversations' to help solve the crisis, and Welby was drafted in as part of a small strategy team to consider what those conversations might look like. The project was led by Francis Bridger (executive director of the Anglican Communion Studies Center at Fuller Theological Seminary in Pasadena) and proposed a 'consensus process' methodology. The idea had been pioneered in the United States by David Satcher (former US Surgeon General) at the Morehouse School of Medicine in Atlanta, who in 2004 initiated the National Consensus Process on Sexual Health and Responsible Sexual Behaviour, bringing together people from divergent ideologies to explore their disagreements in civility without vehemence. Bridger's strategy team explained:

A number of aspects of the 'consensus process' model suggest its appropriateness for adaptation to the needs of the Anglican Communion. Firstly, it is a dynamic conversational process which focuses as much on relational as problem-solving outcomes. Secondly, all aspects of the conversation, from subject priorities and order of the discussion to framing ground rules are established by the participants themselves and therefore the ends are not predetermined. Thirdly, there is no formal voting procedure and yet each member must finally agree to all aspects of the process for it to proceed. In this way, the idea of 'blocks' and 'voting' and 'compromise' are eliminated; and every participating individual – including his or her perspective and the group or viewpoint he/she represents – is fully empowered.[31]

30　Rowan Williams, Advent letter to primates of the Anglican Communion, 14 December 2007, www.rowanwilliams.archbishopofcanterbury.org.
31　'Finding Consensus and Demonstrating Christian Civility within the Anglican Communion with Potential Implications for the Wider Christian World' (project proposal, November 2007), included in Francis Bridger, 'Background and Introduction to the Liverpool Consultation and its Accompanying Documents' (April 2008).

As part of the feasibility study, Welby was deputed to conduct confidential face-to-face interviews with a series of African bishops to hear their interpretations of the Anglican crisis, and he reported back a widespread desire 'to bring internecine warfare to an end'. In April 2008 he hosted a three-day consultation in his large study at Liverpool Cathedral to explore the ideas further. It was chaired by the Archbishop of Canterbury's chief of staff, Chris Smith, and the participants included two global primates, Bernard Ntahoturi (Archbishop of Burundi) and Carlos Touche-Porter (Archbishop of Mexico). The resulting *Liverpool Report* recommended that the Archbishop of Canterbury sponsor an Anglican consensus process for three years 2008–11, around the theme 'New Ways of Being Communion'. Welby was put forward as the best person to help construct the necessary facilitation team. The group recognised, however, that because this approach was pioneered in North America it might be seen as bound to western culture, but they nonetheless recommended the methodology while changing the terminology. In particular, the word 'consensus' might be misunderstood as 'a synonym for compromise or an attempt to subvert historic beliefs', so Archbishop Ntahoturi proposed the term *padare*, a Shona word for a gathering of community elders to discuss difficult issues and seek a common mind.[32] In the event, Archbishop Williams decided not to pursue the idea of a 'global Anglican *padare*'. There was already momentum behind the '*indaba*' process (a similar Zulu word), which was rolled out at the 2008 Lambeth Conference and came to dominate the field. Both approaches were concerned for mutual listening, but *indaba* was less concerned to reach consensus at the end of the conversation. Nevertheless the Liverpool consultation and report was crucial in laying the groundwork for *indaba* by its ethos and researched analysis of key issues. Phil Groves

---

32   Francis Bridger, 'Building Consensus in the Anglican Communion: A Report to the Archbishop of Canterbury Arising from the Liverpool Consultation, April 22nd – 24th 2008' (June 2008).

and Flora Winfield (co-directors of Continuing Indaba 2009–12) were both participants at Liverpool, and the Morehouse School of Medicine became the major financial backer of Anglican *indaba* as the conduit for a $2 million gift from an American donor. Welby surprisingly played no part in Continuing Indaba, but picked up the ideas later in his advocacy of 'facilitated conversations'.[33]

The divisions within the Anglican Communion took institutional shape in summer 2008. Over 200 bishops boycotted the Lambeth Conference, including those from Nigeria, Uganda, Kenya and Rwanda who represented over 60 per cent of the diocesan bishops in Africa.[34] Instead they organised the Global Anglican Future Conference (GAFCON) in Jerusalem, an 'alternative Lambeth Conference', which attracted over 1,100 lay and clergy participants, mostly from the Global South. GAFCON wrote a conservative basis of faith (the Jerusalem Declaration), set up its own primates council and launched the Global Fellowship of Confessing Anglicans.[35] Welby attended neither the Lambeth Conference nor GAFCON, and was distressed at the way the Communion was failing to deal with its deep divisions. He lamented that Anglicans were 'too prone to dodge tough questions' and 'even more prone to have hissing fits and throw the toys out of the pram'. Writing in his Liverpool Cathedral magazine in July 2008 he offered two key principles when faced by theological conflict, again picking up the cathedral's motto of safety and risk interwoven.[36] First, 'other Christians are never the enemy'. 'Too much of the debate in the Communion, and even in this and other cathedrals and churches, use the language of war and

---

33   For a critique of *indaba*, see Francis Bridger and Andrew Goddard, 'Learning from Indaba: Some Lessons for Post-Pilling Conversations', *Anvil* vol. 30 (March 2014), pp. 41–56.

34   George Conger, 'Boycott of Lambeth 2008 is "Most Serious Challenge Yet"', *Church of England Newspaper*, 29 August 2008, p. 5.

35   *Being Faithful: The Shape of Historic Anglicanism Today: A Commentary on the Jerusalem Declaration* (London: Latimer Trust, 2009); *The Way of the Cross: Biblical Resources for a Global Anglican Future* (London: Latimer Trust, 2009).

36   Welby, 'Honouring the Builders', pp. 2–3.

battle. Other Christians are demonised, their view pilloried, their humanity diminished.' Welby insisted that however much Anglicans disagreed, they must recognise in each other the 'essential dignity of human beings', an important concept in Roman Catholic social teaching. They must not

> collude in any conversation or campaign that fails to do so. In the Church of England, the Archbishops and many Bishops are following this principle, but many groups, especially those getting a lot of press coverage, do not. This is the principle that makes for a safe place. Our welcome and hospitality, even to those with whom we disagree profoundly, imitates the grace of God.

Second, it was vital to 'listen carefully to what others say':

> This is where the risk comes in. Listening to views that are disliked, even repellent, carries risk, not least of others thinking we agree with the speaker. At one meeting I was interpreting for a French speaker who was using homophobic language; even saying the words was difficult, but no mediation would have been possible unless he had been allowed to have his say. The Cathedral as a place of Christian reconciliation fulfils its purpose when it enables voices to be heard in a context where people are confronted with the healing power of Christ.

Welby was beginning to strengthen his public voice in applying his years of experience in reconciliation ministry to the global Anglican context. In a series of Bible studies in 2010 he wrote:

> Reconciliation among Christians does not have unanimity at its heart, or tolerance, but the capacity to love despite disagreement, and to differ and be diverse without breaking fellowship. The difficulty is where to draw the boundaries and decide that a difference is of such fundamental importance that a breakdown of fellowship is necessary.

He noted that when the apostles disagreed, even when Peter was in serious error, Paul confronted him head-on but did not divide (Galatians 2). Unity amongst Christians was 'an absolute essential'.[37]

The Lambeth Conference recommended that the Archbishop of Canterbury appoint a small number of 'pastoral visitors' to help resolve disputes within the Communion by maintaining face-to-face communication between estranged parties.[38] The idea was commended by both the Windsor Continuation Group in December 2008 and by the primates meeting in Alexandria in February 2009.[39] They were to be senior Anglican leaders with skills in mediation and reconciliation, and the six chosen by Rowan Williams were Simon Chiwanga (retired Bishop of Mpwapwa in Tanzania), Santosh Marray (retired Bishop of the Seychelles), Colin Bennetts (retired Bishop of Coventry), Chad Gandiya (from Zimbabwe, based at the United Society for the Propagation of the Gospel), Major-General Tim Cross (Britain's most senior soldier in post-war Iraq) and Justin Welby. It was no coincidence that both Bennetts and Welby were closely associated with Coventry's International Centre for Reconciliation, and Welby's extensive knowledge of Nigeria was a significant asset. He was selected for the role because, in Williams' words, he was 'somebody who came with sufficiently clear principles, but also sufficient capacity to command trust amongst diverse groups'.[40]

As a pastoral visitor, Welby built good relationships with a wide range of Anglican bishops across the world. In July 2009 he was sent as Williams' representative to the General Convention of The Episcopal Church at Anaheim in California. In April 2010 he was dispatched to Nigeria, after a

37 Welby, 'The Gift of Reconciliation', pp. 84, 88.
38 *Lambeth Indaba: Capturing Conversations and Reflections from the Lambeth Conference 2008: Equipping Bishops for Mission and Strengthening Anglican Identity* (2008), paragraph 146.
39 *The Windsor Continuation Group Report to the Archbishop of Canterbury* (2008), paragraphs 81–91; 'Deeper Communion, Gracious Restraint', Alexandria Primates Meeting Communiqué, February 2009, paragraph 15.
40 Interview with Rowan Williams, 13 March 2014.

fresh outbreak of rioting in Plateau State, to deliver messages of support from the Archbishop of Canterbury to Benjamin Kwashi (Archbishop of Jos) and Nicholas Okoh (newly installed as Archbishop of Nigeria). There was 'enormous suspicion' of Williams in Nigeria and Okoh flatly refused to accept his letter.[41] It was therefore a very uncomfortable encounter for Welby as messenger. He was told bluntly to go away, though his future meetings with the Archbishop of Nigeria were more cordial. In villages near Jos he met traumatised communities, engaged with local pastors, and prayed beside a freshly dug mass grave with over 360 bodies, mostly women and children, murdered in a raid a few days before. 'The evidence of raw and unconstrained evil was before our eyes, and its consequences all around,' he wrote.[42] 'There is little to say, and tears are better than words.'[43]

Williams looked again to Welby in January 2011 to help facilitate the primates meeting in Dublin, alongside Cecelia Clegg from the University of Edinburgh who had helped to design the facilitation process for Continuing Indaba. The gathering, in keeping with the *indaba* methodology, was deliberately 'short on resolutions, high on intensive discussions', though it did produce statements on climate change, violence against women and girls, and homophobic violence (after the murder of gay-rights activist David Kato in Uganda). However, several primates from the Global South, including Archbishop Okoh and his colleagues in GAFCON, boycotted the event. They refused to 'maintain the illusion of normalcy' and a mere show of Anglican collegiality, protesting that their calls for the Western provinces to repent had fallen on deaf ears and 'those who have abandoned the historic teaching of the church have torn the fabric of our life together

41   Interview with Rowan Williams, 13 March 2014.
42   Justin Welby, 'Material Considerations', *The Treasurer* (December 2010 – January 2011), p. 41.
43   'Dean Justin Visits Nigeria', *LCL* no. 76 (May 2010), pp. 18–19.

at its deepest level'.[44] At the opening session the facilitators put empty seats in the circle, with the names of the absentees, as a silent reminder of the broken relationships. Archbishop Williams was impressed by Welby's 'extremely active' role as facilitator and realised for the first time how significant he would be for the Anglican Communion.[45]

Take Up Your Cross

In a short space of time, Welby had risen to the attention of the movers and shakers in the Anglican world, and was identified informally as a potential future bishop. When Tom Wright stepped down as Bishop of Durham at the end of August 2010, Welby was instructed by Archbishop Sentamu of York to 'put in his papers' so he could be considered for the vacancy. The Crown Nominations Commission typically meets twice for every vacancy – the first time to consider the papers of those clergy on the 'long list' believed potentially suitable for the post and to draw up the 'short list', and the second time to interview the three or four shortlisted candidates. Unless Welby agreed to submit his papers, he could never be considered by the commission. Reluctantly he agreed to do so, only to find himself shortlisted, called for interview at York in April 2011, and offered the job – the fourth most senior bishopric in the Church of England. The Welbys initially 'felt this is wrong', both the wrong time for Liverpool Cathedral in its development and the wrong time for their own family. Justin had been dean for less than three and a half years, and they had promised their teenage children that they would not move again until they had all left school. Caroline felt firmly

---

44   Chris Sugden, 'Worldwide Anglican Update: Sorry, We Cannot Come to Dublin', *Evangelicals Now* (February 2011), p. 7.
45   Interview with Rowan Williams, 13 March 2014.

they must honour that promise and stay in Liverpool, but Justin thought he should take the new post, not least because he had been told to do so. 'For the first time ever in our lives, let alone our ministry,' Caroline revealed, 'we found ourselves on two sides of a wall.' When they met with Sentamu to explain their dilemma, he was typically direct, telling Caroline that 'calling is not something for you, it's for the church – the church has called, so that is the answer'. He reminded her of the call of Jesus to 'take up your cross'.[46] The pragmatic solution they decided was to live in two locations – Justin in Durham diocese, Caroline and the children in Liverpool, though she joined Justin at the weekends. 'Lots of people have to do it', Justin said, 'but it's not a whole load of fun.'[47]

'Caroline and I had always believed we would retire in Liverpool', Justin admitted, 'but clearly God has other plans.'[48] Looking back on their brief time on Merseyside, he concluded that the most significant change in the cathedral's life was its new 'default attitude of saying yes', of refusing to be overly cautious and instead looking 'to make things happen'. Hammering home a favourite theme, his parting words to his congregation were, 'If you don't risk failure you will never have any success.'[49] His final sermon in Liverpool in October 2011 was a passionate exhortation to 'hang on to Jesus ... Do not be ashamed of the gospel.' He warned his congregation, speaking also to himself as he entered the episcopate, against the danger of becoming 'mere straw figures pretending to religion ... Such strawy existence leads us from grace to law, from hospitality to defensiveness, from risk taking in Christ's service to self-preserving in our own interests. It is the danger

---

46 'An Evening with Justin and Caroline Welby', 27 January 2013.
47 *Travellers' Tales*, 31 March 2013.
48 'Dean of Liverpool Announced as Bishop Designate of Durham', *LCL* no. 83 (July – August 2011), p. 6.
49 'Looking Forward', *LCL* no. 84 (September – October 2011), p. 12.

of parishes, the curse of Cathedrals, and the destruction of Bishops.'[50]

---

50   Justin Welby, sermon at Liverpool Cathedral, 2 October 2011, www.liverpoolcathedral.
      org.uk.

Chapter 8

―∞∞∞―

Durham

The beautiful Hautecombe Abbey on the shores of Lake Bourget, near Aix-les-Bains in the foothills of the French Alps, was the location of Justin Welby's eight-day retreat prior to his consecration as Bishop of Durham. Once occupied by the Cistercians and the Benedictines, it was entrusted in the early 1990s to the Chemin Neuf community. Back in England, he was consecrated at York Minster on 28 October 2011 by the Archbishop of York, John Sentamu. By tradition a new bishop is presented by two senior bishops and Welby chose his bosses in Liverpool and Coventry, James Jones and Colin Bennetts, though Bennetts was prevented through illness, so Welby's old friend from HTB, Sandy Millar, stepped in at short notice. (Millar was a missionary bishop in the province of Uganda from 2005, though at the time working as a church planter in Tollington Park in north London.)

The consecration sermon was preached by Bishop Josiah Idowu-Fearon of Kaduna, a significant choice. Idowu-Fearon was one of Welby's close friends, bringing a reminder of global Anglicanism to a quintessentially English event. Like his fellow Nigerian bishops, Idowu-Fearon had boycotted the Lambeth Conference in 2008 and attended GAFCON in Jerusalem instead. He had once been talked of as a possible successor to Peter Akinola as Archbishop of Nigeria, and was not afraid to criticise the Western church. For example, as a guest at The Episcopal Church's General Convention in Minneapolis in August 2003, he warned that the consecration of Gene Robinson as Bishop of New Hampshire would be a departure from Scripture and damage Anglicanism's global witness. Yet

Idowu-Fearon was also seen to be more friendly towards the Western provinces than many of his fellow bishops within the GAFCON movement because of his emphasis on maintaining dialogue at all costs. He was a member of the Lambeth Commission which produced *The Windsor Report* and was honoured by Archbishop Williams in 2007 as a Six Preacher at Canterbury Cathedral. When the GAFCON primates were threatening to boycott the Dublin primates meeting in January 2011, Idowu-Fearon publicly urged them to attend and continue in relationship with those from the West who had grieved them.[1] He preached at Welby's consecration from Ephesians 2:19–22, celebrating the work of 'the peace-making Christ' in redeeming the church as 'a family of brothers and sisters ... a model of human community', built on biblical truth. But he also lamented the 'tragic story' of alienation and discord within the Anglican Communion, once again divided by racism, nationalism, tribalism and clericalism. These Anglican divisions, Idowu-Fearon declared, were 'an offence to Jesus Christ' and 'a stumbling-block to faith'.[2] When Welby moved to Canterbury, Idowu-Fearon was the first person he honoured with the Cross of St Augustine.

A Time of Opportunity

A month after his consecration, Welby was formally enthroned in his cathedral at Durham, on 26 November 2011. In the five days beforehand the new bishop led a prayer pilgrimage through the diocese, to Gateshead and *The Angel of the North*, Sunderland, Durham, Escomb (near Bishop Auckland) and Darlington, inviting the public to join him in prayer or

---

1   Josiah Idowu-Fearon, 'If You Disagree, At Least Be There', *Church Times*, 24 and 31 December 2010, p. 12.
2   I am grateful to Bishop Josiah Idowu-Fearon for a copy of his sermon notes.

to submit prayer requests via Facebook and Twitter.[3] This demonstration of dependence on God was driven home again by the three questions Welby wrote for the start of his enthronement service. Instead of being greeted at the cathedral door by the dean, as was traditional, he was met by the leader of a local community project who asked:

> *Who are you and why do you request entry?*
> I am Justin, a servant of Jesus Christ, and I come as one seeking the grace of God, to travel with you in his service together.
>
> *Why have you been sent to us?*
> I am sent as Bishop to serve you and all people in this Diocese, to proclaim the love of Christ, and with you to worship and love him with heart and soul, mind and strength.
>
> *How do you come among us and with what confidence?*
> I come knowing nothing except Jesus Christ and him crucified, and in weakness and fear and in much trembling.[4]

By this liturgical innovation Welby aimed to set the tone for his episcopal ministry, with a focus upon humble service, whole-hearted discipleship and proclamation of the cross of Christ. The opening interrogation was immediately followed by confession of sin, to underline the emphasis on penitence not triumphalism. The regal word 'enthronement' was eschewed for the more down-to-earth 'inauguration of ministry', a phrase previously used by Tom Wright.[5] The choir anthem by Michael Berkeley had been commissioned by the Welby family in 2010 using the text of one of Rowan Williams' advent poems.

Welby's enthronement sermon expounded the prophet Micah's call to 'do justice, love kindness and walk humbly

---

3   'Praying with the People', *Northern Echo*, 22 November 2011, p. 14.
4   *The Inauguration of the Ministry of the Right Reverend Justin Welby as Bishop of Durham* (order of service, 26 November 2011), p. 9. Welby started a trend: similar questions were asked at the enthronement of Paul Butler as Bishop of Durham in February 2014.
5   I am grateful to David Kennedy (canon precentor at Durham Cathedral) for these insights.

with your God'. In the context of Europe's ongoing financial crisis, the new bishop proclaimed:

> This is a time of opportunity. The idols of our age are fallen, toppled in successive economic and political tempests. All the great institutions (including the institutional church, as we have seen recently) in which we have trusted seem to be caught flat footed with changes in mood and temper so rapid that leaders are constantly running to catch up. ... The idols have fallen, and their fall reveals what still stands, the faithfulness and truth of the Christian gospel.

He acknowledged the desperate need for economic regeneration in the north-east of England, long since stripped of its great industries, but also its primary need for spiritual regeneration. Therefore the Christians of Durham diocese were called 'to be evangelists', harvesters in the Lord's harvest field (Matthew 9:38). All Christians, he explained, were

> commanded to proclaim the extraordinary story of Jesus. It is a huge task, to follow in the giant footsteps of Cuthbert and Aidan and Chad and so many more, intending in the north east to rekindle Christian faith. That is our task, to be those who bring this region to Christ, to spiritual life afresh. It is a great task, a huge task, but it is God's task through us.

Returning to one of his favourite themes, he declared that 'God calls for risk takers' in the extraordinary work of proclaiming this 'revolutionary' gospel.[6] Although Caroline Welby had initially resisted the idea that Justin should become Bishop of Durham, she began to notice a change in her husband after his consecration. In particular, she sensed that 'the authority, God-given, was more and more apparent'.[7]

The bishop's passion for bringing others to faith in Christ was evident again at an Alpha Vision Day in Sheffield in March 2012, organised by Holy Trinity Brompton, and attended by over 700 church leaders from across the north of

6   Welby, 'Enthronement Sermon' (November 2011).
7   HTB Home Focus, 27 July 2013.

Britain. He rearticulated several of the major themes from his enthronement address:

> We are facing in this country the greatest opportunity that God has given us since the Second World War. Every single idol, everything on which human beings in our society have relied on since 1945, has fallen. As those idols fall, all that is left on the horizon to look at is an empty cross and an empty tomb. ... We had government to rely on – they've run out of money. We relied on materialism – it's betrayed us as all idols do. They cannot save us. God has opened up before the Church a moment when no one else can do anything. It is a moment of unique opportunity and the challenge that the Spirit is saying to the Church today is, 'Will you take this moment and reverse the decline that we have seen for the last 70 or 80 years?' You have two tasks: to worship Jesus Christ and to reconvert this country to Christian faith and transform its society.

He noted that there were as many 'active Christians' in Durham diocese in the twenty-first century as there had been in the days of St Cuthbert in the seventh century. Therefore great things were possible. Their task was 'to go out and ... to reconvert our land, to transform its society and all that goes with it'.[8]

Economic Regeneration and Human Flourishing

Welby had only been in his post at Durham for a few days when his skills in conflict resolution were put to the test. The bone of contention was the future of Auckland Castle, in Bishop Auckland, and the Church of England's commitment to economic regeneration in the north-east. The castle had been home to the prince bishops of Durham since Norman times, but its future was under review as not fit for purpose

8   Justin Welby, address to Alpha Vision Day, Sheffield, 3 March 2012, www.htb.org.uk.

in the twenty-first century. Amongst its Renaissance treasures were a set of paintings from the 1640s of Jacob and his twelve sons, by the Spanish artist Francisco de Zurbarán, acquired by Bishop Trevor in 1756 and displayed in his dining room. In November 2010, less than three months after Tom Wright's departure, the *Northern Echo* exposed a plan by the Church Commissioners to auction the paintings at Sotheby's, a revelation which came to the diocese 'like a bolt from the blue'.[9] Bishop Wright wrote in protest at this 'shameful' attempt 'to snatch the North-East's finest cultural artefact, a unique collection in a unique building. Londoners always think art belongs to them. If Durham Cathedral had wheels, someone would want to park it in Kensington.' He described the £15 million which the Church Commissioners hoped to raise by the auction as modest compared to their 'massive assets', like 'a blade of grass in their ten-acre field'.[10] Millionaire Jonathan Ruffer, a highly successful investment-manager in the City of London, stepped forward with a plan to save both the paintings and the castle as a Christian heritage centre, as part of his commitment to urban regeneration in his native north-east. Bishop Auckland would thus become one of a string of pearls attracting tourists to Durham, Jarrow and Lindisfarne (Holy Island). But in December 2011 the deal collapsed.[11] Ruffer blamed impossible conditions from the Church Commissioners, whose actions he called a 'slap in the face' for County Durham.[12] Welby, in only his second week in charge, called on the Church Commissioners to think again and publicly praised Ruffer's 'extraordinary

9   'Secret Plan to Sell Durham Paintings Is Exposed', *Church Times*, 12 November 2010, p. 5.
10 Tom Wright, 'A Powerful Symbol of Justice, Welcome and Civil Rights ... and the North-East's Finest Cultural Artefact', *Northern Echo*, 6 November 2010.
11 'Paintings at Risk as Bishop Auckland Deal Falters' *Church Times*, 16 December 2011, p. 3.
12 Jonathan Ruffer, 'Why I Pulled Out of Zubarán Deal', *Church Times*, 16 December 2011, p. 13.

generosity'.[13] Three days before Christmas he brought both sides together in the City of London, at St Ethelburga's Centre for Reconciliation and Peace (of which Welby was a trustee). In a skilful act of diplomacy, Welby and Sir Paul Nicholson (Lord Lieutenant of County Durham) mediated between the parties until agreement was struck.[14]

In his public teaching Welby turned frequently to the language of 'human flourishing' (again a concept learned from Roman Catholic social thought) to hold together the need for spiritual and material regeneration, or evangelism and socio-political engagement. For example, in an address to the Anglican Alliance for Development in April 2012 he contrasted the holistic mission of the church in seeking justice and mercy for the oppressed with the motivation of secular aid agencies:

> Our good news must be unique, because the radicality of the gospel calls us to a sense of what we are doing and saying utterly different from all other groups. The language of our good news is not GDP [gross domestic product], output and so forth, though they are part of the means, it is human flourishing in a context of love.[15]

Likewise at a service to commemorate the 200th anniversary of the Felling Colliery disaster of 1812, Welby insisted that it was a Christian obligation to 'struggle against evil', whether economic or institutional. The church must campaign against unemployment, debt and social deprivation, not out of 'do-goodery' but because these things 'destroy the opportunity for human beings to flourish'.[16] As one small sign of this commitment, Welby served as patron of the *Northern Echo*'s 'Foundation for Jobs' campaign to create 1,000 apprenticeships and internships in the Darlington region.

13   'Bishop Issues Statement about Auckland Castle and the Zuburans', 8 December 2011, www.durham.anglican.org.
14   Auckland Castle Press Release, 22 December 2011, www.durham.anglican.org.
15   Justin Welby, 'Good News for the Poor', a talk for the Anglican Alliance for Development, 30 April 2012, www.durham.anglican.org.
16   Justin Welby, 'Felling Colliery Address', 24 May 2012, www.durham.anglican.org.

In his inaugural address to the Durham diocesan synod he urged local churches to take a lead in restoring community confidence during times of recession: 'We are on the edge of a precipice of economic crisis which both demands our prayers and will demand heroic action. Food banks, credit unions, job creation should be part of our ministry.'[17] He also used his maiden speech in the House of Lords in May 2012 to advocate economic regeneration in the north-east, and once again 'human flourishing' was a keynote.[18] Nevertheless, although Welby called for Christians to build alliances with politicians, financiers and businesses to usher in justice and community renewal, he warned against the allure of institutional power: 'It is in the Lord we trust, and the House of Lords we use, not the other way round.'[19]

As part of his own social engagement, Welby continued to make use of his financial expertise. During his penultimate year in Liverpool, in January 2010, the cathedral played host to a live webcast of a conference on 'Building an Ethical Economy: Theology and the Marketplace' from Trinity Church, Wall Street in New York (the wealthiest Anglican congregation in the world, which owns part of Manhattan's financial district).[20] He told the *Liverpool Daily Post* that 'Theology has a role in shaping a new economy ... defined by how we care for one another. ... Theology and economics are not two different worlds, they are two ways of living in the same world and we all need to live together.'[21] Welby hoped for a church 'where we talk less about sex and more about money', not the church's lack of money but the way it should be used to support others.[22] In a series of Bible studies on money in 2011, he wrote: 'The economy is a human construction, yet

---

17   Justin Welby, 'Presidential Address', Durham diocesan synod, 26 May 2012, www.durham.anglican.org.
18   Hansard, House of Lords, 16 May 2012, column 423.
19   Welby, 'Good News for the Poor'.
20   'Building an Ethical Economy', *LCL* no. 74 (January 2010), p. 18.
21   'Cathedral and Wall Street Link Up for Ethics Debate', *Liverpool Daily Post*, 6 January 2010, p. 10.
22   Justin Welby, 'Money and Economics', *Guidelines* vol. 27 (May – August 2011), p. 55.

it dominates its originators like Frankenstein's monster. It is occasionally manageable but never mastered. ... In the end, the global economy is hardwired to greed, and greed to idolatry.'[23] But he re-imagined an economy along Christian lines:

> What is an economy that has kingdom values? It is not one in which saving is necessarily very high, because that may degenerate into mere hoarding, a miserly self-protection. Neither is it one that abuses creation and manipulates the poor, even the poor we do not see. It is certainly one that is rich towards God, open-handed, and full of joy and celebration. ... The Bible calls us to a grace-filled economy of generosity and open-heartedness, not to savage fighting with one another over dwindling slices of cake.[24]

Most of Welby's early contributions to the House of Lords concerned the Financial Services Bill, and he spoke of the need to limit directors' pay and establish local credit unions. Lord Lawson (former Chancellor of the Exchequer) drew attention to the fact that it was the first time a bishop in the House of Lords had 'come out as a former derivatives trader'.[25] The *London Evening Standard* celebrated: 'At last, a bishop who understands capitalism.'[26]

Welby's financial nous brought him to the attention of the government and in July 2012 he was appointed to the Parliamentary Commission on Banking Standards, a cross-party group of ten MPs and peers. Their brief was to investigate professional standards and culture within the United Kingdom's banking sector in the wake of the Libor (London Inter-Bank Offered Rate) scandal which had exposed widespread fraud and malpractice. The bishop quickly won plaudits for his no-nonsense approach, sharp questioning and withering put-downs. He tackled Stephen Hester (chief executive of the Royal Bank of Scotland) on the bank's social

23   Welby, 'Money and Economics', pp. 43, 49.
24   Welby, 'Money and Economics', p. 56.
25   Hansard, House of Lords, 11 June 2012, column 1162.
26   'Archbishop with the City on his CV', *London Evening Standard*, 9 November 2012, p. 46.

responsibility and dismissed his answers as 'motherhood and apple pie'.[27] He criticised George Osborne (Chancellor of the Exchequer) for deploying 'an army of straw men'.[28] There was fun at the Chancellor's expense when Osborne referred to the sword of Damocles but deferred to the bishop for the precise biblical allusion, to which Welby shot back in a flash, 'I think it is a Greek myth. Not my branch.'[29] When it was the turn of Andrea Orcel from the Swiss giant UBS, Welby blasted the investment bank as 'a corrupted organisation'.[30] This work with the Banking Standards Commission catapulted Welby to widespread public attention, not least amongst the Westminster elites, and was an important opportunity to contribute to national debate and to shape legislation. Nevertheless when it was still rumbling on at the end of 2013, a year behind schedule, after hours of testimony and thousands of pages, he admitted he would be 'more than delighted when it is buried, ideally with a stake through its heart and garlic between its teeth!'[31]

Welby remained optimistic about the future shape of the banking and financial services industry, which though flawed and fallible had the potential to 'make a major contribution to the society in which we live, for the common good'.[32] He himself sought to model good practice as chair from 2011 of the independent Committee of Reference which vetted the ethical investment funds of F&C, an international asset management company with headquarters in the City of London.[33] Once again, Welby understood this work within

27   Parliamentary Commission on Banking Standards [PCBS], *Changing Banking for Good* (June 2013), vol. 3, oral evidence, 13 November 2012.
28   PCBS, oral evidence, 21 November 2012.
29   PCBS, oral evidence, 25 February 2013.
30   PCBS, oral evidence, 9 January 2013.
31   Justin Welby, 'Presentation', *General Synod Report of Proceedings* vol. 44 (November 2013), p. 4.
32   Justin Welby, 'Good News in Troubled Times', *The Treasurer* (December 2012 – January 2013), p. 14.
33   For reflections on F&C as an example of ethical investment, see Justin Welby, 'L'Investissement responsable' in Paul H. Dembinski (ed.), *Pratiques financières, regards chrétiens* (Paris: Desclée de Brouwer, 2009), pp. 265–78.

the theological context of a wider Christian mandate to seek the flourishing of all. As he told Giles Fraser, 'When one group corners a source of human flourishing, it is deeply wicked. It applies to the City, to commodities traders, and to churches who say only this way is right. ... The City is unspeakably powerful. The longer I go on, the more I am aware of the power of finance.'[34] Lecturing in Zurich in October 2012 under the auspices of Paul Dembinski's Observatoire de la Finance, the bishop called for a re-imagining of the European financial sector that it might be resurrected from 'the wreckage of a hubris induced disaster, to retrieving its basic purpose of enabling human society to flourish effectively'.[35]

Turning Everything on Its Head

As rector of Southam in 2000, Welby had begun to develop his thinking on episcopal leadership in a chapter co-written with his former theological college warden, Ian Cundy (Bishop of Peterborough from 1996 until his death in 2009). They wrote in response to *Working as One Body* (the Turnbull Report) which had encouraged the use of modern management theory in diocesan governance. Welby and Cundy likened leadership in the Church of England to 'trying to take a cat for a walk'. They argued that a bishop must set a pattern for his diocese of 'servant leadership' as modelled by Christ, holding authority but refusing to dominate by 'institutional mechanisms of control' or 'top-down management by command, reinforced by status'. In particular, a bishop had the ability to transform diocesan culture by 'releasing the gifts of the people of God' and helping the institution to listen to 'the prophetic

---

34   Fraser, 'The Saturday Interview', p. 37.
35   Justin Welby, 'Repair or Replace: Where Do We Start Among the Ruins?', 26 October 2012, www.durham.anglican.org.

voice', whereas committee-driven organisations struggled 'to accept the possibility of radical change'. Welby and Cundy proclaimed that experimentation and 'entrepreneurial risk' must be encouraged: 'Bishops are able to give space to creative initiatives while retaining an appropriate degree of supervision and oversight. By their nature boards and committees tend to be restrictive or cautious in their response to vision and imagination.' With sharp polemic thrust they concluded: 'The Church remembers many bishops as great pastors, teachers, missionaries and servants: there are no days in our calendar given to ancient boards or committees.'[36] Preaching in Southam in September 1997, Welby had earlier praised Princess Diana and Mother Teresa of Calcutta for modelling the lesson that institutions must bend to serve people not vice versa. Both women, he declared, 'should make any institution shudder, perhaps foremost a Church of England that so often fails to be flexible, transparent and open'.[37]

Throughout his ministry Welby eschewed a desire for promotion to positions of greater power within the institution. Whether at the original Church of England 'selection conference' in 1988 or the Crown Nominations Commission in 2011, his interviewers were caught off guard by his apparent disinterest in the job. In most cases Welby preferred the line of work he was already in rather than the new opportunities being offered. This was not the false humility of *nolo episcopari* ('I don't want to be a bishop'), but his genuine contentedness with his current sphere of ministry which did not hunger after increased influence. Although he was well connected, with a background at Eton, Cambridge and the City of London, he was not in thrall to the establishment nor easily impressed by holders of power.

---

36   Ian Cundy and Justin Welby, 'Taking the Cat for a Walk? Can a Bishop Order a Diocese?', in G. R. Evans and Martyn Percy (eds), *Managing the Church? Order and Organization in a Secular Age* (Sheffield: Sheffield Academic Press, 2000), pp. 43–4, 47–8.
37   Justin Welby, 'Thought for the Month', *SPCN* (October 1997).

One indication of the way in which Welby sat lightly to status was his attitude to episcopal dress. Like Rowan Williams, he avoided the purple shirt in favour of the more catholic black. His episcopal ring was a simple silver band, without any jewel stone, engraved with the cross of Liverpool Cathedral and the cross of St Cuthbert. His pectoral cross was the Cross of Nails which he had worn since Coventry days. His robes were inherited from Bishop Cundy, to whom they had been given by the students and staff of Cranmer Hall.[38] Although he enjoyed dressing up, and once confessed 'I quite like all this episcopal bling',[39] he had no time for pomposity and would frequently quote Sandy Millar's question, 'What would the man in the sandals say?' Welby recalled that his installation as Dean of Liverpool took place 'with all the pomp the Church of England can manage – and we really do pomp(ous) well'.[40] He poked fun at his own appearance, acknowledging that Anglicanism's quirky traditions might raise doubts about whether it was living in 'the real world': 'There was I last Christmas, dressed in a Victorian cope (a large carpet-like thing) embroidered in purple cloth with nativity scenes. I looked like a self-propelled toadstool: small, colourful, and seldom still.'[41] Likewise when dressed in a mitre he said he resembled 'a self-propelled tulip' or 'a self-propelled curtain with a pointy hat'.[42] The media were provided with a golden photo opportunity in November 2012 when he spontaneously swapped his mitre with the helmet of a nearby policeman.[43] In his maiden speech in the House of Lords he spoke of his amusement at standing before them dressed in 'a white nightie and a black dressing gown'.[44] Nevertheless he enjoyed the sheer fun of it all, like being

---

38   'Archbishop Justin Will Wear "Cundy Cope"', *Crosskeys* (Peterborough diocesan newsletter), Spring 2013, p. 4.
39   Justin Welby, 'Sermon at Chrism Service on Maundy Thursday', 5 April 2012, www.durham.anglican.org.
40   Justin Welby, 'On Feeling Very Important', *The Treasurer* (December 2007), p. 41.
41   Welby, 'When the Bubble Bursts', p. 45.
42   Welby, 'Sermon at Chrism Service'; Welby, 'Good News in Troubled Times'.
43   'Hats Off To You!', *MailOnline*, 13 November 2012, www.dailymail.co.uk.
44   Hansard, House of Lords, 16 May 2012, column 422.

allowed to address his stepfather, Lord Williams of Elvel, in the House of Lords as 'my noble kinsman'.

In Durham, Welby quickly set about inverting the diocesan structures to promote growth. His two major initiatives concerned 'parish share' and evangelism. Like all dioceses, ministry was funded almost entirely by contributions from local congregations. The diocese would set the annual budget and then tell parishes how much they must pay in 'parish share'. But this system was widely in disrepute across the Church of England, criticised as a tax, and it resulted in many parishes feeling placed under pressure, guilty and sometimes hostile to diocesan demands.[45] In Durham diocese finances were particularly stretched, partly because of economic depression across the region, especially in the post-coal-mining districts of east Durham and the cities of Sunderland and Gateshead. The Anglican demographic was largely older than the general population and there was a shortage of clergy. Welby had ten parishes he was unable to fill and led by example by becoming the first Bishop of Durham for centuries to survive without a domestic chaplain. Only about 85 per cent of the budgeted parish share was collected and as many as 40 per cent of parishes could not, or would not, pay the full amount which was asked. Therefore Welby decided to turn the system on its head. Instead of the diocese setting a budget and telling parishes what to contribute, parishes would decide how much they could offer and then the budget would be set accordingly. This new strategy was clearly 'much higher risk' than the old approach, because it might result in less cash in the coffers, but it would also lead to better morale and unity in the diocese.[46]

Welby noted the close link between money and mission. Stable finances were essential not merely to make ends meet but because growing churches needed to be properly resourced.

---

45   For the importance of financial resources for church growth, and critique of the 'parish share' system, see Bob Jackson, *The Road to Growth: Towards a Thriving Church* (London: Church House Publishing, 2005), pp. 149–216.
46   Justin Welby, memorandum to Bishop's Council, 19 January 2012.

The church's attitude to its bank balance revealed its true priorities. As he told his first diocesan synod in his presidential address in May 2012, 'Everything to do with money is merely theology in numbers.'[47] Therefore the new approach to parish share came hand in hand with Welby's second strategy of a major push in parish evangelism. Numbers attending church had fallen so dramatically throughout the twentieth century that the bishop believed the future of Durham diocese itself was an open question. Rates of church attendance in the north-east were amongst the lowest in the country. Out of 1.46 million people in Durham diocese only 14,300 were in an Anglican church on a typical Sunday, less than 1 per cent of the population – lower than any of the 43 dioceses in the Church of England, except Birmingham.[48] As Welby told his Bishop's Council:

> Big buildings and big institutions fall down slowly, but there comes a point when the roof really does fall in and we move from being Durham Cathedral to Fountains Abbey. ... My own gut feeling is that there will be serious questions of viability before I retire, probably camouflaged in pastoral reorganising at diocesan level. Say 7–10 years.[49]

Yet he was convinced that the decline could be halted, and indeed reversed. He pointed to the growth of global Christianity as the normal Christian experience, observing that the Church of England was 'one of the weaker members of the Anglican Communion'. If Anglican churches could grow dramatically in Nigeria, why not then in Durham too? Welby pointed to David Goodhew's recent research on church growth in Britain, and to the flourishing of cathedrals, to show that the situation could be turned around: 'Our hope of revival is based on the resurrection. Again and again in church history churches far worse off than us have, with clear leadership, found new life,

47   Welby, 'Presidential Address' (May 2012).
48   *Church Statistics 2010/11*, pp. 10–12.
49   Justin Welby, memorandum to Bishop's Council, 20–21 March 2012.

and finding it have seen astonishing growth. Personally, I believe passionately that it is possible.'[50]

Church growth had been a central theme throughout Welby's ministry, whether in his Warwickshire parish or his cathedral at Liverpool. At the Alpha International Week at Holy Trinity Brompton, in June 2011, he spoke of his conviction that 'however big our weaknesses', God was able to grow the church:

> If we really put our trust in him, if we preach the Gospel, keep it straightforward and simple, make it easy for people to find Christ, don't put barriers in the way, churches will grow. And the point about growing churches ... is that as people are converted and are transformed by the grace of God, that grace overflows into the world around them, and we transform the world around us. And, my goodness, we need that.[51]

Therefore in Durham, Welby set about changing the local Anglican culture, 'the DNA of the Diocese', which could only be achieved by 'a prolonged period of episcopally led evangelism'. His idea was for the two bishops (Welby and his suffragan, Bishop Mark Bryant of Jarrow) to begin a rolling programme of three or four deanery missions a year. The style would be locally determined, not imposed from above – it might be five people round a kitchen table rather than 500 at an event. Welby emphasised that evangelism was not only the work of clergy or other specialists but of the whole people of God. 'We are looking for Cuthberts, not Billy Graham.' Their evangelism would not be 'crass and manipulative, but profound and Godly, not bums on seats, but seeds of hope bearing fruit'. Therefore parishioners must grow in confidence to share their faith. The Alpha Course and the Emmaus Course (a more catholic alternative to Alpha) were recommended as key tools. There were many strengths of the Anglican parish system, the bishop agreed, but 'we fish badly':

50   Justin Welby, memorandum to Bishop's Council, 20–21 March 2012.
51   Alpha International Week (Justin Welby interviewed by Nicky Gumbel), 7 June 2011.

The church is good at contact and presence but too often poor at bringing people to faith in Jesus. ... We are excellent at building bridges into the community and into society and rather less good at getting the gospel across the bridge, and bringing people back. Or to put it another way our net holds many but we land few.

Once again this change of church culture, with high targets for numerical growth, was a 'high risk' strategy because it might end in failure. But Welby insisted: 'I believe with passion that the God who raised Jesus from the dead can also raise our church to new, different and vibrant life and growth, and am happy that this is one of the measures of my years here. ... I will measure myself, among other things, in terms of numbers.'[52]

These new priorities concerning parish share and evangelism, both locally determined, necessitated an entire reorientation of the diocesan structures and hierarchical mind-set. Those in authority must resist the temptation 'to lead like the lords of the gentiles, to give orders', and the structures must embody servanthood not power:

So we serve by not *telling* people what to pay in parish share, but trusting to maturity and prayer; we serve by evangelism being decided locally and supported from the centre, not by centralised top down initiatives. We believe in subsidiarity, in taking people at the value of their vows, baptismal and ordinal.[53]

To his diocesan synod Welby reiterated that both the parish share and the evangelism strategies aimed 'to turn everything on its head', to make clear that local congregations were the centre of the diocese not the bureaucracy or bishops:

You could say that I believe in holy anarchy. It is anarchy within organisation, a sense of diversity of freedom and empowering that must move us away from a top down centralised approach,

---

52   Justin Welby, memorandum to Bishop's Council, 20–21 March 2012.
53   Welby, 'Sermon at Chrism Service'.

the curse of the Church of England, towards freedom to be the people whom God has called us to be.[54]

These early reforms during Welby's first year in Durham diocese revealed again his characteristic approach, as previously seen in Southam and Liverpool. It was decisive leadership, interwoven with collegiality and consensus. Change was driven forward by Welby himself but locally owned by congregations and clergy. Flexibility, generosity, and a passion to see people turn to Christ were again dominant motifs, and a buoyant confidence in the grace and power of God in a day of opportunity.

Treasure in Clay Jars

Preaching at Durham Cathedral in April 2012 on 'treasure in jars of clay' (2 Corinthians 4:7), the bishop declared:

> If anything was clay-like at present it is the Church of England, and the Anglican Communion. We are divided, often savagely. We are battered. We are weak. ... The church is not a rest home for saints, it is a lifeboat for sinners. And when you stick loads of sinners together, perhaps especially Anglican sinners, you don't get a saintly church ... if you want evidence read the *Church Times* or the *Church of England Newspaper* letters columns.[55]

Outside the diocese an increasing amount of Welby's time was spent seeking reconciliation between estranged Anglicans in the national church and worldwide. He continued in his role as one of the Archbishop of Canterbury's 'pastoral visitors', with a particular focus upon relationships in Nigeria and the United States of America.

54   Welby, 'Presidential Address' (May 2012).
55   Welby, 'Sermon at Chrism Service'.

The security situation in Nigeria deteriorated dramatically during 2011–12 with a campaign of terrorism unleashed by Boko Haram, a radical jihadist group in the north of the country, linked to Al-Qaeda. Thousands were killed, especially in Kaduna and Jos, including many Christians whose churches were bombed. Welby visited on behalf of Archbishop Williams in June 2011 and January 2012, to stand alongside the Church of Nigeria, but his own life was put in danger. On the first trip Welby's car crashed and was surrounded by an angry mob which threatened to lynch the occupants, and he had to be whisked away by a government car. Archbishop Sentamu reported to the Church of England's General Synod that 'my heart is in my mouth every time he goes to Nigeria'.[56] Welby's maiden speech to synod, in February 2012, brought forward a motion expressing support for Nigerian Christians and calling upon the British government to use its influence 'to protect religious minorities of all faiths'. He declared that the church in northern Nigeria was 'systematically, deliberately and progressively being eliminated' and admired the courage of Archbishop Okoh for resisting calls to retaliation. He praised Nigerian Anglicans for their determination in 'winning people to faith in Christ', but observed that 'there is no position on this earth lonelier than being the victims of mass attack in a nation so often forgotten by our media'.[57] A few weeks later Welby hosted a meeting at the House of Lords to enable Okoh to speak directly to British politicians about the security situation in his country.[58]

In March 2012 Welby was the only foreign guest at the House of Bishops meeting of The Episcopal Church (TEC) in Camp Allen, Navasota in Texas. At the end of the five-day gathering, he was invited to offer brief reflections on what he had observed, and responded warmly:

56   General Synod, *Report of Proceedings* vol. 43 (February 2012), p. 184.
57   General Synod, *Report of Proceedings* vol. 43 (February 2012), pp. 176–8. See also Justin Welby, 'Recent Violence in Nigeria' (GS 1861), February 2012.
58   'Presentation by the Primate of the Church of Nigeria at the House of Lords, Tuesday, April 24th [2012]', www.anglican-mainstream.net.

> I found integrity and openness on issues, graciousness under pressure, and towards others who have not been gracious, catholicity, complexity and inclusion. I have found some myths demythologised. For example the myth that TEC is only liberal, monochrome in its theological stand, and the myth that all minorities of view are oppressed. There is rather the sense of a complex body of wide views and many nationalities addressing issues with what I have personally found inspiring honesty and courage, doubtless also with faults and sins, but always looking to see where the sins are happening. The processes are deeply moving even where I disagreed, which I did on a number of obvious issues, but the honesty of approach was convincing, the buy into and practice of Ndaba [sic] superb.

He believed that TEC was ahead of the Church of England in its ability to disagree well. Concerning the wider Anglican Communion, Welby suggested to his American counterparts that 'we need to fit our structures to the reality of our changing and complex relationships, not try and shape reality to structures. Start with relationships, and seek forbearance, charity and love. BUT we will not see it happen for a long time.' In parting, he prayed that Anglicans might 'grow in the ability to live in complexity. That we are able to have diversity without enmity. God has made the churches full of diversity, that is the miracle of unity, praise God for diversity, when lived in love and integrity.'[59]

Women Bishops

Meanwhile closer to home, within the Church of England, Welby found himself called upon to bring reconciliation between hostile factions over the consecration of women as bishops. After years of acrimonious debate and numerous

---

59   Justin Welby, 'Reflections to House of Bishops', March 2012, www.collegeforbishops. org.

Collation at Coventry Cathedral before Welby's installation as residentiary canon, 2002. Bishop Colin Bennetts and Dean John Irvine are wearing the yellow copes.
[© Martin R. Williams]

Welby and Andrew White on satellite phones in the compound of Saddam Hussein's palace, Baghdad, May 2003. With them is General George Sadda, author of *Saddam's Secrets*.
[© Andrew White]

Welby and White at the re-opening of St George's, Baghdad. With them are the caretaker, Hanna Younan, and his daughter Marriam. [© Andrew White]

Palm Sunday, 2007, in the ruins of Coventry's medieval cathedral. The robes were designed by John Piper. [© Martin R. Williams]

The Dean of Liverpool with
Nicky Gumbel at an Alpha
International Conference.
[© Holy Trinity Brompton]

Abseiling down Liverpool
Cathedral in aid of the cathedral
centenary fund.
[© Liverpool Cathedral]

Sorting food at Sunderland Minster for 'One for the Basket', an ecumenical food bank in Durham diocese. [© Aegies Associates/Keith Blundy]

Seated in the chair of St Augustine at Canterbury Cathedral, March 2013.

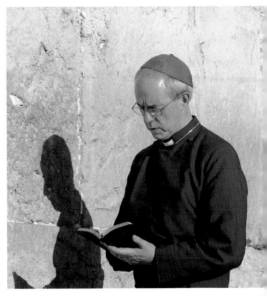

With Prince Charles at the enthronement ceremony. [© Richard Black]

Reading Psalm 15 at the Western Wall, Jerusalem.

Sharing a joke with the Archbishop of York at General Synod.
[© Aegies Associates/Keith Blundy]

With Archbishop Mouneer Anis at the Al-Azhar Al-Sharif mosque in Cairo.

Flying from Nairobi with the Mission Aviation Fellowship, with Caroline Welby (second left), Joanna Udal (centre) and Archbishop Eliud Wabukala of Kenya (second right).

A welcoming party in Dodoma, Tanzania.
[© Mission Aviation Fellowship]

Praying at a mass grave in Bor, South Sudan.
[© Mission Aviation Fellowship]

Barefoot torchlight procession on the 'Holy Mile' to the Anglican Shrine of Our Lady of Walsingham, during the annual youth pilgrimage. [© Graham Howard]

Children at New Wine pray for the archbishop, July 2013.[© New Wine Trust]

official reports, this development seemed increasingly certain. As a result, some traditionalists within Durham diocese felt unable to remain within the Anglican family. Most of the congregation at St James the Great in Darlington decided to join the Personal Ordinariate of Our Lady of Walsingham, established by Pope Benedict XVI to welcome former Anglicans into full communion with Rome while retaining some of their Anglican heritage. The first wave of departures, during Holy Week 2011, saw 1,000 lay people and 60 clergy from across England enter the Ordinariate. The Darlington group were part of the second wave at Lent 2012, led by their parish priest, Ian Grieves, who felt pushed out of Anglicanism by 'this politically correct Church and liberal agenda which grinds on and on'. Welby was 'deeply sad' at the congregation's decision but was determined that this parting of friends would be without acrimony.[60] He had known Grieves for 20 years since undertaking a training placement at St James while a student at Cranmer Hall, one of his early encounters with the catholic tradition, and praised his former supervisor as a 'quite exceptional priest ... a teacher of great gifts'. In a poignant public act of friendship, Welby preached at the congregation's final mass in February 2012, on the eve of their departure, announcing that 'This is not a time for apologies. It is a time for repentance. ... Our repentance is for being part of a church which is in such a state. What do we do now? Bless not curse.'[61]

Welby's personal commitment to the consecration of women as bishops was not in doubt. In a pastoral letter to his diocese in July 2012 he made it clear that he held these views

> as a result of careful studies of the scriptures, and examination of the tradition and ways in which the Church globally has grown into new forms of ministry over the two thousand years of its existence. They are not views gained simply from a

60   Edward Malnick, 'The Parish Torn Apart as Latest Waves of Traditionalists Defect to Rome', *Sunday Telegraph*, 1 April 2012, pp. 14–15.
61   'Church Prepares to Change Allegiance', *Northern Echo*, 20 February 2012, p. 3.

pragmatic following of society around us, but are ones held in all conscience and with deep commitment.

At the same time he was 'passionately committed' to a theological understanding of the church as a redeemed fellowship not a self-selecting group:

> To put it in crude terms, because God has brought us together we are stuck with each other and we had better learn to do it the way God wants us to. That means in practice that we need to learn diversity without enmity, to love not only those with whom we agree but especially those with whom we do not agree.

Therefore he strongly supported the need for those in conscience theologically opposed to the ordination of women to be ensured a 'proper place' in the Church of England, though he acknowledged that it was 'a difficult square to make into a circle'.[62] In conversation with Giles Fraser he spoke of 'a circle with sharp bits on it'.[63] The bishop told his diocesan synod that he personally would 'spare no effort' in seeking to find a way for the Church of England to demonstrate, not only in words, that it valued everyone.[64]

These themes recurred in Welby's contribution to the debates in General Synod in July and November 2012 on women in the episcopate. He urged support for the Bishops and Priests (Consecration and Ordination of Women) Measure believing it to be 'as good as we can get'.[65] But he lamented the manner in which Anglicans had debated the issue with a 'fire-fight of words, articles, letters and emails', drawing parallels with the sectarian violence he had often witnessed in Africa and the Middle East. Followers of Christ, he proclaimed, should behave differently, as 'reconciled reconcilers' and a witness to the world.[66] Returning to one of his favourite mottos, Welby

62   Justin Welby, 'Pastoral Letter', July 2012, www.durham.anglican.org.
63   Fraser, 'The Saturday Interview', p. 37.
64   Welby, 'Presidential Address' (May 2012).
65   General Synod, *Report of Proceedings* vol. 43 (November 2012), p. 110.
66   General Synod, *Report of Proceedings* vol. 43 (July 2012), pp. 221–2.

exhorted the Church of England to prove its commitment to 'diversity in amity, not diversity in enmity': 'The Church is, above all, those who are drawn into being a new people by the work of Christ and the gift of the Spirit. We are reconciled to God and to one another, not by our choice but by his. That is at the heart of our testimony to the gospel.' Welby himself had been converted, he explained, in churches that could not accept women bishops (a reference to his conservative evangelical heritage at the Round church and Bash camps in Cambridge days). Therefore he was 'personally deeply committed' to ensuring that the promises of General Synod to conscientious objectors would be 'carried out faithfully, in spirit as well as in letter – expressing in attitude and by our actions that we more than respect but also love one another'. This Anglican inclusivity was 'a foundation stone for our mission in this country and the world more widely. We cannot get trapped into believing that this is a zero-sum decision, where one person's gain must be another's loss. That is not a theology of grace.' Instead of going to war against one another over such issues, the bishop urged that Christians must 'carry peace and grace as a treasure for the world. We must be those who live a better way; who carry that treasure visibly and distribute it lavishly.'[67]

Behind the scenes Welby brought together the most vocal participants in the debate by creating a safe space for 'mutual listening'. At the request of the archbishops he convened a private gathering at the Community of the Cross of Nails at Coventry Cathedral in August 2012 for 'facilitated conversations'. The two-day event was facilitated by David Porter, the man who had replaced Welby at the International Centre for Reconciliation, using an approach to disagreement that was soon embedded into the life of the Church of England as both men took on a national role the following year. The aim was 'reconciliation', by which Welby meant not

---

67   General Synod, *Report of Proceedings* vol. 43 (November 2012), p. 110.

unanimity or even broad agreement, 'but the transformation of destructive conflict into constructive conflict'.[68] But in 2012 these conversations were too little and too late. In an acrimonious environment at General Synod in November, the women bishops measure won strong backing amongst the bishops and clergy, but fell six votes short of the necessary two-thirds majority in the House of Laity. Welby tweeted that it was a 'very grim day'.[69] He wrote to his diocese of his 'deep sense of sadness' that the measure had failed. But he ended with a note of optimism: 'God is still at work. The Church has gone through more difficult times and had bigger crises. This is a time for prayer, lament and petition for our divided and troubled church.'[70]

68   General Synod, *Report of Proceedings* vol. 43 (July 2012), pp. 221–2.
69   Justin Welby tweet, 20 November 2012, @Bishopofdurham.
70   Justin Welby, message on Durham Diocesan Forum, 21 November 2012, www. durham.anglican.org.

Chapter 9

---∞∞∞---

Canterbury

When Rowan Williams announced in March 2012 his intention to step down as Archbishop of Canterbury at the end of the year and return to academia, Justin Welby had been a bishop for only four and a half months. He had little media profile outside the north-east of England and barely figured in the early speculations about Williams' successor. Better-known bishops like John Sentamu (York), Richard Chartres (London), Christopher Cocksworth (Coventry), Graham James (Norwich) and Steven Croft (Sheffield) were the frontrunners.[1] Every diocesan bishop was required to 'put in his papers' to the Crown Nominations Commission, so Welby duly complied, laying out his vision for the Church of England and the Anglican Communion. But he ended his written submission by telling the commission frankly that it would be 'a joke' and 'perfectly absurd' to appoint him because he had such little episcopal experience.[2]

The first person publicly to canvass Welby's candidacy was Giles Fraser (president of Inclusive Church) in a profile for the *Guardian* in July 2012.[3] Soon others began to appreciate the unique combination of his skills and experience, and by the autumn Welby had emerged as a candidate with a remarkable breadth of support. In a debate for *Channel 4 News* he was named as first choice by both Fraser and Rod Thomas (chairman of the conservative evangelical group

1   'Contenders: Sentamu is the Early Favourite' and 'Dr Williams's Successor Faces an Almighty Task', *Daily Telegraph*, 17 March 2012, pp. 4, 25.
2   'An Evening with Justin and Caroline Welby', 27 January 2013. This section was later cut from the recording.
3   Fraser, 'The Saturday Interview', p. 37.

Reform), men of antithetical convictions about the future of Anglicanism, which left the interviewer surprised that 'peace has broken out in the Church of England'.[4] Likewise in informal soundings taken from around the Anglican Communion, Welby was recommended by both Nigeria and the United States, usually warring parties. He was shortlisted by the Crown Nominations Commission and interviewed, in strict secrecy in a convent in Woking, on 22 September. When Downing Street announced his nomination as Archbishop of Canterbury seven weeks later, the news was enthusiastically welcomed across the world.

Welby's appointment signalled a distinct break with the past. He had far more business experience than any of his predecessors and was ordained relatively late, at the age of 36, older than any Archbishop of Canterbury since the Reformation, all of whom were ordained in their twenties. Not since the seventeenth century had an archbishop had less episcopal experience before appointment to the top job. His sudden rise through the ecclesiastical ranks had been meteoric, from canonry to archbishopric in just five years. Suddenly he was thrown onto the international stage as a global religious figurehead. Labour peer Andrew Adonis believed Welby had 'what it takes to be a great leader of what has become virtually a leaderless institution'. He told the new archbishop: 'You have the chance, if you seize it, to become a national leader rather than simply a church spokesman like your recent predecessors.'[5] Similarly a Tory peer said Welby was 'the best person we've had for ages'.[6]

Yet it was Welby's personal character which most won him favour. The Crown Nominations Commission had been struck by the fact that of all the candidates he was the most

4　　'Who Will Be the New Archbishop of Canterbury?', 25 September 2012, www.channel4news.com.
5　　Andrew Adonis, 'Your First Sermon Theme: "Back Me or Sack Me"', Times, 5 February 2013, p. 24.
6　　Quoted in Robert McCrum, 'Justin Welby: From Mammon to Man of God', Observer, 27 January 2013, p. 33.

'comfortable in his own skin'. Charles Moore, who had met four archbishops at Lambeth Palace, found Welby 'by far the most relaxed'.[7] Dominic Lawson found him 'genuinely modest and completely unpretentious'.[8] Likewise when Lucy Kellaway interviewed the archbishop over lunch for the *Financial Times*, she was struck by his modesty:

> This endless self-deprecation is very Etonian. So far he's told me that he is useless compared to his predecessor, that he has a second-class mind, that he gets hopelessly nervous before big speeches, that he's not holy and that he's probably boring me rigid. But, actually, I don't think he fits the Etonian model at all. That comes from superiority, while his, I'm fairly sure, is something rarer: genuine humility.[9]

Kellaway called Welby a master of 'self-dissing'. 'In a way it was all hogwash,' she concluded. 'Yet it made me putty in his hands.'[10] Welby's relaxed down-to-earth style, especially his easy manner of handling the press, was an asset. Where Rowan Williams often seemed ill at ease in front of the glare of cameras and microphones, Welby rolled up his sleeves at his opening press conference, began with prayer and got briskly down to business. After a few months in harness, he cheerfully confessed, 'I love the job.'[11]

Enthronement

As in Durham diocese, Welby began his new ministry in March 2013 with a five-day 'journey of prayer' through

---

7   Moore, 'I Was Embarrassed'.
8   Lawson, 'So Many Crosses to Bear', p. 24.
9   Lucy Kellaway, 'As Easy-Going as the AB of C', *Financial Times*, 11–12 May 2013, *Life & Arts*, p. 3.
10   Lucy Kellaway, 'Why it is Very Clever to Pretend to be Stupid', *Financial Times*, 11 November 2013, p. 14.
11   Kellaway, 'As Easy-Going as the AB of C'.

the province of Canterbury, to six cathedrals in five cities –
Norwich (close to the Norfolk coast so significant in Welby's
childhood), Coventry (where he had been a canon), London
(both St Paul's and Southwark), Truro, and Chichester
(recently troubled by allegations of historic child abuse). The
pilgrimage was organised with the help of the 24-7 prayer
movement, an international network led by Pete Greig
(director of prayer at HTB), and included prayer activities
from the full range of Anglican spiritualities, including 'prayer
trees', 'labyrinths', 'prayer maps', *lectio divina*, Celtic prayers,
silence and adoration of the eucharist.[12] As the archbishop told
Songs of Praise, 'prayer has to be at the centre of absolutely
everything we do, otherwise it's a waste of space'.[13] It also
had an evangelistic dimension, drawing in surprisingly large
crowds, estimated at 12,500 people in total. This dwarfed his
previous prayer pilgrimage in Durham which attracted only a
few hundred people.

Welby's enthronement at Canterbury Cathedral took place
on 21 March, a serendipitous date as it was the feast day of
two of his heroes – his favourite monk, Benedict of Nursia, and
the Reformation martyr, Archbishop Thomas Cranmer. The
grand pageant, in front of the world's television cameras, was
attended by 2,000 invited guests including Prince Charles, the
Duchess of Cornwall, the Prime Minister and numerous other
dignitaries. A notable figure in the vast procession of church
leaders was Rick Warren (pastor of Saddleback, a mega-church
in California), one of the best-known global evangelicals who
had given the invocation at Barack Obama's presidential
inauguration in 2009. Surrounded by famous personalities, the
event was carefully crafted to send some important theological
messages. Welby was determined that the first voice should be

---

12 'Journey in Prayer', press release, 4 March 2013, www.archbishopofcanterbury.org.
    For the history and priorities of the 24-7 prayer movement, see Pete Greig and Dave
    Roberts, *Red Moon Rising* (Eastbourne: Kingsway, 2004); Andy Freeman and Pete
    Greig, *Punk Monk: New Monasticism and the Ancient Art of Breathing* (Ventura,
    California: Regal Books, 2007).
13 *Songs of Praise*, 24 March 2013.

that of a young woman from the Global South, because that was the profile of the average Anglican. He also wanted to emphasise Christ-like service, not authority. Therefore he was greeted at the West Door not by the Dean of Canterbury but by Evangeline Kanagasooriam, a 17-year-old Christian from Sri Lanka, who asked him the same three innovative questions he had devised for his Durham enthronement, about serving and proclaiming Christ crucified.

Despite the careful choreography there was a deliberate lack of pomposity. Again as at Durham, the word 'enthronement' was conspicuously absent, shunned because of its regal overtones. Although the word 'throne' did creep once into the rubrics of the service order, the event was called an 'inauguration of ministry' and Welby was 'installed' in his diocesan seat and the Chair of St Augustine.[14] Concerning this symbolic change of language, he later quipped: 'You either sound like a fake king, or like a photocopying machine!'[15] The international dimension was enhanced by loud Ghanaian drummers in traditional costume who accompanied the gospel procession, just as there had been African drummers at Rowan Williams' enthronement ten years before.[16] The blessing over the archbishop was another reminder that Anglicanism is not restricted to the English-speaking world, pronounced in French by Bernard Ntahoturi from Burundi, a significant choice. He was a conservative African, chairman of both the Inter-Anglican Standing Commission for Unity, Faith and Order (IASCUFO) and the Council of Anglican Provinces of Africa (CAPA), and his connection with Welby stretched back a decade.

As in Durham, there was a new choir anthem from Michael Berkeley, specially commissioned for the occasion by Welby's mother and stepfather, based on words from the Rule of St

---

14   *The Inauguration of the Ministry of the One Hundred and Fifth Archbishop of Canterbury, Justin Portal Welby* (order of service, 21 March 2013), p. 25.
15   Interview at New Wine Conference, 29 July 2013.
16   Shortt, *Rowan's Rule*, p. 260.

Benedict. Other hymns were evangelical classics from Isaac Watts, Samuel Stone, Charles Wesley and Stuart Townend. Reconciliation was a keynote of the service, not least in the New Testament lesson (2 Corinthians 5) read by Vincent Nichols (Roman Catholic Archbishop of Westminster). Welby's sermon was an exhortation to wholehearted, courageous discipleship: 'A Christ-heeding life changes the church and a Christ-heeding church changes the world ... Let us provoke each other to heed the call of Christ, to be clear in our declaration of Christ, committed in prayer to Christ, and we will see a world transformed.'[17] The sermon showed, according to the *Guardian*, that the new archbishop was 'a cold-shower man rather than warm-bath one. His is a muscular, unapologetic faith.'[18]

Disagreements in the Anglican family meant that the primates had not been in the same room since 2009, because several African conservatives refused to take part whenever the North Americans were present. Welby hoped the goodwill surrounding his enthronement might enable these adversaries to put their divisions aside temporarily and enjoy some 'collegial time' together after the event. Nevertheless, there was no invitation for Archbishop Robert Duncan, primate of the Anglican Church in North America (ACNA), a conservative province and not part of the Anglican Communion. This left the GAFCON primates with a dilemma because Duncan was a member of the GAFCON primates council alongside six Africans, Eliud Wabukala (Kenya), Henri Isingoma (Congo), Stanley Ntagali (Uganda), Valentine Mokiwa (Tanzania), Nicholas Okoh (Nigeria) and Onesphore Rwaje (Rwanda), and one Chilean, Tito Zavala (Archbishop of the Southern Cone). The three most influential archbishops in this group, Wabukala, Okoh and Ntagali, agreed that they should attend Welby's enthronement to 'show our commitment to the

17   Justin Welby, sermon at Canterbury Cathedral, 21 March 2013, www.archbishopofcanterbury.org.
18   'Archbishop of Canterbury: Good and God', *Guardian*, 22 March 2013, p. 52.

Anglican Communion' but not participate in the 'collegial time' afterwards. In a private letter to his colleagues, Wabukala explained: 'there is every indication that Primates who have led the way in promoting false teaching will be received as in good standing'. He continued:

> Since collegiality has been so seriously undermined by the failure to discipline those who have chosen to abandon apostolic faith and practice, I am of the mind that by participation, we could easily cause confusion for those in the GAFCON movement. We know that the Anglican Communion Office loses no opportunity to portray consensus based on 'conversation' rather than the faith we are called to confess.[19]

They feared, for example, that photographs of them standing with Katharine Jefferts Schori (Presiding Bishop of TEC) or Fred Hiltz (Archbishop of Canada) would be misused for Lambeth's PR agenda. To avoid misunderstanding of their partial boycott, Wabukala drafted a letter to Welby, which he hoped would be signed by all the GAFCON primates and published before the enthronement.[20] It praised the 'strength and sincerity' of Welby's commitment to mission, reconciliation and unity, but declared that decisions about the Anglican Communion must be taken 'on the basis of a shared commitment to orthodox Anglican doctrinal and moral teaching, not on the basis of unlimited dialogue between those who happen to have a shared ecclesial history.' The letter expressed sadness that Duncan was excluded from the enthronement service, 'a lost opportunity to demonstrate that your commitment to reconciliation initiatives is more than institutional management'. It also criticised the Church of England's new willingness to accept men in same-sex civil partnerships as bishops: 'This does not help us to be confident that processes which are led from England will be able to deal

19   Eliud Wabukala to GAFCON primates, 28 February 2013.
20   GAFCON primates to Justin Welby, February 2013 (draft).

robustly with the moral and doctrinal confusion which has
overtaken us.' The draft letter concluded:

> Please be assured that we continue to honour the historic See of
> Canterbury in thankfulness for the inheritance of faith that we
> share, as our presence at your enthronement will demonstrate.
> Not to participate as fully as you would have hoped gives us
> no pleasure and we want to assure you of both our readiness
> to meet you and our continued prayers for the godly unity of
> our beloved Communion as well as for you yourself as you
> assume this weighty office.

In the event, the GAFCON primates had no time to organise
a co-ordinated response and this letter was never sent.
Nevertheless Archbishops Wabukala, Okoh and Ntagali
made a quick exit from Canterbury soon after the service,
despite pleas from Mouneer Anis (primate of Jerusalem and
the Middle East) that they should stay.

When Rowan Williams was appointed to Canterbury he
was loudly criticised by some British evangelicals and there
were demands that he step down even before he was enthroned.
Welby, by contrast, was carried to Canterbury on a wave of
national adulation on all sides. Dissentient voices were few
and far between. There were high hopes that he was the man
of the hour who would usher in a new style of leadership and
public engagement. But Welby knew that these expectations
were bound to be dashed. On Easter Sunday, ten days after his
enthronement, he spoke against the cult of the 'hero leader',
warning that they always fail:

> Papers reported on Friday that only 40% of churchgoers are
> convinced that the new Archbishop of Canterbury can resolve
> the problems of the Church of England. I do hope that means
> the other 60% thought the idea so barking mad that they did
> not answer the question. ... Put not your trust in new leaders
> ... Human sin means pinning hopes on individuals is always a

mistake ... Setting people or institutions up to heights where they cannot but fail is mere cruelty.[21]

Although Welby's honeymoon period was soon over, he continued to win high approval ratings. A *Church Times* survey conducted in the summer and autumn of 2013 showed that 73 per cent of readers had confidence in his leadership, and only 7 per cent did not.[22] As so often throughout his ministry, Welby continued to emphasise his own fallibility. He told his friends at HTB:

> I'm going to make a lot of mistakes, necessarily. I'm a human being; like everybody else I will get things wrong. Sometimes I'll do it by stupidity, sometimes by cowardice, sometimes by exhaustion – sometimes they'll look like mistakes but they'll be the right thing. ... Don't believe everything you hear. When you hear bad things, just do pray more.

He appealed: 'Pray for wisdom for me to know what to do, for patience to know when to do it, and for courage to do it properly and not holding back.'[23]

Evangelical Baggage

By 2014 four of the five top bishoprics in the Church of England were in the hands of evangelicals – Canterbury (Welby), York (Sentamu), Durham (Paul Butler) and Winchester (Tim Dakin). The Bishop of London, Richard Chartres, though more catholic in his outlook was also theologically conservative. It was perhaps the first time that evangelicals dominated so many of the top posts since the reign of Elizabeth I, though it was the continuation of a late twentieth-century trend. For

---

21   Justin Welby, sermon at Canterbury Cathedral, 31 March 2013, www. archbishopofcanterbury.org.
22   'Poll: Lack of Trust in Synod', *Church Times*, 7 February 2014, p. 2.
23   HTB Home Focus, 27 July 2013.

a brief period in the late 1970s, for example, Canterbury (Donald Coggan), York (Stuart Blanch) and Winchester (John V. Taylor) had evangelical bishops, though they were balanced by the liberalism of John Habgood at Durham and later York.

Nevertheless, evangelical archbishops have typically been ambivalent about their evangelical identity. Coggan worked for the Inter-Varsity Fellowship and as principal of an evangelical theological college, but was recommended to Prime Minister Harold Macmillan in 1960 as a good archbishop because 'He is too big a man to have any definitive party allegiance, and has grown from an evangelical background into a central churchman.'[24] Likewise in George Carey's first book after his appointment to Canterbury in 1991 he was at pains to point out that he had not 'stopped travelling theologically' and it was difficult to put him into 'a theological box'.[25] A few years later he stated:

> I've changed a lot over the years. My theological colouring has changed. I started out from a very definite, conservative, evangelical, Protestant, Anglican church, and I'm nowhere near that now. ... no one will ever hear me calling *myself* an evangelical ... For me the most important thing is being a Christian, then being an Anglican, and those are the two most important words in my vocabulary.[26]

Carey described David Watson, who had been a help to Welby at Cambridge in the 1970s, as 'in essence an ecumenical charismatic rather than an evangelical'.[27] This ability to connect with a range of spiritualities, especially in the catholic and charismatic traditions, was one of the reasons Carey was chosen for Canterbury.

24   David Stephens (Prime Minister's appointments secretary) to Harold Macmillan, 7 September 1960, National Archives, PREM 5/443, quoted in 'A Quiet Word about the Next Archbishop', *Church Times*, 9 January 2009, p. 19.
25   George Carey, *I Believe* (London: SPCK, 1991), p. 7.
26   Mary Loudon, *Revelations: The Clergy Questioned* (London: Hamilton, 1994), pp. 252–3.
27   George Carey, 'Parties in the Church of England', *Theology* vol. 91 (July 1988), p. 269. See further, Andrew Atherstone, 'Archbishop Carey's Ecumenical Vision', *Theology* vol. 106 (September 2003), pp. 342–52.

Welby's outlook had broadened considerably since his days at Bash camps and the Cambridge Inter-Collegiate Christian Union. Nevertheless, he told the *Church Times* in 2013, 'I'd still describe myself as a conservative Evangelical if I had to put a label on it, but the trouble with the label is it brings so much baggage.'[28] Interviewed by the BBC, he elucidated further:

> The word evangelical has a vast amount of baggage ... it means something different everywhere. I would describe myself as an orthodox Christian, to put it in simple terms – I say the creed without crossing my fingers at any point. I'm perfectly happy to be described as an evangelical in terms of my theology, with a small 'e', but I don't pick up all the baggage of all the bits of evangelicalism around the world. And I've always been someone who draws on the widest tradition of the church. I'm very relaxed about an open and joined-up approach to church traditions.[29]

Asked the same question at the Evangelical Alliance, Welby was hesitant. He did admit to being an evangelical in theology, because 'I believe that Scripture properly interpreted is the final authority in all matters of faith and practice.' Yet he also made clear,

> Am I an evangelical in party terms? Absolutely not, because the Bible tells me we're not to have parties and groups and factions within the church. So I don't buy into a party, but I do have a high view of Scripture and I'm deeply committed to proclaiming the gospel.[30]

This approach to evangelical nomenclature was typical of HTB. Both Sandy Millar and Nicky Gumbel spoke of their dislike of 'unhelpful and divisive labels' and stereotypes such as 'evangelical' and 'charismatic', in favour simply of the title

---

28   Ed Thornton, 'You Don't Have to Agree to be in the Same Church', *Church Times*, 22 March 2013, p. 19.

29   *Enthronement of the Archbishop of Canterbury* (Justin Welby interviewed by Huw Edwards), BBC 2, 21 March 2013.

30   'Question and Answer Session with the Archbishop of Canterbury' (audio recording), Evangelical Alliance, 28 August 2013, www.eauk.org.

'Christian'.[31] Gumbel even went so far as to declare: 'I hate the word evangelical! If you torture me, I'm Anglican.'[32]

Although tentative about evangelicalism, Welby was far happier to affirm charismatic theology as 'central to my own spirituality'.[33] He saw it as complementary to the Benedictine movement, because charismatics emphasised God's imminence and empowering presence, while Benedictines emphasised contemplative awe. 'They're two wings of spirituality that keep everything flying,' he suggested.[34] Likewise Caroline spoke of her own refreshing discovery of the Spiritual Exercises of Ignatius of Loyola which she explained fitted particularly well with charismatic evangelicalism 'because it's all to do with the Bible and it's all to do with the Spirit. It's about contemplative imagination of Scripture and just getting into the stories of the Bible in a way that sometimes bypasses the brain and really touches at the heart.'[35] The archbishop's own daily pattern of prayer was certainly rigorous. An early riser by nature, he began with private prayer, often in 'tongues', and lengthy meditation on Scripture with the help of a demanding modern commentary to benefit from the best scholarship. He often prayed further during a morning run through the streets of Lambeth. The Anglican office provided formal liturgical structure with a regular diet of corporate devotion at morning prayer, midday holy communion, and evening prayer.[36] He went on retreat annually for longer periods of focused prayer and Bible reading, for example to France at Dombes Abbey

---

31   Sandy Millar, *All I Want Is You: A Collection of Christian Reflections* (London: Alpha International, 2005), pp. 107–8; Nicky Gumbel, 'Alpha Plus', in Caroline Chartres (ed.), *Why I Am Still an Anglican: Essays and Conversations* (London: Continuum, 2006), p. 96.

32   Matthew Bell, 'Q: What Makes All of the Above Alpha Males? A: They May Not All Clap Happily and Speak in Tongues, But They Are All Part of an Evangelical Tide: A Global Anglican Phenomenon Called Alpha', *Independent on Sunday*, 31 March 2013, p. 51.

33   Interview at New Wine Conference, 29 July 2013.

34   *Private Passions*, 22 December 2013.

35   HTB Home Focus, 27 July 2013.

36   HTB Home Focus, 27 July 2013.

(Chemin Neuf) and Bec Abbey (Benedictine) in 2013 and 2014 respectively.

Criticism of Welby's broad spirituality came mainly from evangelicals outside the Church of England. For example, the *Evangelical Times* maintained that his conservative evangelical mentor, E. J. H. Nash, must be 'turning in his grave'. The newspaper declared: 'Justin Welby has become the usual highly confusing Anglican mix – a typical Anglican "mess"! Whatever sort of evangelical he is, he is not currently the robust type.' It urged readers to pray for the archbishop, 'that God will lead him back to his spiritual roots and give him grace to make a bold stand for "the faith once delivered to the saints"'.[37] The *English Churchman*, a small-circulation Protestant newspaper, likewise greeted Welby's appointment with the front-page headline: 'CANTERBURY NEEDS A BOLD MAN OF GOD – Not a New Evangelical'. After explaining why every part of his background was a cause for concern, it proclaimed: 'The worst case scenario is that our suspicions are correct and that Welby is a New Evangelical of a rather liberal, charismatic, modern and ecumenical persuasion. He may have success in increasing church attendance but the cost will be high.'[38]

Welby navigated nimbly through many different ecclesial environments. For example, over five days in July 2013 he spoke at four summer events with a range of spiritualities from charismatic to catholic, though weighted towards the charismatic – the Hillsong annual conference in London's O2 arena; the HTB church holiday ('Home Focus') in Lincolnshire; the New Wine conference in Somerset; and the annual youth pilgrimage to Walsingham in Norfolk. The events were deliberately chosen because of their emphasis on youthful vibrancy and commitment to social transformation. The archbishop enjoyed encountering 'a real rainbow of churches', which stretched from high-volume Pentecostal worship with a

---

37   Roger Fay, 'Archbishop Justin Welby', *Evangelical Times* (September 2013), p. 21.
38   *English Churchman: A Protestant Family Newspaper*, 16 and 23 November 2012, p. 1.

crowd of 8,000, to walking barefoot but mitred in penitential procession with a crowd of 800, kneeling in silence at a candlelit vigil before a Marian shrine and concelebrating at the mass. Welby was 'encouraged and uplifted by all traditions' and observed that these extremes were 'held together by Jesus Christ'.[39]

The Lambeth Revolution

Goals and strategy, familiar buzz words from the world of business management, are increasingly ubiquitous amongst Anglican church leaders. For example, the House of Bishops and the Archbishops' Council hit upon the idea of quinquennial goals for the Church of England, which for the period 2010–15 were numerical and spiritual growth, re-imagining ministry, and serving the common good.[40] When Welby took up the reins at Lambeth he likewise announced three emphases for his archiepiscopate: prayer and renewal of the religious life; reconciliation within the church and wider society; and evangelism, by which he simply meant 'telling people the good news of Jesus Christ'.[41] These oft-repeated headlines were clearly conceived and easy to grasp. They could be summarised in just three words and gave Welby's ministry a sense of purpose and vigour as he laid out his vision from numerous platforms. David Ford (Regius Professor of Divinity at Cambridge), who served as an advisor to both Robert Runcie and George Carey, said of the new archbishop: 'I haven't seen this level of strategic thinking in relation to

---

39   Justin Welby, 'When Christ is Present, Our Differences Break Down' (blog), 4 August 2013, www.archbishopofcanterbury.org.
40   *Challenges for the New Quinquennium: A Report from the House of Bishops and the Archbishops' Council*, January 2011 (GS 1815); *Challenges for the New Quinquennium: Next Steps*, June 2011 (GS Misc 995).
41   *Enthronement of the Archbishop of Canterbury*, 21 March 2013.

both the Anglican Communion and the Church here in any of his predecessors.'[42] Rowan Williams himself acknowledged: 'Justin is, frankly, immeasurably better than I ever was at prioritising. He clearly knows where he wants to put his primary energies, and I was always much too ready to say Yes to this and Yes to that.'[43] Likewise the chief of staff at Lambeth Palace, Chris Smith, reflected on their contrasting leadership styles:

> Rowan would be more accepting of many things. Justin arrived with some fairly strong ideas. ... Justin is a bit of a Joshua; Rowan would be rather more of a Samuel. ... Joshua's on the front foot, 'This is where we're going. These are the battles we've got to fight. This is what we do now.' Rowan would work more along the lines of 'What have we got? Where can we go to with this?'[44]

Where Williams talked in visionary terms and left his staff to formulate the practical plans, Welby's strategic abilities were better developed. One of Williams' classic comments was 'I can live with that', but Welby was less patient.

To serve his strategy, Welby set about dismantling the entire Lambeth Palace team and replacing them with his own appointees. When Williams entered office in 2003 he had faced far great restrictions, as he explained:

> When I came in the understanding was that the staff at Lambeth was a given. I explored whether I could bring my chaplain from Wales [Gregory Cameron] with me to Lambeth and was told very firmly, 'No! There's no money for an extra member of staff. The staff at Lambeth is the staff at Lambeth, that's it.' So it took a while to have any sense that there was a staff to mould or reshape. ... Over the years the Church Commissioners did see that that's not necessarily the most helpful message to give an incoming archbishop, so Justin's

42 Interview with David Ford, 5 February 2014.
43 Interview with Rowan Williams, 13 March 2014. On Williams' ambivalence to 'strategy', see Goddard, *Rowan Williams*, pp. 303–4.
44 Interview with Chris Smith, 16 December 2013.

had quite a free hand in a way that I didn't. ... I could bring in nobody when I arrived.[45]

Two reviews of the staffing at Lambeth, *To Lead and to Serve* (the Hurd Report, 2001) and *Resourcing Archbishops* (the second Mellows Report, 2002), both recommended clearer management structures overseen by a lay chief of staff. Since Robert Runcie's days in the 1980s the chief of staff had been the Bishop at Lambeth, usually a senior diocesan bishop who acted as the conduit between the archbishop and his episcopal colleagues. But Williams heeded the advice and abolished the post, recruiting instead Chris Smith, an evangelical layman who brought business and accountancy experience as the former manager of Hoare's Bank in Fleet Street (the oldest independent private bank in Britain). Together they slowly restructured the team, though it took several years. Williams admitted, 'I'm not much of a systems man', so Smith took leadership responsibilities for line management, agendas, diaries and finance. Under him there were four major departments – ecumenical, interfaith, international development and Anglican Communion – each with their own senior secretary or 'principal'. The interfaith work had become a 'monumental priority' since the terrorist atrocities of 11 September 2001, and the international development team (launched in 2005) was Williams' own brainchild to keep the Anglican Communion pulling together in practical relief work when all their theological conversations had turned toxic.[46] The Lambeth operation grew considerably during the tenures of Carey and Williams, almost doubling in size, but as *Resourcing Archbishops* put it: 'The demands upon and expectations of the Archbishops are at the very limit of what is realistic. The jobs are approaching the point at which they will become impossible.'[47]

45   Interview with Rowan Williams, 13 March 2014.
46   Interview with Rowan Williams, 13 March 2014.
47   *Resourcing Archbishops: The Second Report of the Archbishops' Review Group on Bishops' Needs and Resources* (London: Church House Publishing, 2002), p. 1.

Archbishop Welby began the shake-up as soon as he arrived. On *Songs of Praise*, the week of his enthronement, he spoke of the need to challenge 'the driving power of systems in big institutions, like churches', and the courage to refuse to be pushed around by them.[48] With a sense of urgency he set about creating a new Lambeth ethos. Smith was a key ally, having known Welby for 30 years since they served on the HTB church council together in the 1980s. Smith helped to lead the restructuring before himself moving to new pastures in October 2013, so that, as he put it, 'the arrows could be in my back, and then to leave things on a more peaceful basis'.[49] Amongst the other senior staff who left Lambeth's employ within Welby's first 12 months were the ecumenical secretary, the international development secretary, the interfaith secretary, the Anglican Communion secretary, the press secretary, the patronage secretary and the chaplain. It was nothing less than root-and-branch reform. It was called 'a purge', leaving 'a lot of people hurt'.

The interfaith and development work survived in a new shape, but merged into the Anglican Communion Office and no longer directly answerable to the archbishop. The ecumenical work was dismantled, ending a tradition which stretched back to the 1920s of ecumenical specialists at Lambeth who could advise the archbishop on global issues. Instead ecumenical responsibilities were parceled out to individual bishops and to the Church of England's Council for Christian Unity, which Welby hoped would be both cost-effective and liberate 'fresh impetus and imagination' in ecumenical ministry.[50] These various staff were replaced by a new structure and a smaller team, but some prominent advisors expressed concern that such a sudden loss of expertise and corporate wisdom from Lambeth would damage the Archbishop of Canterbury's ability to function effectively in the long term. There was a

48 *Songs of Praise*, 24 March 2013.
49 Interview with Chris Smith, 16 December 2013.
50 Welby, 'Presentation' (November 2013), p. 3.

danger, for instance, that the new arrangements would mean lack of co-ordination and continuity in the ecumenical work. One senior advisor said it was 'completely reckless' to abolish such posts and for Welby 'to either try to wing it on his ecumenical encounters or to "outsource" to experts':

> Because he is very able, he may feel that he can manage unassisted. But in my view there is no substitute for expert briefings, recce visits by staff and being accompanied and guided on his journeys, especially to the Vatican and the East. Given the sensitivities on those fronts, something major could easily go wrong.

Almost no domain escaped Welby's rigorous review. His work as honorary patron or president of several hundred organisations and institutions was cut back. He had no desire to be merely a name on a letterhead and preferred to focus his time on his key priorities. This pruning was largely quiet, though Welby was berated in the press for snubbing an invitation to be vice-patron of the Royal Society for the Prevention of Cruelty to Animals (RSPCA), with environmentalist Bill Oddie and animal ethicist Professor Andrew Linzey amongst his critics.[51]

The downsizing of the Lambeth enterprise was partly driven by finance. Welby was under firm pressure from the Church Commissioners to slash the budget. It also enabled him to set an example of self-restraint to his diocesan bishops, good PR for the church in an age of austerity. The archbishop was painfully conscious of the public impression created by living in a medieval palace on a 13-acre estate, even though the Welbys' own accommodation was only a flat within the complex. The similarities between the archbishop and Pope Francis were striking. Enthroned in the same week, both men were evangelists and reformers, impatient with bureaucracy and keen to break free from the traditional expectations of their office. Both came with atypical backgrounds and

---

51 '"Is That Your Excuse?" Bill Oddie Ridicules Welby for Turning Down Role with RSPCA', *Daily Telegraph*, 19 August 2013, p. 1; 'Welby "Wrong" to Turn Down RSPCA', and letter from Dominic Walker, *Church Times*, 23 August 2013, pp. 3, 12.

brought fresh ideas. Both were unpretentious, subverting the culture of deference.[52] At the Vatican, Pope Francis refused to live in the papal apartments, ate in the communal refectory, modelled compassion for the poor and began a shake-up of the curia, challenging vested interests. The two men met for the first time in June 2013 in Rome, an encounter which Welby called 'probably one of the highlights of my life'.[53] He described the pope as 'obsessive and passionate about Jesus Christ', someone of 'the most absolute simplicity and humility ... full of love, not standing on his position or his dignity. He is the most extraordinary gift of God to the global church.'[54] The archbishop agreed wholeheartedly with the pope that 'simplicity has got to be the style we set'.[55] He knew that 'people are fed up of grandstanding and grand behaviour'.[56]

So a scaled-back Lambeth operation not only saved money. It chimed with contemporary trends towards small government and leaders with the common touch, and might even be seen as a Christian imperative. Unlike his predecessors, Welby preferred to travel around London by public transport, often on the bus or the Underground, and he enjoyed the walk to the House of Lords, so the Lambeth chauffeur decided to leave after two decades of loyal service. The archbishop also set about changing the image of 'Fortress Lambeth', with its austere gatehouse and high boundary walls which seemed more in keeping with a Victorian prison. As a first step in making Lambeth more hospitable, the gatekeepers, not noted for their effusive welcome, were retrained and dressed in a smart new livery, complete with the Lambeth crest.

Most radical was the new management structure which the archbishop introduced, a completely new way of operating.

---

52 Damian Thompson, 'Here Comes the God Squad: Evangelicals Have Taken Charge in the Vatican and Lambeth Palace', *Spectator*, 6 July 2013, pp. 12–13.

53 Justin Welby, Christmas message for Vatican Radio, 25 December 2013, www.archbishopofcanterbury.org.

54 St Mellitus College, 2 December 2013.

55 Interview at New Wine Conference, 29 July 2013.

56 Macrory, 'Archbishop's Move', p. 62.

It was based around a more flexible, less hierarchical inner cabinet, the so-called 'Lambeth Seven'. These were the archbishop, chaplain, director of reconciliation, advisor on evangelism, chief of staff, Bishop at Lambeth, and director of communications. Kay Brock, who took on the reconfigured chief of staff remit (with responsibility for public affairs, Lambeth Palace administration, and relations with parliament and the royal households), was the only member of the senior team to survive from the previous regime. Welby began to hand-pick his colleagues before he had even been enthroned. As his chaplain and closest confidante he chose an old friend from Durham days, Jo Bailey Wells, who had recently returned to England after seven years in the United States. They had been members of the same tutor group at Cranmer Hall in the early 1990s. By appointing Wells to his right hand, Welby signalled again his firm support for the ordination of women. More significant, however, was their similarity of approach to the Anglican crisis. After a stint teaching the Old Testament at Ridley Hall in Cambridge, Wells had founded in 2005 the Anglican Episcopal House of Studies (AEHS) at Duke Divinity School in Durham, North Carolina. Coinciding with the fall-out in The Episcopal Church from the consecration of Gene Robinson, the name of the AEHS was carefully chosen. It aimed to train students across the whole breadth of the Anglican and Episcopal spectrum, both those who stood with TEC and those who had broken from it. Wells refused to take sides in the conflict, describing herself as 'a hard-to-pin-down piggy-in-the-middle'. AEHS sought to be a model of reconciliation:

> What we created at Duke was, essentially, a kind of Indaba – to enable the listening learning process in the way students interacted at worship, in lectures, over meals and in practical service ... people could see that we disagreed yet we loved one

another. ... Overall it's about pursuing honesty and overcoming fear – fierce conversation. So hard yet so freeing.[57]

This sentiment chimed closely with Welby's own concerns, essential in a trusted advisor who would help to set the tone for the Lambeth community. Wells was given responsibility to pursue the first of Welby's priorities, to promote prayer and the revival of the religious life.

As director of reconciliation, the archbishop's second emphasis, he head-hunted David Porter from Coventry Cathedral. Porter made his name in the 1990s as director of the Evangelical Contribution on Northern Ireland (ECONI), a non-denominational organisation which sought to build peace in Ulster, linked to the Evangelical Alliance. In opposition to the ideologies of Paisleyism and Orangeism, ECONI pursued reconciliation and social justice but was unafraid to challenge evangelical shibboleths. It self-consciously developed an identity which was non-defensive and inclusive, adopting an ethos according to its historian of 'embrace rather than exclusion', with a preference for 'minimal orthodoxy rather than maximal dogmatism'. In 1999 ECONI was rebranded as the Centre for Contemporary Christianity in Ireland (CCCI), deliberately eschewing the evangelical label.[58] Porter, a political activist, had served on the Northern Ireland Civic Forum and been involved in dialogue with paramilitaries. Like Jo Bailey Wells, he brought international experience to Welby's team, and as a Baptist he was not easily linked to any of the Church of England's multitudinous networks or pressure groups. Initially Porter was seconded to Lambeth half-time, but this soon became full-time because he was crucial to Welby's strategy. The archbishop looked to provide Porter with a team

---

57   Jo Bailey Wells, 'Resilient Tents of Meeting: Conflict Resilience and Reconciling Presence', Faith in Conflict Conference, Coventry, 28 February 2013, www.coventrycathedral.org.uk.

58   Patrick Mitchel, *Evangelicalism and National Identity in Ulster, 1921–1998* (Oxford: Oxford University Press, 2003), pp. 279–80, 282. See also, Gladys Ganiel, *Evangelicalism and Conflict in Northern Ireland* (Basingstoke: Palgrave Macmillan, 2008).

of his own, funded through the Lambeth Partners, a group of wealthy donors who support the archbishop's ministry headed by his old friend Ken Costa (investment banker and churchwarden of HTB).[59] As evident throughout his ministry, Welby knew that strategy must be resourced by the right people and properly funded.

To help keep evangelism on the agenda, he turned to another old friend from Durham University days, Chris Russell, the godfather to one of his children. Russell was vicar of St Laurence, Reading, with a particular ministry to young people, and a contributor to the Church of England report, *Mission-Shaped Youth* (2007). He became Welby's part-time (two days a week) advisor on evangelism and witness. To conduct a review of Lambeth communications, Welby drafted in Mark Elsdon-Dew (the experienced head of communications at HTB and married to the archbishop's cousin) who was seconded to Lambeth for four months from March to July 2013. These first four staff appointments – Wells, Porter, Russell and Elsdon-Dew – revealed the three major networks of influence in which Welby was most deeply embedded: Durham, Coventry and HTB. All of them were evangelicals. These formational relationships stretched back many years but continued to shape his decision-making as archbishop.

Welby kept a lay chief of staff but also revived the Bishop at Lambeth, a role given to Nigel Stock, aged 63, the former Bishop of St Edmundsbury and Ipswich, chosen both for his experience and his more catholic churchmanship. The final place in Welby's new cabinet was the director of communications, the only post open to a competitive application process.[60] Ailsa Anderson, former press secretary to the Queen, was appointed. Nevertheless, the archbishop's team was not quite

---

59   For a critique of the Lambeth Partners, see Sean Farrell, 'Partners in Profit, Partners in Prayer', *Independent*, 29 October 2011, p. 57.

60   'Archbishop's Director of Communications' (advertisement), *Church Times*, 5 July 2013, p. 53.

complete. He hoped that the 'Lambeth Seven' might become the 'Lambeth Eight', with the appointment of a senior figure to be his liaison with the wider Anglican Communion, preferably an African bishop. This was highly sensitive, politically, for global Anglicanism and after a year the right person had still not been identified.

Since the 1980s a small group of Anglican nuns had been part of the Lambeth Palace community, another Runcie innovation. They were responsible for prayer life in the Crypt Chapel (three services a day), and also served in various ways outside the palace walls in Southwark parishes, such as helping with drop-in centres or night shelters. They were drawn over the years from the Order of the Holy Paraclete, the Community of the Holy Name, and the Sisters of the Love of God, but like many Anglican orders they were mostly elderly and dwindled in numbers. Welby saw another opportunity for an overhaul. One creative suggestion was to invite the Melanesian Brotherhood, an Anglican community with houses in the Solomon Islands, Vanuatu, Papua New Guinea and the Philippines. They seemed a perfect fit, because their emphases were reconciliation, peace-making and prayer. They had sprung to international prominence when seven brothers were martyred in civil unrest in the Solomon Islands in 2003, and would bring to Lambeth a vibrant reminder of the global Communion. Welby, however, preferred his favoured religious community of the moment, Chemin Neuf. His hopes to establish a Chemin Neuf house in Liverpool in 2011 had not come to fruition, but Lambeth was an even better location. They brought all the advantages of youth, ecumenism, charismatic renewal and a new model of religious life, as well as mirroring Welby's priorities of prayer, reconciliation and evangelism. The first four members arrived in February 2014 – a married Anglican couple (Alan and Ione Morley-Fletcher), a German Lutheran ordinand training at St Mellitus College (Oliver Matri), and a Polish Roman Catholic (Ula Michlowicz). Though drawn from different denominations,

Chemin Neuf was Roman Catholic by foundation, so to be put in charge of the chapel of a Protestant archbishop was previously unthinkable. The significance was not lost on the community's Jesuit founder, Laurent Fabre, who looked back to Henry VIII's break with Rome in 1534, and declared '480 years of waiting is long even for God. This is a first step of something new.'[61] Welby, in another context, called the Reformation 'one of the greatest tragedies of Christian history' because it split the church.[62]

Doing Theology

Although Welby had better skills than Rowan Williams as a strategist and pioneer leader, he was conscious that he could not match his predecessor's depth as a theologian. Indeed at both Durham and Canterbury, Welby followed academics of international repute, Wright and Williams. It was symptomatic of a wider trend in the Church of England. When Geoffrey Rowell (Bishop of Gibraltar in Europe) retired in November 2013 it marked the end of an era – he was the last diocesan bishop to have taught theology full-time at a university (outside a theological college) or to have held a fellowship at Oxford or Cambridge. The current trend was for new bishops with hands-on experience of managing organisations or growing local churches. Nevertheless, Welby was eager to be resourced theologically. Asked on different occasions to name his favourite theologian, the people who came most quickly to mind were David Ford, Anthony Thiselton, Karl Barth, Emil Brunner, Stanley Hauerwas and Miroslav Volf.[63]

61   'Father, Make Them One: Chemin Neuf Community Comes to Lambeth Palace', 20
      February 2014, www.archbishopofcanterbury.org.
62   Lawson, 'So Many Crosses to Bear', p. 29.
63   Thornton, 'You Don't Have to Agree', p. 20; St Mellitus College, 2 December 2013.

To help his own thinking, Welby established a small retreat group to meet a couple of times each year to 'do theology' together. In addition to the archbishop there were ten members (half of them university professors) from a range of denominations and theological disciplines, including biblical studies, historical and systematic doctrine, ecumenism, interfaith relations, liturgy, evangelism and pastoral care. They were seven Anglicans – Jo Bailey Wells, David Ford, Julie Gittoes, Paula Gooder, Mike Higton, Graham Tomlin and James Walters – alongside a Methodist (Tom Greggs), a Roman Catholic (Paul Murray), and a Presbyterian (John Swinton). One of their number, Professor Ford, reflected on the impact of personal suffering in shaping Welby's theology and public engagement:

> It's not a triumphalistic theology. It recognizes that the cross is utterly intrinsic. It gives him a freedom as a person. He's not just creating a position or defending it, he can be vulnerable, not self-protective and therefore devastatingly honest. My goodness he can be! He just cuts through fluff or flab in a way that can be rather shocking. He won't put up with pious nonsense. ... There's a freedom from fear, and therefore he isn't always looking over his shoulder, he isn't always asking whether 'my PR people' can clear this statement. He's got the capacity to be a very unusual public figure. ... The press haven't turned on him yet. They haven't quite got a caricature to puncture. They did caricature Rowan. Justin's much more mobile, much less easy to pin down.

Concerning the archbishop's character as a leader and his activist nature, Ford observed:

> There's no side. He's just absolutely direct, very sharp. He knows how to nail issues. He came late in life to theological training, but my goodness he absorbed it. He really does love to engage with Scripture. ... He's unafraid of the world. We're going to see sparks flying, I suspect, in various ways. He takes teaching the faith very seriously and that involves applying it to contemporary issues in a very direct way. ... He's oriented to action. It isn't primarily getting the statement right that

concerns him, he'll want to always follow through. There will be a flow of proactive things from Justin over the next ten years, that's how he's always been.[64]

The archbishop's skills in navigating moral and political controversy were frequently put to the test as he sought to capitalise on his media profile as a Christian leader to shape the national debate. In Rowan Williams' words, he would need 'the constitution of an ox and the skin of a rhinoceros'.[65] Five previous Archbishops of Canterbury died violently, at the hands of the mob or burned at the stake, but Welby joked that the worst he had to face was 'execution by the daily newspapers'.[66] Sex and money absorbed most public attention, and sparks did fly as Welby stepped into the arena.

64   Interview with David Ford, 5 February 2014.
65   Rowan Williams, interview with Press Association, 16 March 2012.
66   *Private Passions*, 22 December 2013.

Chapter 10

Sex, Money and Power

One of the guiding principles which shaped the Alpha Course at Holy Trinity Brompton was a desire to teach the core doctrines of the Christian faith as believed by most churches around the world. Its focus was 'mere Christianity', in the style of C. S. Lewis.[1] Therefore HTB emphasised areas of broad Christian agreement, such as the death and resurrection of Jesus Christ, and was at pains to avoid more divisive topics. This is seen, for example, in the shifting pattern of public pronouncements concerning sexual ethics. Nicky Gumbel's *Searching Issues* (1994), one of the Alpha Course's best-selling books, included a chapter on 'What is the Christian Attitude to Homosexuality?' It was written under the assumption that it was possible to describe '*the* Christian attitude', but within two decades any broad consensus amongst the churches had disappeared, in the Anglo-American world at least.

Comparison of the various editions of Gumbel's book demonstrates the shift in culture. The first edition argued concisely that homosexual practice was sin which needed to be repented, and that homosexual orientation could be healed by 'the supernatural power of the Spirit' or by psychiatric therapies. Gumbel proclaimed that the church must speak out against homosexual practice: 'It is wrong to promote a homosexual lifestyle in schools. It is wrong to ordain unrepentant practising homosexuals into Christian leadership.'[2] The 2001 edition of *Searching Issues* carried

---

1   Charles Foster, 'From Knightsbridge to the Nations: The Alpha Movement and the Future of Christendom', *Contemporary Review* vol. 288 (Autumn 2006), pp. 320–3.
2   Nicky Gumbel, *Searching Issues* (Eastbourne: Kingsway, 1994), pp. 86, 90.

substantially the same argument, though with some softening of tone. Gumbel was now at pains to make clear that 'We should reject and resist all forms of irrational prejudice', and that sins like greed and dishonesty were equally condemned by the Apostle Paul.[3] References to the destruction of Sodom and the Old Testament condemnation of homosexual practice as 'detestable' were deleted, as was Gumbel's criticism of 'the defiant attitude of some of the leaders of the gay movement today'. Leanne Payne's controversial book, *The Healing of the Homosexual* (1984), was likewise removed from Gumbel's recommended reading list, though his basic teaching did not change.[4] A decade later, however, he had grown far more circumspect. For the revised edition of *Searching Issues* in 2013 the chapter on homosexuality was entirely erased, as was the chapter on sex before marriage.[5] HTB withdrew previous editions of the book from sale from all its worldwide distributors in its multiple translations, because the subject had become toxic and was damaging the Alpha brand and its ecumenical appeal. The HTB attitude to the rights and wrongs of homosexuality, or sexual morality more broadly, was now a studied silence.

Welby's priority of Christian unity, and his understanding of the nature of core doctrine, was influenced by his friends at HTB. Perhaps, like Gumbel, he would have preferred not to become embroiled in the tumultuous public controversy about homosexuality and to focus only on areas of agreement. However, as Archbishop of Canterbury, he did not have the luxury to remain silent. Indeed on this topic every word he uttered was under close scrutiny.

---

3   Nicky Gumbel, *Searching Issues* (Eastbourne: Kingsway, 2001), pp. 71, 73.
4   Gumbel, *Searching Issues* (1994), pp. 78–9, 91.
5   Nicky Gumbel, *Searching Issues* (London: Alpha, 2013).

Human Dignity and Homophobia

In his opening statement as archbishop-designate in November 2012 Welby affirmed the right of the state to define civil partnerships and insisted that 'We must have no truck with any form of homophobia, in any part of the church.' He promised to

> listen very attentively to the LGBT communities, and examine my own thinking prayerfully and carefully. I am always averse to the language of exclusion, when what we are called to is to love in the same way as Jesus Christ loves us. Above all in the church we need to create safe spaces for these issues to be discussed honestly and in love.[6]

These 'safe spaces' would enable Christians to listen to each other and recognise one another's essential humanity and integrity, even if no agreement was reached, and Welby affirmed that it would be 'very much part of what I do'.[7]

Previous incumbents at Lambeth were especially wary of Peter Tatchell, the gay-rights activist and a genius at attracting press attention by high-profile confrontations with the church hierarchy. In April 1997, for example, he notoriously scaled the walls of Lambeth Palace garden with fellow members of *Outrage!* to confront Archbishop Carey and a group of African and Asian bishops who were planning the next Lambeth Conference.[8] The following year, Tatchell and his co-conspirators stormed the pulpit at Canterbury Cathedral while Carey was preaching his Easter sermon.[9] His relationship with Rowan Williams was less abrasive but still cool. In March 2013, Welby's former statements about homosexuality during his ministry in Southam were revealed by the first edition of this biography, *The Road to Canterbury*, and attracted some

---

6   Lambeth Palace press conference, 9 November 2012, opening statement, www. archbishopofcanterbury.org.
7   Lambeth Palace press conference, 9 November 2012, reply to a question.
8   'Gay Rights Protesters Confront Archbishop', *Times*, 21 April 1997, p. 5.
9   'Tatchell is Charged over Pulpit Stunt at Cathedral', *Times*, 13 April 1998, p. 6.

newspaper comment.[10] Tatchell reacted by publishing an open letter to the archbishop on the eve of his enthronement, denouncing his 'harsh homophobic opinions':

> You claim that you are not homophobic but a person who opposes legal equality for LGBT people is homophobic – in the same way that a person who opposes equal rights for black people is racist. ... You say that you are listening to the concerns of the LGBT community but you continue to ignore and reject our claim for equal marriage rights. It does not feel like you are listening. Or perhaps you [are] listening but not hearing?

It was immoral, Tatchell maintained, to sacrifice LGBT rights in order to appease conservative Anglicans and to prevent a split in the Anglican Communion. He had frequently spoken out against the persecution of Christians, and he asked the archbishop to reciprocate by showing 'true moral leadership' in the stand against homophobic discrimination.[11] To diffuse a potentially explosive confrontation, Welby promptly invited Tatchell for a private dialogue. It was the first time Tatchell had entered Lambeth Palace through the front door, though he was wary of walking into an Anglican PR stunt and demanded 'more than tea and sympathy'.[12] During their face-to-face encounter, he urged the archbishop to apologise on behalf of the Church of England for centuries of persecution of gay people. Although it was meant to be off the record, Tatchell quickly issued a press statement summarising their conversation: 'I got the impression that he wants to support gay equality but feels bound by church tradition. ... He struck

10   Andrew Atherstone, *Archbishop Justin Welby: The Road to Canterbury* (London: Darton, Longman and Todd, 2013), pp. 59–60; 'When Archbishop Spoke Out Against Gay Sex and Adoption', *Daily Telegraph*, 8 March 2013, p. 17.

11   'An Open Letter to Justin Welby from Peter Tatchell', 21 March 2013, www.newstatesman.com.

12   'Archbishop Welby to Meet Tatchell', 16 April 2013, www.petertatchellfoundation.org.

me as a genuine, sincere, open-minded person, willing to listen and rethink his position.'[13]

Welby's attitude to homosexual relationships is difficult to pin down, perhaps deliberately so, and is open to a variety of interpretations. The *Independent* called him the 'Ambiguous Archbishop'.[14] He generally avoided the subject in platform speeches, but did give unscripted answers to interview questions when asked. When the interviewers were his friends, like John Mumford, Nicky Gumbel, Mark Melluish, Graham Tomlin and J. John, they declined to put the question, to prevent a media storm.

Most obvious is Welby's consistent opposition to same-sex marriage. The episcopal bench in the House of Lords voted against the Marriage (Same Sex Couples) Bill in June 2013, though in one of the best-attended debates in living memory they were overwhelmed by the strength of support for the bill, which passed its second reading by 390 votes to 148. Welby argued that the bill undermined marriage:

> The result is confusion. Marriage is abolished, redefined and recreated ... The concept of marriage as a normative place for procreation is lost. The idea of marriage as covenant is diminished. The family in its normal sense, predating the state and as our base community of society ... is weakened.

The archbishop did, however, support the concept of civil partnerships because 'It is clearly essential that stable and faithful same-sex relationships should, where those involved want it, be recognised and supported with as much dignity and the same legal effect as marriage.' He acknowledged that the Church of England had not always well served the LGBT communities, expressing his 'sadness and sorrow for that considerable failure', and denounced 'homophobic language' as not only wrong but 'sickening'.[15] Elsewhere Welby described

---

13 'Archbishop Welby is Struggling to Support Equality', 18 April 2013, www.petertatchellfoundation.org.
14 'An Ambiguous Archbishop', *Independent*, 22 March 2013, p. 18.
15 Hansard, House of Lords, 3 June 2013, columns 953–4.

the family as 'the fundamental building block of society ... not just the nuclear family, the extended family, the whole network of family, which goes back before the creation of the state. And that is not something that the Church should experiment with.'[16] He called the bill 'a bad piece of legislation'. 'This is a radical change to one of the most fundamental building blocks of society ... A law that changes marriage from being about covenant to being about contract is a weakening of the glue that holds society together.' Nevertheless he added, 'You can tell, I'm quite uncomfortable. ... I'm still thinking my way through this.'[17]

This hesitation was typical of Welby's public comments, perhaps a deliberate attempt to deflect criticism by suggesting that his views were still a work in progress, and to keep the conversation open. If his opposition to same-sex marriage was clear, his view on same-sex relationships per se was more obscure. For example, interviewed by the BBC he stated that some same-sex partnerships 'are just stunning in the quality of the relationship'.[18] Likewise on LBC radio he affirmed: 'I know plenty of gay couples whose relationships are an example to plenty of other people, and that's something that's very important.' It would be 'completely absurd', he said, to suggest the love between gay couples was somehow less than the love between straight couples: 'I think we need to find ways of affirming the value of the love that is in other relationships without taking away from the value of marriage as an institution.'[19] He tried to articulate his 'fairly nuanced' position for the *Church Times*:

> It's perfectly clear ... that you find relationships within the LGBT communities that are deeply loving, profoundly committed, and stable. It's equally clear that you find some relationships within marriage that are dysfunctional,

16   *Sunday* (Justin Welby interviewed by Trevor Barnes), BBC Radio 4, 17 March 2013.

17   Lawson, 'So Many Crosses to Bear', p. 29.

18   'Justin Welby Speaks of Same-Sex Challenges for Church' (Justin Welby interviewed by Robert Pigott), 21 March 2013, www.bbc.co.uk/news.

19   LBC Radio (Justin Welby interviewed by Iain Dale), 11 March 2013.

damaging, harmful. So the idea that the quality of affection in all straight relationships is always better than in all gay relationships is obviously contrary to the evidence. But it remains absolutely clear that the Christian ideal for the upbringing of children is in a stable relationship between a man and a woman, committed in marriage to one another for life, and to the nurture and support of members of that family.[20]

The archbishop sought to hold in tension both the church's historic teaching that 'marriage is a lifelong and exclusive relationship between one man and one woman', but also the 'essential dignity' of all human beings whatever their sexuality.[21] He argued that the church's pastoral practice must reflect both these truths:

And so when you're dealing with gay couples, or straight couples, people who are cohabiting, people who are married – the numerous different combinations of relationships, former relationships, that there are – you always come to people seeking to show them the love of Christ. And you will deal pastorally with people where they are, because that's how God deals with us, with me.[22]

So there was 'a very big difference', he explained, between Christian ideals and pastoral realities. Asked whether this was the same as turning a blind eye to official Church of England policy, Welby responded: 'It's not a blind eye. It's about loving people as they are and where they are. And you'll find that in every church ... because it imitates the practice and the character of Jesus himself.'[23]

Some wondered, therefore, whether the archbishop was opposed to same-sex marriage but willing somehow to affirm same-sex unions. He did not repeat the blunt language he had

20   Thornton, 'You Don't Have to Agree', p. 19.
21   *Sunday*, 17 March 2013.
22   'Archbishop of Canterbury Enthroned' (Justin Welby interviewed by Eamonn Holmes), Sky News, 21 March 2013.
23   'Archbishop of Canterbury: Love People as They Are' (Justin Welby interviewed by Robert Pigott), 21 March 2013, www.bbc.co.uk/news.

used at Coventry Cathedral ten years earlier, that homosexual practice is 'against the will of God' and 'not permitted by Scripture'. The closest he came to it was in an interview for the *Sunday Times Magazine*:

> I have no sense of moral outrage over sexuality in any particular direction. I'm far too conscious of my own weaknesses to start hurling rocks at people. My understanding of sexual ethics has been that, regardless of whether it's gay or straight, sex outside marriage is wrong. ... The trouble is in the Church we get totally hooked on sexual sin. It's not the thing that most concerns me. People move in together, they have partners, they're not legally married; but there is a profound sense of commitment to each other, which is of intrinsic value.[24]

This classic affirmation that 'sex outside marriage is wrong' needed further glossing when it became legal for people of the same gender to marry. In a phone-in on LBC radio in April 2014, Welby clashed with Ann Widdecombe (former Tory MP), who had converted from Anglicanism to Roman Catholicism in 1993 because in her view the Church of England was 'always ready to sacrifice faith to fashion and creed to compromise'.[25] She pushed the archbishop: 'just answer straightforwardly, is homosexuality wrong?' 'It's a complex question,' he replied. 'People can't help being gay. And every human being's dignity has to be respected. ... And if you put the same question to the pope you get the same answer.' He insisted that the Church of England's teaching was perfectly clear, that sex outside marriage is wrong, and marriage is between a man and a woman. 'I think we just try and say things with a certain amount of charity and respect of the complexity of issues that people in this world face.'[26]

The natural corollary of Welby's theology of human dignity was his opposition to 'homophobia'. This became a repeated

---

24   Lawson, 'So Many Crosses to Bear', p. 29.
25   Ann Widdecombe, *Strictly Ann: The Autobiography* (London: Weidenfeld and Nicolson, 2013), p. 238.
26   LBC Radio (Justin Welby phone-in, with James O'Brien), 4 April 2014.

refrain. Reflecting at General Synod on the bishops' defeat in House of Lords, he observed:

> I am not proposing a new policy, but what I felt then and feel now is that some of what was said by those supporting the Bill was uncomfortably close to the bone. ... We may or may not like it, but we must accept that there is a revolution in the area of sexuality, and we have not fully heard it. The majority of the population rightly detests homophobic behaviour or anything that looks like it – and sometimes they look at us and see what they do not like. I do not like saying that. I have resisted that thought. However, in that debate I heard it, and I could not walk away from it.[27]

As a form of practical action, the archbishop asked the Church of England's Board of Education to update its policies and resources on bullying in schools, specifically to stamp out homophobic bullying. It was not, contrary to press reports, a collaboration with Stonewall (the gay-rights campaigners), though Stonewall was amongst the various specialist organisations consulted for advice on best practice.[28]

In August 2013 the archbishop officially opened the new buildings of the Evangelical Alliance at King's Cross in central London, and in his address warned that the contemporary church made a bad impression 'because we're seen as against things ... we come across too easily as negative'. People often said, for example, 'I don't want to hear about a faith that is homophobic.'[29] Quizzed on this afterwards by Andrew Brown (a journalist at the *Guardian*), Welby was asked whether in retrospect he regretted his vote against the same-sex marriage legislation. Rather than shut down an awkward question, or provide a succinct answer, the archbishop offered some lengthy off-the-cuff musings. He reflected:

27   Justin Welby, 'Presidential Address', *General Synod Report of Proceedings* vol. 44 (July 2013), p. 19.

28   'Stonewall Row', *Church Times*, 29 November 2013, p. 5; letter from John Pritchard, *Church Times*, 6 December 2013, p. 17.

29   'Address by the Archbishop of Canterbury at Official Opening' (video recording), Evangelical Alliance, 28 August 2013, www.eauk.org.

> The church has not been good at dealing with homophobia
> ... in fact we have, at times, as God's people in various places,
> really implicitly or even explicitly supported it, and we have to
> be really, really repentant about that because it is utterly and
> totally wrong. But that doesn't mean that redefining marriage
> is the right way forward ...

He was 'absolutely committed' not to exclude anyone in the
Church of England who took a different view. 'We're not going
to get anywhere by throwing brick bats at each other.' So he
would vote against the legislation again, but was continuing
'to think and listen very carefully'. He concluded:

> We have to face the fact that the vast majority of people under
> 35 think not only that what we're saying is incomprehensible
> but also think that we're plain wrong and wicked, and equate
> it to racism and other forms of gross and atrocious injustice.
> We have to be real about that. I haven't got the answer, and
> I'm not going to jump one way or the other until my mind is
> clear on this. I'm not going to get into the trenches on it.[30]

These comments made front-page headlines and some
believed that Welby was softening his stance. Brown wrote
that the archbishop had grown more adept at handling the
press, but had words of caution: 'the tendency to ramble in
front of an audience is compelling. But anyone with a gift for
hearing what their audience wants to be said, and then saying
it, is going to get into trouble when they are overheard.'[31] It
was typical of Welby to do his thinking in public in this way.
In other interviews he confessed, 'The old rule with me ... is
when I don't know what to say, I talk until I work out what
I need to say.'[32] He realised that 'my old habit .... of thinking
aloud', on various subjects, misled people into assuming he
was stating new policies. Nevertheless, he found it a difficult
habit to break. His status as archbishop meant that 'quite

30   'Question and Answer Session with the Archbishop of Canterbury' (audio recording),
      Evangelical Alliance, 28 August 2013, www.eauk.org.
31   Andrew Brown, 'Welby and the Press: A Progress Report', *Church Times*, 6 September
      2013, p. 18.
32   'Facing the Canon', 13 March 2014.

casual comments .... have far more weight than one wants
them to have'.[33] Challenged during a BBC interview that his
words at the Evangelical Alliance proved he was adopting
'a more Western, liberal interpretation' of sexuality, Welby
quickly and firmly denied it. He explained that he was merely
'commenting on the change in culture, not on my personal
position on the issue. The change in culture is undeniable, it's
a simple fact of the world in which we live', though that did
not mean a change in Church of England teaching.[34]

Each time Welby tackled the subject, his tone was
deliberately reticent and conflicted, recognising the public
strength of feeling and that the church's historic teaching
was increasingly unpalatable. In March 2014, on the eve
of England's first same-sex marriages, he cautiously told a
congregation in Bury St Edmunds that it was one of the few
questions which kept him awake at night:

> It is unbelievably difficult, unbelievably painful and
> unbelievably complicated. ... I haven't got a quick one-liner
> that solves the problem. I wish I had. I would dearly love there
> to be one; there isn't. ... The church does look very bad on
> this issue to many people in this country, particularly younger
> people, and we're mugs if we think anything else. We need to
> be really blunt about that.

Nonetheless he reaffirmed the church's historic understanding
of Scripture that sexual activity is only for heterosexual
marriage. The archbishop called on English Christians to listen
to the global church on this issue and to engage in constructive
dialogue with each other: 'rather than shouting that one side's
homophobic and the other side's betraying the gospel, we need
actually to listen to each other as human beings'.[35]

33   Thornton, 'You Don't Have to Agree', p. 20.
34   *HARDtalk* (Justin Welby interviewed by Zeinab Badawi), BBC News Channel, 27
      January 2014.
35   'Archbishop of Canterbury Speaks about Same-Sex Marriage During Bury Visit'
      (video recording), 29 March 2014, www.buryfreepress.co.uk.

Good Disagreement

'By nature I am a conflict avoider,' Archbishop Welby declared, 'I like to keep my head down and get on with the job.'[36] It was a surprising admission from someone who had spent so much of his ministry in conflict zones where others feared to tread. But he recognised that the path to reconciliation was not to dodge conflict, but 'to go deep into it and face it in its most painful places'.[37] That applied equally to Church of England polemics as to African civil wars. Giles Fraser was one of those who hoped for decisive action, and shortly before Welby's enthronement he gave his impressions of the new archbishop:

> He's tough, streetwise and might turn out to be a real nettle-grasper. ... It's a clever appointment. He's much more conservative than people realise. But only Nixon can go to China and my hope is that it will take a conservative to make the necessary progressive moves.[38]

Welby cautioned that he had 'no magic wand' to solve Anglican conflicts.[39] He was determined not to be pushed around, or to be pressurised into taking sides in partisan disputes. 'It's a rule of thumb that ... most often the main lobbying groups won't be right', he observed. 'Everybody tells you what they're saying is what God's saying. It's not always the case.'[40] Nevertheless, reconciliation was a top priority.

The first nettle which Welby grasped was women bishops. Rowan Williams' last General Synod in November 2012 had ended in debacle and mutual recriminations as the legislation to introduce women bishops fell at the last hurdle. One distressed

---

36   Justin Welby, 'Moving the Frontiers' (blog), 7 March 2013, www.archbishopofcanterbury.org.

37   Justin Welby, 'The Crooked, Straight Path of Reconciliation' (audio version), Faith in Conflict Conference, Coventry, 28 February 2013, www.archbishopofcanterbury.org.

38   McCrum, 'Justin Welby: From Mammon to Man of God'.

39   'Archbishop Compares C of E to Shouting Family', *Church Times*, 1 March 2013, p. 5.

40   Justin Welby, 'Recognising the Prompting of the Holy Spirit When Making Decisions' (August 2013), video recording, www.new-wine.org.

synod member called it 'a train crash of epic proportions'.[41] It looked as if the process had potentially been set back several years, and there were murmurings in the House of Commons that parliament should take decisive action to resolve the impasse if synod would not. Welby quickly got to work and assured MPs that he was addressing the problem as a matter of urgency. His main strategy was to prioritise 'facilitated conversations' to foster mutual listening and civil dialogue. In his final years in office, Rowan Williams had invited small groups from General Synod to Lambeth Palace to discuss their differences. Under Welby this approach was rolled out in a more systematic way, using the professional facilitation skills of David Porter and his team. In February and April 2013 a House of Bishops working party met for conversations with representatives from pressure groups like Forward in Faith, Reform, Church Society and WATCH (Women and the Church), plus other invited individuals. In July 2013 the whole General Synod engaged in the experiment. In a radical departure from the normal synodical procedure of adversarial debate in front of a watching media, the delegates broke into small groups behind closed doors to discuss their feelings and even took part in role play. Porter's protocols for the facilitated conversations were significant in shaping their purpose and tone. The protocols explained: 'How we occupy shared space with those who differ from us is as important as the matter under discussion. ... We seek to be an inclusive space where all views are heard and diversity encouraged.' The emphasis was upon listening sensitively, telling personal stories, accepting the legitimacy of other people's feelings, and remaining committed to a shared future.[42] By November 2013 there was already a new legislative package on the table, again discussed in small groups at synod, and it sailed through the first stages

41   'Church Leader Survives Vote of Confidence over Female Bishops', *Guardian*, 19 January 2013, p. 4.
42   David Porter, 'St Michael's House Protocols: Guidelines for Seminars and Conversations', Coventry Cathedral (November 2011).

of the new process. At his most succinct, Welby affirmed that 'this is the right thing to do, and we need to get on with it'.[43] It seemed likely that he would deliver the first women bishops to the Church of England by 2015, a remarkable turn-around in a few short months. The legislation sought to make some space for opponents of women bishops, the main bone of contention, but the archbishop was unconcerned by the messiness of the situation and the inevitable illogicalities. He told General Synod:

> Let us be clear, it is an untidy Church. It has incoherence. It has inconsistency between dioceses and between different places. It is not a Church that has a simple set of rules that says, 'We do this and do not do that'; it is a Church that says, 'We do this and we do that'. Actually, quite a lot of us do not like that, but we are still going to do it because of love and grace. It is a Church that speaks to the world and says that consistency and coherence are not the ultimate virtues. Holy grace is what we hold to.

Nonetheless he recognised that there would need to be 'a massive cultural change' if the Church of England was really to live out its commitment 'to the flourishing of every tradition'.[44]

The archbishop's favourite metaphor for the Christian church was the family, a concept which profoundly shaped his understanding of Christian disagreements. For example, he told the *Church Times*:

> One of the problems of the Church of England is that we have our arguments very loudly in public. Lots of other groups have the same level of argument, but in infuriated whispers in private. We shout at each other quite a lot. You find families like this: some families argue by yelling; other families sulk,

43   *Good Morning Sunday* (Justin Welby interviewed by Clare Balding), BBC Radio 2, 20 April 2014.
44   Justin Welby, 'Presidential Address', *General Synod Report of Proceedings* vol. 45 (February 2014), pp. 158–9.

silently. It is by no means clear that yelling is worse: it is just rather more obvious.[45]

Welby's commitment to the dysfunctional church family was rooted, in part, in his own childhood experience of being raised in a divided family. Reflecting in August 2013 on the complexities of his father's side of the family, he told a congregation in Barbados:

> Families are strange things. We may get on well or not get on at all. Or it may be, for most of us somewhere in the middle. But once a family exists, whatever we do we cannot escape it, and when that family is the family of God, its future is clear and the only question for each of us is whether we co-operate with what God wants and find all the good things in store for us, or whether we try and hide away, forget the family, and lose sight of our destiny, our hope and our salvation. ... We cannot forget that in every age and every place the church is human, and humans make terrible mistakes and do terrible wrongs. But it is still the family of God.[46]

Likewise preaching in Hong Kong he stated:

> There's an old saying in England, you choose your friends but you're stuck with your family. And believe it or not, you and I are family. We are of the family of God, and you're stuck with me and I'm stuck with you, not just now, not just in this life, but for all eternity – so we'd better get used to each other.[47]

This family framework underpinned Welby's repeated assertion that no one would be 'chucked out' of the Church of England or the Anglican Communion for minority opinions that contradicted official church policy.[48] It was inconceivable that Christians would want anyone to be chucked out of a family.

---

45   'Archbishop Compares C of E to Shouting Family'.

46   Justin Welby, 'Building Communities of Hope', sermon at Christ Church, Barbados, 9 August 2013, www.archbishopofcanterbury.org.

47   Justin Welby, sermon at St John's Cathedral, Hong Kong, 27 October 2013, www. archbishopofcanterbury.org.

48   Macrory, 'Archbishop's Move', p. 62.

Reconciliation, in Welby's theology, meant learning to live with difference. 'It's not exactly startling that we have disagreements,' he said in a BBC interview. 'What I'm trying to do is not to get everyone to agree – because I don't think we're going to agree – it is to try to transform bad disagreement to good disagreement.'[49] Indeed he saw diversity of doctrine as a virtue. He did not want Anglicans to be 'a bunch of clones who all think the same', but people who thought very differently and yet loved each other.[50] Preaching in Iceland in October 2013 at a gathering of the Porvoo Communion (an ecumenical partnership between the Anglican churches of Britain and Ireland with the Lutheran churches of Scandinavia and the Baltic), the archbishop contrasted unity and unanimity:

> Unanimity amongst us is first of all a mirage and secondly a diversion. Unanimity is too busy with checking whether the other person is doing the right thing to hear the call of the widow – unity sees and hears her and puts aside our own preferences to stand in solidarity and cry with her. Unanimity is tidy, it's all organised, and bears no fruit – unity is irregular, confused, relational, it is an improvisation of celebration and lament, of the prayer for justice, and solidarity with the poor. You make it up as you go along.[51]

At the Faith in Conflict Conference he proclaimed:

> Circling the wagons and self-defining ourselves as those who are of one mind against the rest of the world has a noble feeling. Hollywood inspired, it gives us the feeling that this is a good day to die hard – hard of heart and hard in action. By contrast the process of reconciliation seems weak and unprincipled, alienating us from everyone involved in quarrel. I find myself often doubting myself deeply: have I become totally woolly, taken in by the niceness of bad people or bad theology, trapped in an endless quest for illusory peace rather than tough answers? That is a question that all involved in

49   HARDtalk, 27 January 2014.
50   'Archbishop Compares C of E to Shouting Family'.
51   Justin Welby, 'The Widow, the Crook and the Power of Persistence', sermon at Dómkirkjan Cathedral, Reykjavik, Iceland, 21 October 2013, www.archbishopofcanterburyorg.

reconciliation should be asked, and held accountable to, but it is also part of the process.[52]

Rowan Williams had spent much of his archiepiscopate seeking areas of core theological agreement around which Anglicans could coalesce, most notably in the failed Anglican Covenant. Welby's project was different: not the pursuit of theological agreement but learning to live with theological disagreement.

Welby's welcome of diverse opinions extended beyond ecclesial questions like the consecration of women bishops, to the realm of sexual ethics, including homosexuality. Since it was not an issue of Nicene orthodoxy it was not therefore, in his view, a reason for division. He had modelled 'good disagreement' in his public conversation with Adrian Daffern at Coventry Cathedral in 2004 and continued in his conviction that a 'reconciled' church would include contradictory viewpoints. In May 2013 Waheed Alli (media entrepreneur and Labour peer), a gay Muslim, met with Welby to discuss same-sex marriage. Alli argued that the bishops in the House of Lords should not present a united front nor claim to speak for the whole Church of England. Nicholas Holtam (Bishop of Salisbury) was happy to break ranks by criticising current church policy, though he did not have a seat in the Lords. Alli persuaded him to write a public letter in favour of the bill, but he first asked if Holtam would have Welby's blessing. 'Absolutely', the archbishop replied, 'And that goes for any bishop'.[53] In his speech during the debate, Welby praised Holtam's 'strong and welcome contribution', to the consternation of conservative clergy in the Salisbury diocese.[54]

Facilitated conversations had successfully altered the tone of the clash over women bishops, and Welby was keen that the same methodology be applied to Anglican disputes

---

52   Welby, 'The Crooked, Straight Path of Reconciliation' (text version).
53   Oliver Wright, 'I Was Called Sinful and Dirty. And that was in a Lords Debate', *Independent*, 3 June 2013, pp. 22–3. See further, Nicholas Holtam to Waheed Alli, 29 May 2013, www.salisbury.anglican.org.
54   Hansard, House of Lords, 3 June 2013, column 953.

over homosexuality. Sir Joseph Pilling (chairman of the House of Bishops working group on human sexuality) took advice from the archbishop and the working group's report, published in November 2013, was an extended argument for learning to live with disparate interpretations of Scripture. It proposed a two-year process of dialogue within the Church of England aimed at mutual trust and mutual flourishing. It had in view not to settle the substantive issue, but rather 'a facilitated process of listening to each other so the journey can continue in an atmosphere of respect for difference'.[55] Only one member of the working group, Bishop Keith Sinclair (Welby's predecessor at Holy Trinity, Coventry), dissented, arguing that the Bible's teaching on same-sex relationships is clear. He believed that if the report was adopted it would 'cut the Church adrift from her Scriptural moorings and, by depriving her of a prophetic vision, allow her to be swept along by the currents of Western culture'. Sinclair warned that the proposed conversations rested on the 'false premise' that Scripture was inconclusive and that 'the jury is still out' on what Anglicans should teach, a premise he did not accept.[56] The main report quoted Welby several times, thus implicitly aligning the Pilling process with the archbishop's agenda. The College of Bishops also echoed his language when it said the Pilling process was a search for 'good disagreement', and it anticipated facilitated conversations about homosexuality not just within the Church of England, but ecumenically and across the Anglican Communion.[57] At General Synod, Welby rejected the accusation that this approach to reconciliation was 'soft and wishy-washy':

> 'Facilitated conversations' may be – and I feel is – a clumsy phrase, but it has at its heart a search for good disagreement.

---

55 *Report of the House of Bishops Working Group on Human Sexuality* (London: Church House Publishing, 2013), pp. 104–5.
56 'A Dissenting Statement by the Bishop of Birkenhead', in *Report of the House of Bishops Working Group on Human Sexuality*, pp. 131, 137, 141.
57 Statement from the College of Bishops, 27 January 2014, www.churchofengland.org.

It is exceptionally hard-edged, extraordinarily demanding and likely to lead in parts of the world to profound unpopularity and dismissal.

The creation of 'safe space' for dialogue was vital. Indeed the archbishop suggested that, regardless of the outcome, 'the very process is a proclamation of the gospel'.[58]

Political Engagement

Bishop Richard Chartres was optimistic that Welby's new style of leadership would help to shift the Church of England's agenda decisively away from 'this false narrative of division and faction' concerning women bishops and gay marriage, towards compassion for the poor and responsible citizenship.[59] The archbishop recognised that a church bitterly divided made unattractive headlines, 'it is poison to the mind of those who are outside the church – it anesthetizes them against the gospel'.[60] He told the New Wine Conference in July 2013:

> I think one of the things that worries me most is the remorseless power of negative religion in this country. The more we harp on the negative and fail to show love for one another, and for Jesus Christ, to proclaim service to the poor, ministry to the poor, the more we give in to those who oppose the gospel.[61]

Social transformation, by contrast, was a good news story. He observed:

> When the church has spent its time looking inwards and discussing with increasing passion and decreasing unity and common vision what I call the 'below the belt issues',

58   Welby, 'Presidential Address' (February 2014), p. 159.
59   Martin Vander Weyer, 'Delphic Wisdom for Bankers from the Bishop in the Library', *Spectator*, 11 May 2013, p. 28.
60   'An Evening with Justin and Caroline Welby', 27 January 2013.
61   Sermon at New Wine Conference, 29 July 2013.

nobody's interested. When the church in one way or another is seen as engaging with its community, speaking about poverty, challenging the accepted customs of our society, the materialism, suddenly a lot of people are beginning to pay attention. It's happening all over the country.[62]

Therefore it was important to resist the temptation to sort out the church before changing the world. Indeed the church would never be sorted: 'Dream on sunshine, we're human, and that means it'll always be a mess.'[63]

Welby insisted that religious faith was not 'separate and private', or to be kept behind closed doors, but was 'stitched into our public life'.[64] His father was an aspiring Tory MP; his stepfather was a Labour peer. Not surprisingly, perhaps, Welby was 'a classic floating voter'.[65] As archbishop he tried to steer clear of party politics, while nonetheless throwing himself into political engagement. He explained the distinction by pointing to both Scripture and papal encyclicals:

> The point is, the church does not stand for a party. ... There isn't a party-political programme in the Bible. What there is, is a clear and absolute imperative of the common good, of solidarity, of subsidiarity – the great heritage that we have of Catholic social teaching that's come from Rome. And we have to hold on to that. That will overlap with party-political programmes at some point. It's political, not party-political.[66]

Seeking the common good and fighting against injustice were 'absolutely central to what it means to be a Christian. ... Loving God and loving our neighbour go together like the warp and the weft of a piece of fabric.' No amount of 'religious observance or pious comment' could replace the pursuit of justice.[67] He reiterated, 'When I read my Bible I

62   St Mellitus College, 2 December 2013.
63   Interview at New Wine Conference, 29 July 2013.
64   Justin Welby, 'Love Thy Neighbour', *Radio Times*, 11–17 May 2013, p. 9.
65   Moore, 'I Was Embarrassed', p. 19.
66   *Sunday*, 17 March 2013.
67   Justin Welby, speech at Church Urban Fund conference, Stratford, London, 13 November 2013, www.archbishopofcanterbury.org.

find that Jesus commands me to be very outspoken about the pressures on the poor.'[68]

Unlike Rowan Williams, who attended the House of Lords just once a month, Welby made it a high priority in his diary. He enjoyed the cut and thrust of political debate, and focused his energies on issues of social deprivation and economic prosperity. His favourite subjects were banks, remuneration, ethical investment, benefits, credit unions, payday loans and food banks. Some commentators thought this was the wrong remit for an archbishop. One critic complained, 'Welby is junked out on publicity, like some drug-crazed rock star. He should forget his grandstanding over banks and get on with his day job.'[69] The *Independent* said he had 'no business in mainstream politics'.[70] A more sympathetic observer, Andrew Brown, commented: 'It worries me that the Archbishop seems to want to make news. He should learn from his predecessor's unhappy experience that no one cares about opinions that cannot be backed with actions.'[71]

One of Welby's first political interventions as archbishop was a direct challenge to the government's welfare reforms which were being steered through parliament by Iain Duncan-Smith (Secretary of State for Work and Pensions). Forty-three Anglican bishops published an open letter in the *Sunday Telegraph* in March 2013 criticising the Welfare Benefits Up-rating Bill for its disproportionate impact on families, which they argued would push 200,000 children into poverty. Welby gave the bishops his full backing, and declared: 'As a civilized society we have a duty to support those among us who are vulnerable and in need. ... Politicians have a clear choice.'[72] The *Daily Mail* took up the cudgels, retorting that there was

68   *HARDtalk*, 27 January 2014.
69   Quoted in Kellaway, 'As Easy-Going as the AB of C'.
70   'The Church Should Keep to Matters Spiritual', *Independent*, 27 July 2013, p. 36.
71   Andrew Brown, 'Perils of Wanting to Make News', *Church Times*, 25 October 2013, p. 34.
72   'Archbishop Joins Urgent Child Poverty Call', press release, 10 March 2013, www. archbishopofcanterbury.org.

'nothing remotely Christian' about trapping families in welfare dependency and what parents needed most were incentives to go out to work. But its main rebuke was to Welby himself for endorsing 'a woolly socialist attack' upon the government:

> How profoundly depressing. … After years of drift and decline in the Church of England, this paper had high hopes that Mr Welby would offer a clear spiritual lead to a nation in moral decay. By launching this half-baked political attack on Mr Duncan Smith – without even raising the subject when they met last week – the Archbishop has made a truly disappointing start.[73]

Daily Mail columnist, Max Hastings, derided Welby's statement as 'wet enough to earn him a place on a fishmonger's slab'.[74] The archbishop defended his right to question the government, insisting that he was not making 'a great, grand political gesture' but merely raising reasonable concerns shared by many people.[75]

The next major intervention from Lambeth Palace was an attack upon payday lenders. When Rowan Williams sponsored a House of Lords debate in April 2008 about child poverty and tighter controls of credit agencies, it attracted modest attention. But when Welby addressed the same topic it was front-page news. In the Lords he denounced the payday lenders who charged interest rates equivalent to 2,500 per cent, or more, and demanded an end to 'legal usury' on the high street.[76] One of the biggest culprits was Wonga, sometimes charging over 5,000 per cent interest. In an interview for *Total Politics*, published in July 2013, the archbishop happened to mention that he had told the head of Wonga, 'We're not in the business of trying to legislate you out of business, we're

73   'Preaching the Gospel of the Half-Baked Left', *Daily Mail*, 11 March 2013, p. 14.
74   Max Hastings, 'Our Coffers are Empty, Yet Still the Compassion Industry Squeals for More Money', *Daily Mail*, 12 March 2013, p. 14.
75   Justin Welby, 'Universal and Specific' (blog), 11 March 2013, www.archbishopofcanterbury.org.
76   Hansard, House of Lords, 20 June 2013, column 485.

trying to compete you out of business.'[77] This throw-away line captured the public imagination. His idea was for the Church of England, which had local branches in every community, to establish its own credit unions to rival the payday lenders. The archbishop admitted:

> It was a casual comment. I wish I could say that I had a grand strategy, but I didn't. It was an accident. But it was an accident in which God was involved. Because it has created such momentum that there is a great new movement to change the way we do community finance.[78]

In this instance Welby's habit of 'thinking aloud', as he made casual comments to an interviewer, did lead to practical policy decisions. But it was policy created on the move, before wide consultation, and left the staff in the Mission and Public Affairs department at Church House struggling to catch up. The press enjoyed the image of a daring archbishop going into battle single-handed against the corporate leviathan. The *Sun* ran with the front-page headline, 'The Lend is Nigh', and applauded 'his admirable crusade to stop money lenders fleecing desperate families'. 'Bold. Imaginative. Forward-looking', its editorial began, 'Not words often used in the same sentence as Church of England.'[79]

There was temporary embarrassment when it was revealed by the *Financial Times* that the Church Commissioners had invested in Accel Partners, an American venture capital firm which raised funds for Wonga in 2009.[80] The Commissioners' stake, part of their pension provision, was only £85,000 out of their £5 billion portfolio, but it smacked of hypocrisy. Welby won respect for personally facing John Humphrys on the *Today* programme where he frankly confessed the 'very embarrassing' mistake and promised it would not happen

77   Macrory, 'Archbishop's Move', p. 66.
78   Justin Welby, 'The Widow, the Crook and the Power of Persistence'.
79   'Praise Him', *Sun*, 26 July 2013, p. 8; 'Not Wronga', *Sun*, 27 July 2013, p. 8.
80   'Church of England Admits Links to Wonga after Archbishop's Attack', *Financial Times*, 26 July 2013, p. 1.

again.[81] Andrew Brown was impressed by the 'dazzling' way Welby played his hand and thus averted a potential PR disaster. 'Again, this was a matter of tone as much as substance,' observed Brown. 'Instead of adopting the traditional vicarish tone of sounding apologetic even when making assertions ... he managed to sound assertive, even while apologising.'[82] Church of England credit unions would take at least ten years to establish properly, so it was a long-term project, possibly longer that Welby's archiepiscopate, but an example he said of 'putting our money where our mouth is'.[83] He acknowledged he was now under pressure to produce concrete results: 'talk is cheap – and my job involves a lot of it – but the challenge is in delivery ... mere words won't do ... it's actions that count.'[84] The Wonga controversy taught Welby that if the church stopped talking about sex, or arguments about Anglican polity, it was possible to make good headlines. At last the Church of England was saying something which the nation wanted to hear. His comments struck a chord and the flow of usually abusive letters received at Lambeth Palace was largely positive for a change.

A poll for *Prospect* magazine in January 2014 showed a 'precipitous decline' in Christian belief amongst the British population compared with the 1950s, but also a greater acceptance that senior church leaders like the Archbishop of Canterbury should be free to express their views on social and political questions rather than keep to religion. Commenting on the findings, Peter Kellner (president of YouGov) teased that the Church of England should 'abandon religion and become a political party':

> In short, we have more respect for what the Archbishop says about greed and poverty than what he says about faith and

81   *Today*, BBC Radio 4, 26 July 2013.
82   Andrew Brown, 'Splinter from a Wooden Sword', *Church Times*, 2 August 2013, p. 24.
83   Macrory, 'Archbishop's Move', p. 66.
84   Justin Welby, 'Turning Words into Reality' (blog), 12 August 2013, www.archbishopofcanterbury.org.

theology. Perhaps he should consider spending Easter not in a cathedral but at a political conference, pondering resolutions and not the resurrection.[85]

Welby replied pithily with his usual refrain that politics and religion 'cannot be separated'.[86] At the Church Urban Fund's 'Tackling Poverty Together' conference he praised the Christian vision of early twentieth-century social reformers like William Beveridge, R. H. Tawney and Archbishop William Temple who helped to lay the foundations of the Welfare State, and he argued that British society 'cannot be picked apart into secular and spiritual' because Christian ethics were so deeply woven into national life.[87] Likewise he told the National Housing Federation that the dignity of every human being, whatever their economic or social potential and regardless of their faith, was not only a Christian doctrine but also one of the marks of a civilised society:

> Jesus made a point of going wherever there were people in need – he healed people from his own community and outside it, he healed the grateful and the ungrateful, and he healed the downright hostile. He did whatever he could wherever there was need, and he didn't set conditions. That's the example that we're trying to follow. Churches at their best in areas of deprivation are faith-blind: not setting aside our own faith, but blind to the faith positions of those they seek not to do things to, but to share life with and enable and empower.[88]

It was not do-goodery, as he reminded the Methodist Conference. 'We do not want to be useful. We want to be the revolutionary, society-changing, transforming, extraordinary, Spirit-filled Church of God.'[89]

---

85   Peter Kellner, 'Ye of Little Faith', *Prospect* (January 2014), pp. 40–1.
86   Justin Welby, sermon at Canterbury Cathedral, 25 December 2013, www.archbishopofcanterbury.org.
87   Welby, speech at Church Urban Fund, 13 November 2013.
88   Justin Welby, speech at the National Housing Federation conference, Birmingham, 20 September 2013, www.archbishopofcanterbury.org.
89   Justin Welby, speech at Methodist Conference, 10 July 2013, www.archbishopofcanterbury.org.

Chapter 11

A Global Communion

The final years of Rowan Williams' archiepiscopate brought a gloomy stalemate in global Anglican relationships. The formal 'instruments of communion' had proved ineffective, with high-profile boycotts of both the 2008 Lambeth Conference and the 2011 primates meeting, the last in the series. The plans for an Anglican Communion Covenant had hit the buffers. *The Tablet* observed that the new archbishop would need 'superhuman qualities' to meet the formidable challenges of a fissiparous Communion.[1] In one of the bleakest assessments, Archbishop Okoh of Nigeria said that Williams was 'leaving behind a Communion in tatters: highly polarized, bitterly factionalized, with issues of revisionist interpretation of the Holy Scriptures and human sexuality as stumbling blocks to oneness, evangelism and mission all around the Anglican world'. The new man at Lambeth would need to be a leader who 'pulls back the Communion from the edge of total destruction'.[2]

Welby failed in his first attempt to persuade all the primates to gather for informal 'collegial time' after his enthronement. To summon a formal primates meeting would be futile. He therefore developed a new way of working, which placed personal relationships before organisational structures. He aimed to visit every primate in person within his first 18 months, by October 2014, to foster good relations and understand their local context and concerns. It was a highly ambitious target in such a short space of time. Rowan

---

1   'Wanted: Superhuman Anglican', *The Tablet*, 24 March 2012, p. 2.
2   Statement by Archbishop Nicholas Okoh, 18 March 2012.

Williams typically made six international trips each year – two Anglican, two ecumenical and two interfaith. He tended to be reactive, responding to formal requests to visit other Anglican provinces, and did not go where he was not invited. Of the 37 other provinces in the Anglican Communion, eight were never visited during Williams' decade in charge and, significantly, four of these were amongst the most conservative, Nigeria, Uganda, Rwanda and the Southern Cone (South America).[3] When Williams did travel on formal provincial visits it was with an entourage. Welby's approach was radically different. He proactively solicited invitations and travelled with Caroline, only occasionally with a member of staff, staying with the primates in their homes. He wanted to get behind the public personas, position statements and official receptions, to build friendship.

The first primate with whom the Welbys stayed, in May 2013, was Eliud Wabukala in Nairobi, chairman of the GAFCON primates council and a vocal critic of Canterbury. It was a significant gesture of friendship towards a stronghold of conservative Anglicanism and they were warmly welcomed. In honour of their arrival the kerbstones at Bishopsbourne, the Archbishop of Kenya's residence, were freshly painted white. From Nairobi the Welbys flew in company with Wabukala to Dodoma for the enthronement of the new Archbishop of Tanzania, Jacob Chimeledya; and then on to Uganda. Over the next 11 months they visited the primates of Jerusalem and the Middle East (in Cairo), the West Indies (in Barbados), Central America (in Guatemala), Mexico, Hong Kong, Japan, Korea (combined with the tenth assembly of the World Council of Churches in Busan), Sudan, Burundi, Rwanda, Congo, Canada and the United States. Along the way Welby continued to break new ground. He was the first ever serving Archbishop of Canterbury to visit Mexico, for instance. The visit to South Sudan in January 2014 was particularly harrowing. That new

3   Interview with Rowan Williams, 13 March 2014.

nation had spiralled into brutal civil war, leaving thousands dead and hundreds of thousands displaced from their homes. The Welbys were advised not to travel but were determined to go to support the local churches. During the trip they were flown by the Mission Aviation Fellowship from Juba to Bor, capital of Jonglei state, a city in ruins with buildings burned to the ground and corpses lying unburied on the streets. At St Andrew's Cathedral, the archbishop was asked to bless a mass grave before they buried 5 clergy and 20 lay leaders whose bodies were in white bags at his feet.[4] It was 'a profoundly shattering visit'. On the same trip he travelled to the Congo and a camp for 25,000 internally displaced people which he described, in the style of Dante's *Inferno*, as 'the last circle of hell', but he encouraged them that 'Jesus Christ is the same yesterday, today and forever'.[5]

GAFCON

A confidential briefing sent by Wabukala to his fellow GAFCON primates in April 2013, shortly after Welby's enthronement, argued that the heart of Welby's approach to Anglican unity was 'reconciliation without repentance'. His experience in war zones, the briefing maintained, had led him into 'a confusion of categories in which theological differences about truth claims are treated as if they are like civil, industrial or political conflicts. The essential doctrinal and moral truths of the Christian faith are clearly not matters that can be negotiated in this way.'[6] Therefore when the second

---

4   'MAF Flies Archbishop to War-Torn Community', 5 February 2014, www.
     maf-uk.org; Justin Welby, sermon to General Synod, 11 February 2014, www.
     archbishopofcanterbury.org.
5   'Facing the Canon', 13 March 2014.
6   'Archbishop Justin Welby: Questions and Concerns' (briefing to GAFCON primates),
     April 2013.

GAFCON conference was summoned to Nairobi in October 2013 it laid particular emphasis on the need for repentance before reconciliation, drawing lessons from the East African Revival. There were over 1,300 delegates from 27 Anglican provinces. By far the largest contingent was Nigeria with 470 delegates, including 150 bishops, followed by Uganda with 176 delegates. Archbishop Ntagali of Uganda wrote:

> We have a new Archbishop of Canterbury who is born again and has a testimony. I have personally met him and I like him very much. But, the problems in the Communion are still there, and they don't change just because there is a new global leader. In fact ... the crisis has deepened.[7]

Welby made a flying visit to Kenya the day before the conference began, partly to offer condolences after the recent terrorist attacks by Somali militants on Nairobi's Westgate shopping mall which had left 67 dead. He also met with the GAFCON leadership and preached in All Saints Cathedral, exhorting the congregation to keep the Bible at the centre of the church's life. Concerning global Anglican relationships, the archbishop declared:

> I have thought and said for a long time that there is a need for new structures in the Anglican Communion. ... We need a new way of being together as the Communion, a way that reflects the twenty-first century and not the old colonial pattern. ... We must have a structure for the future that is not for ourselves, for the power of some middle-aged English clergyman based in London ... but as in the Acts of the Apostles so that the work of declaring the gospel may go forward and that many people may become disciples of Jesus Christ. We want a world won for Christ.

He went on to address the church's perennial struggles over power, sex and money. Welby reminded his Kenyan audience that he had spoken against same-sex marriage in the British parliament 'at great personal cost' and had become 'the object

7   'Ugandan Primate Calls for GAFCON Support', 14 August 2013, www.gafcon.org.

of much hatred'. He had done so 'because we seek to honour marriage, not because we hate or fear anyone, whatever their sexuality. To hate or fear is not the teaching of Scripture.' He called on his hearers to repent of the ways in which they were dishonouring marriage, whether through violence, lack of respect, adultery or pornography, since Christians should 'not pretend that we are right and the rest of the world alone sins'.[8]

The GAFCON conference focused primarily on evangelism, education, family life, socio-political engagement, and lessons from the suffering church. Nevertheless, the future of Anglicanism was never far from the surface. In his welcome speech, Wabukala told the delegates, 'we're in a spiritual battle for the future, not just of Anglicanism, but of the entire Christian faith', so it was time for the GAFCON movement to commit itself to obedient action.[9] Miguel Uchoa (Bishop of Recife, a conservative breakaway from the Anglican Episcopal Church of Brazil) proclaimed, 'never forget that too much caution – Anglican caution – is the reason why we are here'.[10] Likewise Peter Jensen (former Archbishop of Sydney) observed that the old structures of the Communion 'could not contain the powerful new wine of today's confessional Anglicanism'. He announced that GAFCON was 'a new way of being Anglican, a way which insists on standards of belief and behaviour, a way which does not need to go through Canterbury to be Anglican'.[11] This ecclesiology might have surprised Welby who, when asked in March 2014 what makes somebody an Anglican, explained succinctly that Anglicans are Christians who have 'a link with the Archbishop of Canterbury'.[12]

Although Welby did not attend GAFCON itself, he sent video greetings, saying he was 'so thrilled' the conference

---

8   Justin Welby, sermon at All Saints Cathedral, Nairobi, 20 October 2013, video recording, www.anglicanink.com.
9   Welcome by Eliud Wabukala, GAFCON, 21 October 2013.
10   Miguel Uchoa, exposition of Ephesians 6, GAFCON, 26 October 2013.
11   Opening remarks by Peter Jensen, GAFCON, 21 October 2013.
12   'Facing the Canon', 13 March 2014.

was taking place. He spoke of the need for 'confidence in the gospel' but also for contextual theology which allowed for different approaches to moral questions in different parts of the globe:

> To carry out the task of telling people about Jesus Christ, we need to be a Church that is holy. And for us as individuals and for us as churches right round the world that is always a massive challenge. We all live in different contexts and the challenge overlaps but is slightly different wherever we live. We are dealing with very rapid changes of culture in the Global North and the issue of sexuality is a very important one. How we respond rightly to that – in a way that is holy, truthful and gracious – is absolutely critical to our proclamation of the gospel. ... Wherever we are, there's a different context; but wherever we are, in our own context, in the right way, we have to live as a Church that is holy.

Welby also reiterated the challenge of Christian unity, not unanimity, 'that we demonstrate by our love for one another that Jesus is the Son of God and therefore people are drawn to believe in him'. He concluded:

> I pray for you this week that you will meet Jesus afresh with elation and joy and celebration; that you will hear his voice; and that you will find the determination, together with all other Christians, in passionate unity and love for one another, expressing disagreement graciously yet with powerful truth, to proclaim that Jesus Christ is Lord and there is no other.[13]

The archbishop's video message received a lukewarm reception amongst GAFCON delegates. It was criticised from the platform by William Taylor (rector of St Helen's, Bishopsgate), part of the Church of England delegation, who wondered aloud what video greeting the Apostle Paul would have sent. No doubt, like Welby, the apostle would have smiled warmly, expressed his regret at being absent, and exhorted them to holiness and unity, said Taylor, but he would also

13   Justin Welby, message to GAFCON, 23 October 2013, www.archbishopofcanterbury. org.

have insisted 'that where churches or bishops or dioceses or provinces are seeking to deceive us with empty words into the shameful behaviour of disobedience – *do not be partners with them*'.[14] Another conservative commentator, Professor Gerald Bray, dismissed Welby's message as 'decidedly anaemic'. He recognised that the archbishop 'means well' and that 'his heart is with GAFCON in many ways', but exhorted him to stand up and be counted.[15]

The Nairobi Communiqué issued by GAFCON reiterated that Anglican divisions would not be healed without 'a change of heart from those promoting the false gospel', and promised to defend those marginalised from their dioceses because they were 'standing for apostolic truth'. To that end it formally recognised a new initiative in the Archbishop of Canterbury's own backyard, the Anglican Mission in England (AMiE), as 'an expression of authentic Anglicanism both for those within and outside the Church of England'. The draft communiqué thanked Welby for his video message, but the final version thanked him for sending a video message, a subtle distinction. The draft also commended Welby for opposing same-sex marriage in the House of Lords, but this was deleted because some delegates felt his statements on the subject had not been sufficiently robust. Reporting back to the Church of England's General Synod, Welby summarised his encounter with the GAFCON primates as 'a great pleasure and, as always, an education'. Although the views expressed about the Anglican Communion, and about himself, were 'not invariably warm and cuddly', he remained encouraged.[16]

14   William Taylor, exposition of Ephesians 5:1 – 6:9, GAFCON, 25 October 2013, www.gafcon.org.
15   Gerald Bray, 'A Canterbury Tale', *Churchman* vol. 127 (Winter 2013), p. 292.
16   Welby, 'Presentation' (November 2013), p. 3.

Lessons from Virginia

In May 2012, while still Bishop of Durham, Welby attended a lunch at Holy Trinity Brompton, hosted by Nicky Gumbel, to meet two Anglican clergymen from Virginia. He went at the request of Rowan Williams, and found the meeting 'emotional ... profound, God's very presence was around us, we sensed the power of God'.[17] The clerics in question were Tory Baucum (rector of Truro Church, Fairfax, Virginia) and Shannon Johnston (Bishop of Virginia), on opposite sides of the rift in North American Anglicanism.

Baucum was ordained in The Episcopal Church in 1989 and served his early ministry in the dioceses of Arkansas and West Missouri. Like Welby, he was an early adopter of the Alpha Course and helped introduce it to the congregation of St Andrew's, Kansas City, where he was an associate minister for evangelism. In 1995 St Andrew's hosted one of America's first Alpha conferences led by Nicky Gumbel and Sandy Millar. Baucum joined the faculty of Asbury Theological Seminary, a Methodist seminary in Kentucky, but continued to travel widely teaching Alpha. After the consecration of Gene Robinson, he was transferred by the Bishop of West Missouri and licensed in 2005 by Bishop Chartres of London for his work as an Alpha missioner in the United States, which angered the local Bishop of Lexington. Baucum stood unsuccessfully for election as Bishop of Albany in 2006 (one of TEC's more conservative dioceses) and the following year was appointed rector of Truro, a large charismatic congregation. It had seceded from TEC to join the Convocation of Anglicans in North America (CANA), a missionary initiative sponsored by the Church of Nigeria, and in 2009 was subsumed into ACNA. Baucum's associate rector, Tim Mayfield, was an old friend of Welby's from HTB days who served a summer placement with him at Southam while training for ordination.[18]

17   Justin Welby, 'Pentecost Sermon' (27 May 2012), www.durham.anglican.org.
18   Tim Mayfield, 'What Made Me Decide to Become a Vicar?', SPCN (August 1998).

On his appointment to Truro, Baucum discovered 'a cataract of litigious rage' between congregation and diocese, and the congregation was forced to relinquish its buildings after losing an acrimonious legal dispute.[19] Nevertheless, in early 2011 the rector reached out to Bishop Johnston and the two men began to meet each month to pray together and work towards reconciliation, despite widespread criticism from their natural allies. Baucum explained his rationale:

> I still love the Episcopal Church, I've grown to love Shannon, I do consider him a friend, I do consider him to be a brother – but a brother who I think has taken a wrong turn. That's not the same thing as ceasing to be Christian. ... He does worship the same resurrected Christ that I worship, and believe the same Nicene faith that I believe. There's a lot of common ground that I can work with. ... I'm completely committed to doctrinal orthodoxy, I totally believe it, but I'm equally committed to relational orthodoxy. ... I think it really does matter how we view our theological opponent. Even if you don't think they're a brother, they're still made in the image of God and sometimes that isn't on display in our rhetoric.[20]

Welby was impressed by the courage of this Virginian relationship-building and wrote in public support: 'Division, dislike and even hatred are the quickest ways to kill churches. The first to leave is the Spirit of God. Reconciliation and modeling difference without enmity to a world in desperate need of it is both healing spirituality and effective testimony to Christ.'[21] In his Pentecost sermon at Durham Cathedral in May 2012, he argued that one of the chief ministries of the Holy Spirit was to bring unity amongst separated Christians, repeating his favourite motto, 'diversity without enmity'. Because 'self-centredness and sin' had seeped into the church it was habitually divided, whereas Christians should be

---

19   Tory Baucum, 'Coventry in Retrospect: A Personal Reflection', 4 March 2013, www. truroanglican.com.

20   Tory Baucum and Shannon Johnston interviewed by Bill Marsh, Faith in Conflict Conference, Coventry, 26 February 2013, www.coventrycathedral.org.uk.

21   'The Path of Peace: A Precondition of Evangelistc Fruitfulness', 18 September 2012, www.truroanglican.com.

modelling to the world a godly pattern of 'disagreeing in love, and settling our disputes in the unity of the Spirit'. He pointed to Baucum and Johnston as an example of how it should be done.[22]

During the TEC General Convention of July 2012, Welby contributed to *Center Aisle*, the Virginia diocesan journal, offering an antidote to Anglican divisions. He lamented that 'We seem to spend a very high proportion of our time examining in more and more grisly detail the reasons and rationales for our separation.' Instead he argued that reconciliation is achieved not by endless debate, but principally by mission because it

> causes us to look outwards, away from those things that divide us, and to find ourselves shoulder to shoulder with others with whom we may disagree profoundly but with whom we share one unutterably precious thing – that we both love Jesus Christ and for His sake we are doing what we are doing. ... The more we are engaged in these works of mission, carrying in word and action the Good News of Jesus Christ to a world that is more and more in need of Him, the more we find ourselves regarding those with whom we disagree as fellow Christians, who may be wrong but with whom we are called to live, whose love we receive and to whom we owe such love.

Again he praised the model of Baucum and Johnston and quoted a phrase from his mentor Sandy Millar, 'The miracle of the church is not that like-minded people agree but extremely unlike-minded people love each other while managing somehow to live in common service to Christ.' In short, Welby announced: 'If you want to get together, get on with mission, together.'[23]

Baucum was naturally delighted with Welby's appointment as Archbishop of Canterbury, and singled out Welby's desire 'to heal relational wounds', observing that he 'relates to people

---

22   Welby, 'Pentecost Sermon'.
23   Justin Welby, 'The Answer to Division in the Anglican Communion is Mission', *Center Aisle* (9 July 2012), www.centeraisle.net.

out of an optimism of grace rather than a psyche draining, soul sucking hermeneutic of suspicion'.[24] The two Americans spoke about their relationship at the Faith in Conflict Conference at Coventry Cathedral in February 2013, which Welby hailed again as a model of 'transformed conflict'.[25] A few weeks later they returned to England as guests at his enthronement. Ironically, however, that very month the plug was pulled on Baucum and Johnston's tête-à-têtes, because the bishop's commitment to Nicene orthodoxy was compromised when he allowed John Dominic Crossan, a radical New Testament theologian, to give a series of addresses in the diocese. The two-year Virginia experiment was at an abrupt end, but it lost none of its lustre for Welby.

In March 2014 the archbishop appointed Baucum as a Six Preacher at Canterbury Cathedral, citing his commitment to scholarship, evangelism and reconciliation. To grant such an honour to a clergyman from ACNA provoked celebration and consternation in equal measure. Archbishop Robert Duncan hailed it as 'historically significant', and attended Baucum's installation at Canterbury almost exactly a year after he had missed out on Welby's enthronement.[26] Baucum himself had prophesied that with Welby at Lambeth, ACNA would be recognised as in formal relationship with the Church of England, and thus the wider Anglican Communion, within a decade.[27] That was precisely what alarmed ACNA's opponents. A group calling themselves the Progressive Episcopalians of Pittsburgh urged Welby to rescind the appointment which they denounced as 'an affront' to TEC and 'a sop' to the

24   Tory Baucum, 'Why I am Grateful for Bishop Welby's Appointment', 9 November 2012, www.truroanglican.com.
25   Justin Welby, 'Moving the Frontiers' (blog), 7 March 2013, www.archbishopofcanterbury.org.
26   'Canterbury Appoints Anglican Church in North America Priest to Cathedral Post', press release, 16 January 2014, www.anglicanchurch.net.
27   Tory Baucum, 'The Inaugural Service of Archbishop Welby', 24 March 2013, www.truroanglican.com.

Church of Nigeria.[28] Interrogated at General Synod, the archbishop explained that the appointment was his personal decision and had 'no implications in itself as to ecclesial relationships'.[29] Perhaps in an attempt to balance things up, he spoke effusively of Katharine Jefferts Schori in February 2014 when she was granted an honorary Doctor of Divinity degree by the University of Oxford. He praised her 'remarkable gifts of intellect and compassion, which she has dedicated to the service of Christ', and held her up as 'a powerful model for women seeking to pursue their vocations in the church'.[30]

Walking the Precipice

Preaching in Monterrey in Mexico in August 2013, on the feast day of the seventeenth-century divine Jeremy Taylor, Archbishop Welby quoted from Taylor's classic treatise on religious toleration, *The Liberty of Prophesying* (1647). Offering an impromptu history lesson, he explained that during the English Civil War varieties of religious belief had been suppressed, and warned:

> I sometimes worry that as Anglicans we are drifting back in that direction. Not consciously, of course, but in an unconscious way that is more dangerous. Like a drunk man walking near the edge of a cliff, we trip and totter and slip and wander, ever nearer to the edge of the precipice. It is a dangerous place, a narrow path we walk as Anglicans at present. On one side is the steep fall into an absence of any core beliefs, a chasm where we lose touch with God, and thus we rely only on ourselves and our own message. On the other side there is a vast fall into a ravine of intolerance and cruel exclusion. It is for those who

---

28   Elizabeth N. Stifel (vice-president of Progressive Episcopalians of Pittsburgh) to Justin Welby, 23 January 2014, www.progressiveepiscopalians.org.

29   *General Synod Report of Proceedings* vol. 45 (February 2014), p. 47.

30   'Archbishop Congratulates Bishop Katharine Jefferts Schori on Honorary Oxford Degree', press release, 7 February 2014, www.archbishopofcanterbury.org.

claim all truth, and exclude any who question. When we fall into this place, we lose touch with human beings and create a small church, or rather many small churches – divided, ineffective in serving the poor, the hungry and the suffering, incapable of living with each other, and incomprehensible to those outside the church.

He declared that 'the Anglican Communion's great vocation as bridge builder is more needed than ever. ... So what do we do? Archbishops and their wives can go round the world trying to encourage people to be nice, but it does not really work.' The answer he averred was to 'walk in the light': 'There must not be politics in dark corners, but love expressed in the light, even love expressing difference. In that light we will be secure enough to be churches that reach out, serve the poor, and draw others to light, as a lighted house draws the weary traveller.'[31] This theme was developed further in a sermon in Hong Kong two months later. In answer to his own rhetorical questions, 'Why are things so bad? Why is our church divided? Why is our Anglican Communion not in agreement?', Welby issued a call for repentance in the manner of an Old Testament prophet:

> You have sinned, and sin has results – and the only way out of them is repentance; it is to turn round and go in the opposite direction. ... Repentance is when you know you're going the wrong way and, rather than going on, you turn round and go back and take the way that God has shown you. We are to be a repentant church.[32]

However, the archbishop did not go on to elucidate which particular sins he had in mind as responsible for Anglican divisions, nor did he name those guilty of politicking in the shadows. But he made it clear that he wanted to encourage a variety of Anglican expressions and to navigate a safe path

31   Justin Welby, 'Walk into the Light', sermon at Hotel Quinta Real, Monterrey, Mexico, 13 August 2013, www.archbishopofcanterbury.org.
32   Justin Welby, sermon at St John's Cathedral, Hong Kong, 27 October 2013, www.archbishopofcanterbury.org.

between the extremes. He appeared to apportion blame equally to both sides.

All eyes were on Welby in the hope that he could bring a breakthrough in resolving the Anglican crisis, perhaps by redefining the terms of the debate. He agreed that the structures of the Anglican Communion needed 'to flex and adapt' to ensure that they were 'not simply driven by the imperial accident of history'.[33] For a generation the Communion's centre of gravity had been shifting from the West to the Global South. In 1950 there were just 12 Anglican provinces, inhabited largely by the British and their relatives (England, Wales, Scotland, Ireland, the United States, Canada, Australia, New Zealand, South Africa and the West Indies, as well as China and Japan). By 1980 there were 27 provinces, rising to 38 by 1998. By the 1990s there were more Anglicans in Nigeria than the whole of Europe and North America put together.[34] Although Canterbury was the oldest see, established in the sixth century, the role of the archbishop as an 'instrument of communion' for a global network of self-governing churches in the twenty-first century was increasingly questioned. Welby resisted the suggestion that he should exercise global authority. One of his favourite catchphrases was 'I am not the pope'.[35] He made it clear, for example, that he had no intention of telling TEC 'how to do their business'.[36] When lecturing at a peace conference in Oklahoma City in April 2014 he made a special point of thanking Katharine Jefferts Schori and the local diocesan bishop for permission to minister 'in their patch'.[37] The same rule applied in all other Anglican provinces, where Welby had

33   Thornton, 'You Don't Have to Agree', p. 19.
34   Peter Brierley, 'The Anglican Communion and Christendom', in Timothy Bradshaw (ed.), *Grace and Truth in the Secular Age* (Grand Rapids: Eerdmans, 1998), pp. 15–37; Bruce Kaye, *An Introduction to World Anglicanism* (Cambridge: Cambridge University Press, 2008).
35   Cole Moreton, 'Sometimes I Think: This is Impossible', *Sunday Telegraph*, 20 April 2014, p. 17.
36   Lambeth Palace press conference, 9 November 2012, reply to a question.
37   Justin Welby, speech at Reclaiming the Gospel of Peace Conference, Oklahoma City, 10 April 2014, www.archbishopofcanterbury.org.

no right to interfere in their affairs. 'The church works best when it works locally', he affirmed. 'We need to ensure that we do not try and centralize. Command and control just is biblically wrong, administratively useless and strategically vain.'[38] Nevertheless, he did not want to preside over the break-up of the Anglican Communion, which he believed still had potential to be 'a source of remarkable blessing to the world'.[39] After one international visit, Welby reflected: 'The Anglican Communion is extraordinary – a wonderful gift to the world Church. I say that from the bottom of my heart.'[40] In particular he reiterated that the ministry of reconciliation was 'one of the charisms of the Communion', a special Anglican calling, though sadly a charism not always evident.[41]

Although Welby had no formal authority outside England he was painfully aware that every statement he uttered was scrutinised by Anglicans around the world. Decisions taken by the Church of England had 'an impact on Christians we've never heard of far away'.[42] For example, even in South Sudan, amidst the trauma of civil war, his episcopal hosts wanted to quiz him about the Pilling Report.[43] Therefore he appealed for Anglican provinces in the West not to make unilateral decisions without appreciating their impact on other parts of the Communion. This was put most sharply during a phone-in on LBC radio in April 2014. An Anglican school chaplain, Kes Grant, rang to ask the archbishop why the blessing of same-sex marriages could not be left to the conscience of individual clergy in the Church of England. He replied that such actions in England would be 'absolutely catastrophic' for Christians in Africa, referring to the mass grave near Jos where he had wept with traumatised relatives in April 2010, an experience that 'burns itself into your soul'. Those Nigerian Christians

38   St Mellitus College, 2 December 2013.
39   Lambeth Palace press conference, 9 November 2012, opening statement.
40   Justin Welby, 'Listen to their Voices of Pain', *Church Times*, 5 July 2013, p. 13.
41   St Mellitus College, 2 December 2013.
42   St Mellitus College, 2 December 2013.
43   Reported by John Pritchard, *ad clerum* (diocese of Oxford), 25 February 2014.

had been murdered by their neighbours, he suggested, as an unintended consequence of decisions about homosexuality made by the church 'far, far away in America'. He was worried that similar pronouncements from Lambeth Palace might lead to further violence against African Anglicans.[44] He later explained that he did not mean Anglicans in the West should stop doing what was morally right because it would cause trouble elsewhere – that would be 'moral blackmail' – but he was trying to emphasise the Anglican Communion's interconnectedness.[45]

There were already signs that conservative Anglican provinces felt the need to distance themselves from Welby, as they had from Rowan Williams before him. When Welby threw his weight behind 'facilitated conversations' on homosexuality, recommended by the Pilling Report, Archbishop Wabukala replied from Nairobi:

> As with 'Continuing Indaba', without a clear understanding of biblical authority and interpretation, such dialogue only spreads confusion and opens the door to a false gospel because the Scriptures no longer function in any meaningful way as a test of what is true and false.[46]

The Archbishops of Canterbury and York were under pressure in England to speak out against the anti-homosexuality legislation being debated by the parliaments of Nigeria and Uganda, so they wrote a brief letter to the presidents of those nations in January 2014 and to all the Anglican primates. It quoted from the primates' own Dromantine Communiqué of 2005 with its unreserved commitment to pastoral care and friendship towards homosexual people, denouncing their victimisation as 'anathema'.[47] In effect it was a rebuke to two African presidents over the heads of the African archbishops.

44   LBC Radio, 4 April 2014.
45   Cole Moreton, 'The Deadly Dilemma', *Daily Telegraph*, 19 April 2014, p. 27.
46   Eliud Wabukala to the Global Fellowship of Confessing Anglicans, 29 January 2014, www.gafcon.org.
47   'Archbishops Recall Commitment to Pastoral Care and Friendship for All, Regardless of Sexual Orientation', 29 January 2014, www.archbishopofcanterbury.org.

Archbishop Ntagali swiftly reminded the English archbishops that the Dromantine Communiqué also reaffirmed Resolution 1.10 of the 1998 Lambeth Conference, which taught that 'homosexual practice is incompatible with Scripture' and rejected the blessing of same-sex unions. Just as the Church of Uganda had broken with TEC and the Church of Canada, Ntagali warned that it may no longer 'be able to maintain communion with our own Mother Church', the Church of England, if Welby and Sentamu did not 'step back from the path they have set themselves on'.[48] In similar tone, Wabukala proclaimed:

> The good advice of the Archbishops of Canterbury and York would carry much more weight if they were able to affirm that they hold, personally, as well as in virtue of their office, to the collegial mind of the Anglican Communion. At the moment I fear that we cannot be sure. Regrettably, their intervention has served to encourage those who want to normalize homosexual lifestyles in Africa and has fuelled prejudice against African Anglicans. [49]

By these interventions Wabukala won plaudits in Kenya from the Islamic community. For example, a Muslim in Mombasa wrote to the national press, praising Wabukala's stand against Canterbury and urging 'all African nations to reject this cultural abomination with the vehemence it deserves'.[50] When Sentamu visited Butere in western Kenya in February 2014, to celebrate the centenary of the Christian gospel arriving in the region, several of the local bishops boycotted him.

The interdependence of the Anglican Communion, and Welby's role as a lynchpin in these global relationships, meant that he was always speaking to several audiences at once. The

---

48 'Archbishop Stanley Ntagali Comments on Uganda's Anti-Homosexuality Bill, the Church of England's "Pilling Report", and the Open Letter from the Archbishops of Canterbury and York', press release, 30 January 2014, www.churchofuganda.org.
49 Eliud Wabukala, 'A Response to the Statement by the Archbishops of Canterbury and York', 31 January 2014, www.gafcon.org.
50 'Let's Reject Attempts to Defile Africanism', letter from Sharif Hafidh, *Sunday Nation* (Nairobi), 16 February 2014, p. 14.

Pastoral Guidance on Same-Sex Marriage, issued by his own House of Bishops in February 2014, which banned Church of England clergy from entering same-sex marriages or blessing them, was not only intended for an English readership. One of the reasons it was rushed out so quickly, was that Welby and David Porter were travelling to Cairo the next day to meet with the steering committee of the Global South primates, and they needed a document to placate them.[51] Although Welby's fiercest critics came from Africa, he refused to criticise in return and persistently praised them for their firm commitment to Christian discipleship. He called the Anglican Church of Nigeria 'an extraordinary powerhouse',[52] and singled out Nigeria, Kenya and Uganda as 'courageous Churches ... They are not sinless but they are heroic.'[53]

51   'Cairo Meeting Boosts Welby', *Church of England Newspaper*, 28 February 2014, p. 1.
52   *Newsday*, BBC World Service, 6 January 2014.
53   Welby, 'Presidential Address' (February 2014), p. 160.

Chapter 12

⟨⟨⟨⟩⟩⟩

Speaking for Jesus

Archbishop Welby made it a personal rule, whenever speaking on a public platform or in interview, always to talk about Jesus Christ. With access to the great and the good in public life, and a score of speaking engagements every week, he had 'huge opportunity to talk about Jesus with everyone and anyone, at any time, always'.[1] Indeed he saw it as his responsibility as Archbishop of Canterbury 'to enable not just faith, but faith in Jesus Christ, to be at the centre of our conversation, and that will inevitably be controversial, because Jesus was enormously controversial and remains so'.[2]

This emphasis upon Jesus ran right through every part of Welby's ministry, from his days as a junior curate in Chilvers Coton to his global role as *primus inter pares* of the Anglican Communion. Whether running children's holiday clubs, revitalising the ministry of a local parish church, teaching the Alpha Course in Africa, launching Fresh Expressions in a cathedral, or reimagining 'parish share' in a diocese, it all came back to Jesus. When Welby spoke of reconciliation, as he did very frequently, between African tribes or Anglican church parties, Jesus was again the recurring theme – first receiving reconciliation with God through the cross of Christ, and then ministering that grace to others as 'reconciled reconcilers'. His desire to be a risk-taking archbishop, a dominant theme at every stage of his development, had the same Christ-centred underpinning. For example, preaching at Canterbury Cathedral at Easter 2014 he rearticulated the

---

1   St Mellitus College, 2 December 2013.
2   *Songs of Praise*, 24 March 2013.

motto first developed for Liverpool Cathedral, now applied to the universal church: 'The church is to be a safe place to do risky things in Christ's service.' To be a risk-taker was to imitate Jesus who was anointed by a prostitute in the face of religious disapproval: 'when it came to a choice between the righteousness of the graveyard and the warm heat of repentant sin, Jesus was without hesitation. He does not pull his punches, but takes the risks of being anointed and loved by a sex worker.' Welby called for Christians to be 'a people of risk-taking generosity not defensive fear', 'God's salvation makes sense to us and to the world when we become a risk-taking, outward-facing church. Fear corrodes us, the adrenalin of risk draws us close in to Christ.'[3]

As a natural evangelist, Welby looked for every opportunity to proclaim faith in Jesus, one of his central priorities as archbishop. Trained in the HTB school he talked often about church growth, a good news story in more senses than one. He saw it as entirely normal. 'All the churches I have been in, have been a member of, or for that matter been involved in leading, have grown', he said, 'and I know an awful lot of rapidly growing churches. You can do it.'[4] Or again, 'I've always been part of growing churches, and it's not that difficult.'[5] Pithy media comments like this naturally got him into hot water. When discussing the state of the Church of England on Radio 4 in December 2013, the archbishop acknowledged that there were some struggling congregations and that attendances were falling in some places, yet added: 'But the reality is that where you have a good vicar you will find growing churches.'[6] It was an unguarded statement, for which he apologised in General Synod, but it revealed his default assumption about

---

3   Justin Welby, sermon at Maundy Thursday Chrism Service, Canterbury Cathedral, 17 April 2014, www.archbishopofcanterbury.org.

4   Macrory, 'Archbishop's Move', p. 66.

5   'Archbishop of Canterbury: Love People as They Are' (Justin Welby interviewed by Robert Pigott), 21 March 2013, www.bbc.co.uk/news.

6   *Today*, BBC Radio 4, 31 December 2013.

the impact of good leadership.[7] Vicars from static or shrinking churches saw it as a slight on their own ministries. One cleric pointedly observed that by the same logic shrinking dioceses presumably meant a lack of good bishops.[8] Welby's apparent obsession with numbers also drew criticism. 'Numbers mean doodly-squit in the church', insisted Martyn Percy (Principal of Ripon College Cuddesdon), 'Yet we live a culture that is obsessed by measuring things numerically, and judging success from this. ... God's maths is different from ours.'[9]

Nevertheless Welby was determined to promote evangelism with results which could be measured. He spoke at General Synod of the need for a 'fierce determination' not to allow evangelism to be squeezed off the church's agenda.[10] In November 2013, within days of each other, Pope Francis issued an apostolic exhortation, *Evangelii Gaudium* ('The Joy of the Gospel') on the centrality of missional outreach, and General Synod renewed its commitment to 'intentional evangelism'.[11] Welby saw this happy coincidence as a message from the Holy Spirit to the church, 'Go out there with the gospel. Carry the gospel into the world around. Do not hold back. We have the best news there is.'[12] The two archbishops set up a new Task Group on Evangelism to hold the Church of England to this priority and to promote fruitful evangelistic initiatives.

Archbishop Welby confessed that he was 'not a natural optimist'. Indeed, taking a leaf from A. A. Milne's *Winnie-the-Pooh*, 'a lot of people say I'm a sort of Eeyore character, rather than Tigger.'[13] Nevertheless he frequently repeated that

---

7   Welby, 'Presidential Address' (February 2014), p. 158.
8   Letter from Nick Shutt, *Church Times*, 17 January 2014, p. 17.
9   Martyn Percy, 'God's Maths?', *The Door* (Oxford diocesan newspaper), March 2014, p. 15.
10   Welby, 'Presidential Address' (July 2013), p. 20.
11   *Challenges for the Quinquennium: Intentional Evangelism* (GS 1917), October 2013.
12   St Mellitus College, 2 December 2013.
13   *Newsday*, 6 January 2014.

he was 'more optimistic about the Church than I have been at any other time in my life'.[14] He proclaimed:

> When the church is working, it is the most mind-bogglingly, amazingly, extraordinarily beautiful community on earth. ... It heals, it transforms, it loves. It changes society and it brings people face-to-face with God. It's wonderful. God chose to create the church in order to carry on the work of Jesus, so the mission of the church is to build the community as God intended it.[15]

Welby often used the language of 'revolution' to describe the challenges facing the church in the twenty-first century, but sometimes he reinterpreted revolution in explicitly evangelical terms. 'We are in a time of revolution', he said, 'and we need another revolution in the Church. What it looks like, I do not know, but I want to be in it. What it feels like is Jesus-centred, fire-filled, peace-proclaiming, disciple-creating, and the Church word for this revolution is revival.'[16] Revival could be painfully disruptive, a sharper concept than gentle spiritual renewal. It was associated with many people come to faith in Jesus and the knock-on effects of revival were the Christian transformation of society and culture. Inverting the military term 'collateral damage', Welby explained: 'People seeking Christ create collateral blessing. That means changing the world for the better in ways you could not have predicted.'[17] But the starting point was always faith in Jesus, and the unique function of the church was to introduce people to Jesus, as the archbishop reminded his friends at HTB:

> It doesn't matter who you are, there's only one thing we ever do that lasts for eternity and that's to lead someone to faith in Christ – when we do that, that's forever, everything else dies. ... Make new disciples. Not because we're trying to notch up the numbers, but because we know that Jesus loves us so

14   Justin Welby, 'Christians in the World', *Outlook: The Magazine of the Diocese of Canterbury* no. 14 (Summer 2013), p. 13.
15   'Justin Welby' (October 2013), www.alpha.org/journal.
16   Sermon at New Wine Conference, 29 July 2013.
17   Sermon at New Wine Conference, 29 July 2013.

extraordinarily, so amazingly that he died on the cross for us, and for other people to know that will transform their lives and we will change the world.[18]

This fundamental motivation to Welby's ministry put everything else into perspective, whether tussles over women bishops and same-sex marriage, food banks and credit unions, state pageantry or global Anglican politics. 'The best decision that any human being can ever make in their life, anywhere in the world, in any circumstances, whoever they are,' the archbishop declared, 'is to follow Jesus Christ as their Lord.'[19] Welby had personally taken that decisive step as a Cambridge undergraduate in the 1970s, a spiritual encounter which shaped his entire life and ministry, and his perspective on his legacy. When all was said and done it came back again to relationship with his Saviour. 'At the Last Judgment', he noted, 'God isn't interested if I was Archbishop of Canterbury. He couldn't care less. He's interested in whether I put my trust in Jesus Christ.'[20]

18   HTB Home Focus, 27 July 2013.
19   St Mellitus College, 2 December 2013.
20   Interview at New Wine Conference, 29 July 2013.

Index

Accel Partners 233
Adonis, Andrew 186
Akinola, Peter 161
Alexandria Declaration 107, 110
Alli, Waheed 227
Alpha Course 35, 73-4, 83-5, 138, 148-50, 164, 176, 211-12, 244, 255
Anaminyi, Peter 113
Anderson, Ailsa 206
Angel, Gervais 35
Anglican Church in North America (ACNA) 190, 244, 247
Anglican Covenant 133, 227, 237
Anglican Episcopal House of Studies (AEHS) 204
Anglican Mission in England (AMiE) 243
Anis, Mouneer 192
Arafat, Yasser 106-7
Arbuthnot, Andy 38
Arbuthnot, Charlie 35, 38-9, 41, 46-8
Ashafa, Mohammed 114
Ashton, Mark 34
Association of Corporate Treasurers (ACT) 98
Association Internationale pour l'Enseignement Social Chrétien 100
Attlee, Clement 5
Auckland Castle 165-7

Badawi, Zeinab 221
Bagehot, Walter 24

Balding, Clare 224
Barak, Ehud 106
Barnes, Trevor 216
Barrington-Ward, Simon 16, 69-70, 78
Barth, Karl 208
Bash Camps 33-6, 183, 195
Batt, Bill 9
Batten, Susan 9
Baucum, Tory 244-7
Beake, Stuart 123
Behrens, James 35, 41
Benedictines 134-7, 188, 196-7
Benn, Tony 146
Bennett, Dennis 24
Bennetts, Colin 106, 108, 122-3, 134, 137, 140, 156, 161
Berkeley, Michael 12, 163, 189
Betteridge, Simon 72-3, 76
Beveridge, William 235
Bible Society 71
Blanch, Stuart 194
Boko Haram 179
Boyle, Edward 8
Bray, Gerald 243
Bridger, Francis 152
Brock, Kay 204
Brother Andrew 47
Brown, Andrew 219-20, 231, 234
Brunner, Emil 208
Bryant, Mark 140, 176
Bulman, Claire 83
Burundi 112-13, 115, 121, 153, 189, 238

Butler, Adam 9-10
Butler, Montagu 1
Butler, Paul 163, 193
Butler, Rab 1, 8, 13, 17, 23, 27
Buttet, Nicolas 100-1

Callander, Sila, see Sila Lee
Cambridge Inter-Collegiate
Christian Union (CICCU) 28-30,
33, 35, 37, 195
Cameron, Gregory 199
Campbell, Nicky 29
Campus Crusade for Christ 36
Carey, George 93, 106, 121,
194, 198, 200, 213
Cattaneo, Hernan 146
Ceaușescu, Nicolae 49
Centre for Contemporary
Christianity in Ireland (CCCI)
205
Chadwick, Henry 34
Charley, Julian 34
Chartres, Richard 185, 193, 229,
244
Chavasse, Francis 141
Chemin Neuf 150-1, 161, 197,
207-8
Chenevix-Trench, Anthony 13
Children's Society 94-5
Chilvers Coton 69-78
Chimeledya, Jacob 238
Chiwanga, Simon 156
Church Army 71
Church Commissioners 122,
166, 199, 202, 233
Church Missionary Society
(CMS) 16, 21, 23, 69, 71, 74
Church Pastoral Aid Society
(CPAS) 41, 84
Church Planting 60-1, 74, 149-
50, 161
Church Society 223
Church Urban Fund 235
Churchill, Winston 2, 7, 13
Clegg, Cecelia 157
Clinton, Bill 106

Cocksworth, Christopher 185
Coggan, Donald 194
Coles, John 34
Collins, John 34, 59, 61
Commission for Health
Improvement 97
Community of the Cross of Nails
(CCN) 105-6, 113, 133, 136,
183
Community of the Holy Name
207
Congo 113, 190, 238-9
Convocation of Anglicans in
North America (CANA) 244
Costa, Ken 29, 36, 38, 46, 59,
206
Council of Anglican Provinces of
Africa (CAPA) 189
Coventry Cathedral 103, 105-6,
108-9, 121-9, 136-9, 183
Cranmer Hall, Durham 67-9, 72,
103, 173, 181, 204
Cranmer, Thomas 188
Credit Unions 168-9, 231-4, 259
Croft, Steven 185
Cross, Ronald 8
Cross, Tim 156
Crossan, John Dominic 247
Crossman, Richard 5-6
Crown Nominations
Commission (CNC) 158, 172,
185-6
Cundy, Ian 67, 171-3
Czechoslovakia 48

Daffern, Adrian 125-6, 128-9,
227
Dakin, Tim 193
Dale, Iain 216
Dallaglio, Lawrence 95
Dante 239
Davies, Myles 149
Dembinski, Paul 100, 171
Dimbleby, Jonathan 77
Dix, Gregory 135
Dixon, Bob 2

Dixon, Piers 2, 7
Dow, Graham 138
Dresden Trust 123
Dudley-Smith, Timothy 34
Duff, Antony 22-3
Duke, Doris 4
Duncan, Robert 190-1, 247
Duncan-Smith, Iain 231-2
Durham Diocese 161-8, 171-8

Eames, Robin 133
East African Revival 240
Eastern European Bible Mission
(EEBM) 47-9
Eaton, Caroline, see Caroline
Welby
Eaton, Mary 36-7, 53
Eden, Anthony 2, 23
Edwards, Huw 195
Eisenhower, Dwight 2
Eldebo, Runar 134
Elf Aquitaine 42-4, 51, 109, 111
Elf UK 51, 54
Eliot, George 70
Elmore Abbey 134-5
Elsdon-Dew, Mark 75, 206
Emmaus Course 176
Enterprise Oil 54-7, 63-5, 67-72,
99, 114-15, 144
Eton College 13-18, 27-9, 34-5,
187
Eucharistein Community 101-2,
134
Evangelical Alliance 195, 205,
219-21
Evangelical Contribution on
Northern Ireland (ECONI) 205
Evangelism 73-4, 83-4, 137,
147-8, 164-5, 175-7, 206, 255-9
Evans, David 97
Evans, Jonathan 115

Fabre, Laurent 150, 208
Facilitated Conversations 152-4,
183-4, 223, 227-9, 252
Feba Radio 113

Financial Ethics 43-4, 56-9, 98-
100, 167-71, 230-5
Fletcher, David 34
Fletcher, Jonathan 33-4
Flynn, Errol 4
Food Banks 168, 231, 259
Forbes, Patrick 15
Ford, David 198, 208-9
Forster, Peter 67
Forward in Faith 223
Foster, John 8
Fraser, Flora 9
Fraser, Giles 171, 182, 185, 222
French, Bernie 72, 83
French, Jean 72, 83
Fresh Expressions 147-9, 255
Fulton, Bob 53
Fulton, Penny 53

Gandiya, Chad 156
Gardner, Francis 14, 17
Gay Christian Movement 45
Gay Liberation Front 45
Gibbs School, Kensington 13
Gillum, Tom 67
Gittoes, Julie 209
Gladwin, John 30
Global Anglican Future
Conference (GAFCON) 154,
157, 161-2, 190-2, 238-43
Global Fellowship of Confessing
Anglicans (GFCA) 154, 252
Gooder, Paula 209
Goodhew, David 175
Graham, Billy 36-7, 73, 176
Grant, Kes 251
Green, Michael 34
Greggs, Tom 209
Gregory, Clive 140
Greig, Pete 188
Grey, Lady Jane 71
Grieves, Ian 69, 181
Groves, Phil 153
Gumbel, Nicky 24, 28-31, 33-6,
59, 62, 67, 75, 176, 195-6, 211-
12, 215, 244

Habgood, John 194
Hafidh, Sharif 253
Hamilton, John 30
Handford, Clive 140
Harrison, Ian 22
Hastings, Max 232
Hauerwas, Stanley 208
Hester, Stephen 169
Higton, Mike 209
Hills, Nicky 29-32, 35
Hillsong 197
Hiltz, Fred 191
Holmes, Eamonn 217
Holtam, Nicholas 227
Holy Trinity Brompton 9, 36-8,
45-7, 53, 57, 59-63, 67, 69,
73-6, 84, 106, 149-50, 161, 164,
176, 188, 193, 195, 197, 201,
206, 211-2, 244, 256, 258
Holy Trinity, Cambridge 28, 30,
39
Holy Trinity, Coventry 137-9,
228
Holy Trinity, Parr Mount 69, 72
Homosexuality 45-6, 76-7, 94-
5, 124-9, 157, 211-21, 227-8,
251-4
Howard, Dick 105
Howells, Danny 146
Huddleston, Trevor 15
Hughes, John 63-4
Hume, Basil 92-3
Humphrys, John 233
Hussein, Saddam 108

Idowu-Fearon, Josiah 110, 161-2
Ignatian Spirituality 150, 196
Inclusive Church 185
Indaba 117, 153-4, 157, 180,
204, 252
Ingham, Michael 133
Inter-Anglican Standing
Commission for Unity, Faith and
Order (IASCUFO) 189

International Centre for
Reconciliation (ICR) 105-23,
156, 183
Inter-Varsity Fellowship 38, 194
Iraq 108-9, 121
Irvine, Andrea 138
Irvine, John 61, 84, 108, 122-3,
125, 134, 137-8
Irwin-Clark, Peter 76
Isingoma, Henri 190
Israel 106-9

James, Graham 185
James, Nick 38
Jeangrand, Miss 8
Jeger, George 9
Jenkins, Simon 71
Jensen, Peter 241
J.John 32, 215
John, Jeffrey 124-5, 133
Johnston, Raymond 44-6
Johnston, Shannon 244-7
Jones, David 15, 18
Jones, James 142, 161

Kaduna Declaration 110
Kanagasooriam, Evangeline 189
Karumba, Bosco 25
Kato, David 157
Kellaway, Lucy 187
Kellner, Peter 234
Kelly, Phil 21-6
Kennedy, John F. 7
Kennedy, Joseph 6
Kennedy, Patricia 6-7
Kenya 4, 16, 18, 21-6, 30, 69,
113-14, 151, 154, 190, 238,
240, 253-4
Kenyatta, Jomo 23
Kings, Graham 41
Knutsen, Thomas 42
Kwashi, Benjamin 157

Lambeth Conference 117, 153-5,
156, 161, 213, 237, 253
Lambeth Palace 198-208, 213

Lambeth Partners 206
Lawson, Dominic 187
Lawson, Nigel 169
Lee, Nicky 28-9, 62, 67
Lee, Sila 29
Lennon, John 145
Leonard, Graham 63
Lewis, C. S. 211
Linzey, Andrew 202
Liverpool Cathedral 139-55, 158-60
Liverpool Report 152-4
Lucas, Dick 34

McClure, John 62, 69
McCrum, Michael 14
McGowan, Chris 41
MacInnes, David 28-9, 34, 59
MacIntyre, Alasdair 136
Macmillan, Harold 194
Manoogian, Torkom 107
Marray, Santosh 156
Marsh, Bill 245
Matri, Oliver 207
Mayfield, Tim 244
Melanesian Brotherhood 207
Melchior, Michael 106
Melluish, Mark 12, 215
Michlowicz, Ula 207
Millar, Annette 37
Millar, Sandy 36-7, 46, 53, 59-61, 64, 67, 75, 161, 173, 195, 244, 246
Milne, A. A. 257
Mission Aviation Fellowship 239
Mitchell, Harold 4
Mokiwa, Valentine 190
Moore, Charles 29, 187
Morehouse School of Medicine 152, 154
Morley-Fletcher, Alan 207
Morley-Fletcher, Ione 207
Mother Teresa 172
Movement for the Restoration of the Ten Commandments of God 85

Movement for the Survival of the Ogoni People (MOSOP) 112
Moxon, David 134
Mtetemela, Donald 85
Mumford, John 25, 215
Murray, Paul 209

Nash, E. J. H. 33-5, 197
Nashdom Abbey 134-5
National Front 92
National Housing Federation 235
Nationwide Festival of Light 44-6
Newton, Fiona 86-7
New Wine 74-5, 129-31, 197, 229
Nichols, Vincent 190
Nicholson, Paul 167
Nigeria 43, 109-12, 114-17, 121, 128, 133, 151, 154, 156-7, 161, 175, 178-9, 186, 190, 237-8, 240, 244, 248, 250-2, 254
Nissen, George 16
Nixon, Richard 222
Ntagali, Stanley 190, 192, 240, 253
Ntahoturi, Bernard 113, 153, 189
Ntukamazina, Pie 112-13
Nutting, Anthony 23
Nzimbi, Benjamin 151

Oakeshott, Keith 23
Obama, Barack 188
Obasanjo, Olusegun 112
O'Brien, James 218
Observatoire de la Finance 100, 171
Oddie, Bill 202
Oestreicher, Paul 106
Ogunyemi, Abiodun 110
Okoh, Nicholas 157, 179, 190, 192, 237
Ono, Yoko 145
Open Doors 47

Orcel, Andrea 170
Order of the Holy Paraclete 207
Osborne, George 170

Palmer, Hugh 34
Parish Share 87, 98, 174-5, 177, 255
Parliamentary Commission on Banking Standards 169-70
Paulson, Hank 47-9
Payne, Leanne 212
Percy, Martyn 257
Perkin, Paul 34, 57, 61, 106
Philpott, John 71-3
Pigott, Robert 216-17, 256
Pilling, Joseph 228
Pilling Report 228, 251-2
Piper Alpha 57
Policy Exchange 141
Pope Benedict XVI 181
Pope Francis 202-3, 257
Pope Leo XIII 98
Portal, Iris 13
Portal, Jane 1-2, 7-10, 16, 189
Portal, Viscount 1
Porter, David 183, 205-6, 223, 254
Porvoo Communion 226
Primates Meeting 156-8, 162, 237
Prince Charles 27, 77, 96, 188
Prince Harry 96
Princess Diana 172
Pritchard, John 67, 219
Proclamation Trust 74
Progressive Episcopalians of Pittsburgh 247
Pullinger, Jackie 38-9, 50
Pytches, David 60, 74

Queenborough, Baron 4

Reagan, Ronald 45
Redgrave, Lynn 11
Redgrave, Michael 10-12
Redgrave, Rachel 10-12

Redgrave, Vanessa 10-12
Reform 186, 223
Reiss, Michael 35-6
Ridley Hall, Cambridge 30, 204
Riley, Andrew 97
Risk 49, 60, 99, 119, 139, 142-5, 164, 172, 174, 177, 255-6
Robinson, Gene 133, 161, 204, 244
Rogers, Trevor 86
Roman Catholic Social Thought 98-101, 155, 167, 230
Romania 49
Rosse, Earl 8
Round Church, Cambridge 33, 35-6, 39, 183
Rowell, Geoffrey 208
Royal Society for the Prevention of Cruelty to Animals (RSPCA) 202
Ruffer, Jonathan 166
Runcie, Robert 198, 200, 207
Runcorn, David 21
Russell, Chris 69, 206
Ruston, Mark 33-4, 39-40
Rwaje, Onesphore 190
Rwanda 154, 190, 238

Sacramentalism 101-2
St Barnabas Church, Kensington 61-2, 76, 84
St Ethelburga's Centre for Reconciliation and Peace 167
St George's Church, Baghdad 109, 121
St James the Great Church, Darlington 69, 181
St John's Church, Neville's Cross 69
St John's College, Durham 67, 69
St Mark's Church, Battersea Rise 61
St Mary's Church, Astley 71-2
St Matthew's Church, Cambridge 36, 39

St Matthias Church, Burley, Leeds 24
St Mellitus College, London 150, 207
St Michael's Church, Paris 50, 52-3, 69
St Michael's Church, Ufton 78
St Paul's Church, Onslow Square 76
St Peter's School, Seaford 13
Santer, Mark 61
Saro-Wiwa, Ken 112
Satcher, David 152
Schori, Katharine Jefferts 191, 248, 250
Scott, Giles Gilbert 141
Scripture Union 33, 71
Second Severn Crossing 67
Sentamu, John 158-9, 161, 179, 185, 193, 252-3
Sertin, Marilyn 50
Sertin, Peter 50, 53
Sharing of Ministries Abroad 85
Sharon, Ariel 106
Sheppard, David 34
Shilston, Andrew 65
Shutt, Nick 257
Simeon, Charles 33
Simpson, O.J. 90
Sims, Sidney 36
Sinclair, Keith 138, 140, 228
Sisters of the Love of God 207
Skjevesland, Kjell 42
Smith, Chris 153, 199-201
Smith, David 64
Soul Survivor 75
Southam 78-97
South Sudan 238-9, 251
South Warwickshire NHS Trust 96-8
Spence, Basil 105, 137
Stammers, Kay 4
Stock, Nigel 206
Stockwood, Michael 38
Stone, Samuel 190

Stonewall 219
Stott, John 34-6, 45
Stride, Eddy 44
Student Christian Movement 28
Sturzenegger, Doris 4
Swinton, John 209

Tantawi, Muhammad Sayed 106
Tanzania 22, 85, 156, 190, 238
Tarallo, André 43
Tatchell, Peter 77, 213-14
Tawney, R. H. 235
Taylor, Jeremy 248
Taylor, John V. 194
Taylor, William 34-5, 242
Temple, William 235
Thatcher, Margaret 9, 22, 54
The Episcopal Church (USA) 133, 156, 161, 179-80, 204, 244-8, 250, 253
Thiselton, Anthony 67, 208
Thomas, Rod 185
Thuan, Nguyen Van 101-2
Tomlin, Graham 70, 209, 215
Toronto Blessing 75
Touche-Porter, Carlos 153
Toulmin, Alison 86
Townend, Stuart 190
Trevor, Richard 166
Trinity College, Cambridge 17, 27-31, 33, 35, 39
Turnbull, Bill 31
Turnbull, Michael 76-7, 171
Turvey, Raymond 59
Tyndale, William 78

Uchoa, Miguel 241
Uganda 22, 74, 85-6, 154, 157, 161, 190, 238, 240, 252-4
Urquhart, David 138

Vanden-Bempde-Johnstone, Robin 9
Vineyard Christian Fellowship 53, 60, 62, 69, 75

Vogelaar, Hendrik, see Hank
Paulson
Vogelaar, Michael Justin 49
Vogelaar, Mona 49
Volf, Miroslav 208
Von Hügel Institute, Cambridge
98-100
Von Post, Gunilla 7

Wabukala, Eliud 114, 190-2,
238-9, 241, 252-3
Wagner, Peter 60
Wakefield, Wavell 8
Walker, Dominic 202
Walker, Hiram 7
Walsingham 149, 197-8
Walters, James 209
Warren, Rick 188
Watson, David 28, 32, 34, 59,
194
Watson, Tim 151
Watts, Isaac 190
Welby, Bernard 3
Welby, Caroline 36-7, 39, 44-54,
63-4, 68, 72, 76, 82-3, 108, 115,
139-40, 158-9, 164, 196, 238-9
Welby, Edith 3
Welby, Eleanor 79
Welby, Gavin 2-12, 16-18, 25-6,
38
Welby, Hannah 79
Welby, Jane, see Jane Portal
Welby, Johanna 49, 51-3
Welby, Justin 1-259
Welby, Katharine 68
Welby, Peter 68
Welby, Timothy 67

Wells, Jo Bailey 204-6, 209
Wells, Nicky 29
Werrell, Ralph 78-9
Wesley, Charles 190
West, Rosemary 90
White, Andrew 106-9, 116, 121
White, Richard 148-9
Widdecombe, Ann 218
Williams, Charles 37, 42, 134,
174, 189
Williams, Harold 136
Williams, Jane, see Jane Portal
Williams, N.P. 37
Williams, Rowan 124, 133, 148,
151-3, 156-8, 162-3, 173, 179,
185, 187, 189, 192, 199-200,
208-10, 213, 222-3, 227, 231-2,
237-8, 244, 252
Wimber, John 53, 60, 62
Windsor Report 133, 162
Winfield, Flora 154
Women and the Church
(WATCH) 223
Women Bishops 180-4, 222-4
Wonga 232-4
Wood, Maurice 33-4
Woods, Christopher 69, 74
World Council of Churches 238
Wright, Kenyon 106
Wright, Tom 158, 163, 166, 208
Wuye, James 114
Wycliffe Hall, Oxford 62, 67

Youth for Christ 71

Zavala, Tito 190
Zurbarán, Francisco de 166

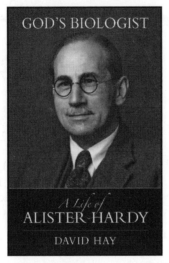

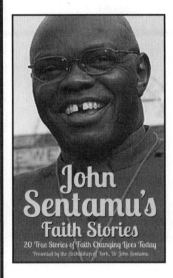
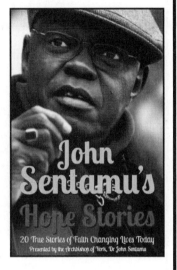

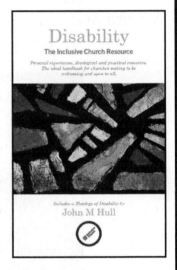

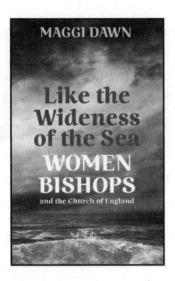